CARRIACOU

∞

STRING BAND SERENADE

CARRIACOU

STRING BAND SERENADE

Performing Identity in the Eastern Caribbean

REBECCA S. MILLER

Wesleyan University Press MIDDLETOWN, CONNECTICUT

Published by Wesleyan University Press, Middletown, CT 06459
www.wesleyan.edu/wespress
2007 © Rebecca S. Miller. First Paperback 2024.
Printed in the United States of America

The publisher gratefully acknowledges assistance from the Dragan Plamenac Publication
Endowment Fund of the American Musicological Society.

Library of Congress Cataloging-in-Publication Data
available at https://catalog.loc.gov/
hardback ISBN 978-0-8195-6858-8
paperback ISBN 978-0-8195-0148-6
ebook ISBN 978-0-8195-0149-3

For my father

and in memory of my mother.

Contents

Figures

Guide to Webpage Music Tracks

To hear audio samples and view video of the music and song in
Carriacou String Band Serenade (1995–1997):

https://serenade.hampshire.edu/

Foreword to the New Edition

I began the research for this book in the early 1990s when Carriacou was a comparatively isolated island culture. Digital technology and the internet were in their infancy globally and, in Carriacou, nearly absent; cell phones were nonexistent. Television broadcasts beamed island and national news; CNN programming had just arrived in Carriacou via Grenada. Tourism was scant: aside from occasional passengers who disembarked for a few hours from small cruise ships to visit Hillsborough, most visitors were European and American yacht owners who dropped anchor in Tyrell Bay for a few days or weeks at a time. Carriacou was far from unknown, however, thanks to several annual cultural events that attracted visitors from elsewhere in the Eastern Caribbean as well as emigrant Kayaks (the local term for Carriacouans) who returned to enjoy the festivities while visiting their extended family and friends. The most popular of these included Carriacou's Regatta Festival in early August, Carriacou Carnival in February, and, in the week before Christmas, the Parang Festival, which captured my attention and became the focus of this book.

With its emphasis primarily on string band music, Hosannah singing, and quadrille music and dance, the Parang Festival was enormously popular and generated huge excitement in the weeks and months leading up to the event. Despite this, many Kayak musicians and cultural leaders at the time worried about the future of these musical traditions. Some were generally concerned about the steady creep of American popular culture. Others noted that young people were not interested in the local string band music, preferring popular pan-Caribbean musics such as soca and ragga. Hosannah singers were faced with similar concerns of cultural obsolescence, but like string band musicians, they gamely recontextualized what had long been a community-based tradition and entered the competition at Parang. In the case of Hosannah bands specifically, the sheer visibility provided by Parang may well have contributed to the survival of the Hosannah band tradition even though the nature of the competition seemed to threaten its future, due to the very real frustration and anger that emerged every year over the judging. Possibly the most fraught of Carriacou's folk traditions was quadrille dancing. With the death of violinist Canute Caliste in 2005,

the future of Carriacou quadrille music, in particular, was in jeopardy because there now existed only two violinists (including myself)—neither of
whom lived in Carriacou—who were familiar with Mr. Caliste's unique
quadrille repertoire.

Fast forward to 2024. Unsurprisingly, the cultural landscape of Carriacou has shifted, given the ubiquity of digital technology and media. As is
the case globally, cell phones and the internet have transformed the ways
that Kayaks communicate and have expanded access to news and culture
well beyond Carriacou and Grenada. Social media offers Kayaks a powerful platform to promote, document, and present traditional culture island-
wide and to outsiders. For example, in 2020 and 2021, when Parang was
canceled in response to the Covid pandemic, the organizing committee—
the Mount Royal Progressive Youth Movement (MRPYM)—ably pivoted to
social media (YouTube and Facebook) to create a mini-Parang; today, those
videos function as a sort of archive of that time and these performances.

Since the 1990s, tourism to Carriacou has increased, as has foreign investment, with a small but growing presence of Europeans and Americans who
live on the island part- and full-time. In late 2017, the Chinese government
partnered with Grenada in the construction of large infrastructural projects. This includes a housing complex in the Carriacou village of Lauriston,
which contrasts both in appearance and social function with vernacular
Kayak housing and which, as of early 2024, remains unoccupied.

Thanks to earlier visits and being privy to local news from my Kayak
friends over the decades, I was well aware of many of the larger shifts in
Carriacou's social and cultural landscape. Nevertheless, upon returning in
early 2024, I was happy to see that many of the dire predictions surrounding the future of traditional music and dance in Carriacou had not been
realized. Folk arts are inherently malleable and subject to change and adaptation. Whether they flourish or fail in the face of economic, political,
and social pressures is dependent on many factors, some of which are well
beyond human control. In Carriacou, the traditions of string band music,
quadrille dance, and Hosannah singing have clearly adapted to changing
circumstances and trends, and, to an extent, are attracting younger Kayaks
to take the place of "older heads" as singers, dancers, and instrumentalists.

Much of this resilience comes from the apparent determination of both
individual artists and community-based groups. For example, in an effort
to encourage and train the next generation of string band musicians, the

Mount Royal Progressive Youth expanded the Parang Festival to include a youth string band category (joining youth Hosannah bands that were well in place since the 1990s). Another community-based group, Shadeau Beni Serenaders, has supported Hosannah singing and serenading traditions since 2016. Experiments with in-school music programs taught by master musicians aim to train a new generation of instrumentalists, and in the L'Esterre Rosary School, instruction in quadrille dance continues as it has over the decades.

The concerns surrounding the future of Carriacou quadrille have largely been laid to rest with the 2010 formation of the L'Esterre Company of Dancers. Representing the next generation of quadrille performers, the group has found creative ways to further the tradition even without a dedicated group of quadrille musicians. Instead, they dance to edited archival recordings of music featuring Canute Caliste and accompanists—a pragmatic solution that poetically connects today's dancers with their predecessors. Also, on occasion, the dancers are accompanied by live music provided by Carriacou string band musicians who play one or two of the quadrille tunes in a somewhat different but entirely compatible and high-energy style. There are other adaptations, such as shortened performances from the original six figures of the English quadrille to just three, in response to the limited stage time often allotted to the group at local and regional performance venues. Despite these changes, the members of the L'Esterre Company of Dancers continue to infuse quadrille dance with energy, rhythmic elegance, and grace.

Other factors inform the vitality of Carriacou's traditions. The island's cultural activities continue to be consolidated under the leadership of a local cultural officer appointed by the Minister of Carriacou and Petite Martinique Affairs—a position held, among others, by Hosannah Band singer Linton Lendore, by string band musician Harrison Fleary, and, as of 2024, by calypsonian/string band musician Andy "Leftist" Matheson. On a national level, the 2013 establishment of the Grenada Tourism Authority included an initiative to increase tourism to Carriacou and Petite Martinique. To this end, the government razed the old market structure in the center of Hillsborough, and in its place built an impressive-looking Visitors' Center. Recognizing the value of traditional culture as a means to draw visitors to Carriacou, the Tourism Authority co-sponsors new events such as the Carriacou Maroon and String Band Festival. Held over a weekend in April, this Festival celebrates the ancestors through local foodways, music, and dance.

Along with these efforts, there has also been the inevitable loss. This foreword is dedicated to the memory of Canute Caliste as well as that of his granddaughter, Cleddie Alexander-Stewart (1978–2024), in addition to dancers and musicians I've written about or with whom I've had the honor of playing music: Sonnelle Allert, Milton "Tailor" Coy, Sharma Dixon, Winston Fleary, Norris George, Enel James, Ronald Jones, Jerry McGillivary, and others. I also note here the grievous passing of calypsonian and Ghetto Boys' lead singer Kenly ("Rhyno") Joseph, who in 2015 was shot to death in Brooklyn, New York. The collective and individual knowledge and musicianship of these artists, as well as their contributions to Carriacou's cultural landscape, are inestimable. What is also amply clear is that their efforts have carried through to the next generation.

That said, the resilience of folk culture is never a given. This is particularly true in small Caribbean nations, many of which rely on tourism as a major source of revenue while also grappling with the destructive forces of overdevelopment and natural disasters wrought by climate change. This last concern became a devastating reality on July 1, 2024, when Hurricane Beryl made landfall on Carriacou as a Category 4 storm. While Carriacou has been in the path of devastating storms in the past—Hurricane Emily in 2005, Hurricane Ivan in 2004, Hurricane Janet in 1955, and others—Beryl broke many meteorological records and was historic in its destructive force. Within a half hour, the hurricane leveled or damaged nearly all homes and buildings, leaving many residents unhoused, and knocked out communications and power. Two Kayaks died as a result of the storm.

While it will take years to rebuild, the hope is that Carriacou's folk traditions will once again flourish, thanks to the historic success of local artists who have adapted and will continue to do so into the future. As readers will see, the processes of artistic change in Carriacou in response to major upheavals are not new. This book presents not only an ethnographic snapshot of Carriacou's recent history, but also a model of the tremendous durability of traditional arts as they both redefine and reinforce cultural identity.

Rebecca S. Miller
July 2024

Acknowledgments

I am grateful for the support and encouragement I received from family, friends, colleagues, and institutions during the various research and writing stages of this project. Because many of the ideas and much of the research for this book arose from the dissertation I wrote between 1997 and 2000, I would like to thank the following institutions that supported this work: the Thomas J. Watson Jr. Institute for International Studies, which awarded me a Pre-Dissertation Research Grant in 1995 to undertake summer field-work; the Fulbright Institute, whose fellowship funded a ten-month stay in Carriacou from 1996 to 1997; and the Music Department of Brown University, whose Research Assistantship in 1997 supported additional library research and the early writing stages of this project. A generous and well-timed Dean's Graduate Dissertation Fellowship (1998–99) and subsequent Dean's tuition scholarship from Brown University's Graduate School (1999–2000) also supported my early writing.

Many colleagues and friends have assisted me in moving this book forward. At Brown University, I would like to thank Professors Marc Perlman, Paget Henry, and Paul Austerlitz for their help and support during the early phases of my research and writing. Special thanks go to Donald R. Hill, Professor of Anthropology, SUNY–Oneonta, for his generous assistance with this project from its earliest stages as well as his enthusiasm for all things Carriacouan. At Hampshire College, I am grateful for Faculty Development Grants in 2002 and 2006, which supported additional research, and for a sabbatical leave during which I rethought much of my original material and rewrote it into book form. Huge thanks go to Michael Dessen, Assistant Professor, University of California, Irvine, for his keen insights regarding African diasporic cultural production and for his expertise and tremendous assistance with Finale transcription software. I am also extremely grateful to Katherine Hagedorn, Michael Largey, Lois Wilcken, and Cheryl Zoll for their critical and thoughtful feedback on the entire manuscript in its various stages, as well as to Daniel Neely and Peter Manuel for their helpful critiques of the quadrille chapter. Deb Gorlin and the late Nina Payne of Hampshire College gave me crucial advice on the craft of writing. I also thank John Gunther, John Bruner, Josiah Erikson, and Dan Parker for their help setting up streaming audio files and the web-page where readers can hear music samples. Additional thanks and gratitude go to Susan Jahoda, Stephen Korns, Michael Heffley, Michael Veal, Von Martin, Raymond Joiner, Krister Malm, Amelia Ingram, Jennie Southgate, and the staff of the Watkinson Library, Trinity College, Hartford, Connecticut, for advice and assistance along the way.

In Carriacou, I offer my deepest thanks to Kervin and Hilda Stiell—friends and confidants who have helped my husband and me over the years in ways too numerous to mention. I am furthermore forever grateful to the late Canute Caliste of L'Esterre: I am honored to have worked closely with him and will always remember his warmth, humor, and music. I thank his daughter, Clemencia Alexander, for her friendship, generous assistance, and advice over the years and for her kind permission to reproduce Mr. Caliste's painting *Dancing and Cudreal in Carriacou* for the front cover of this book. I am also grateful to Clemencia's daughter, Clearine Alexander, for assisting me with interviews. I thank the following individuals for their cooperation and assistance: members of the Mount Royal Progressive Youth

FIGURE O.1   Canute Caliste, violinist/folk artist, L'Esterre, Carriacou, January 1997.

Movement, particularly Wallace Collins; Patrick Compton, Director of the Carriacou Museum; Winston Fleary; and Dennis "Poco" Joseph, formerly of L'Esterre and currently a resident of Brooklyn, New York. I extend great thanks to the many string band musicians in Carriacou, whose generosity and fine music made this study possible, including Harrison Fleary and the Central Serenaders; Albert Fortune and BBH; Kenly ("Rhyno") Joseph and the Ghetto Boys; Anselm James and the Country Boys; Lawrence Chase; Cyrus Doyle; Ronald Jones and his late wife, Katie; the late, great violinist Norris George; Milton "Tailor" Coy and his sons, Maitland and Scofield; Welcome Cummins; Enel James; Peter Quashie; Godwin "Mose" Moses; Desmond Dixon; and Jerry McGillivary.

I also offer my deepest thanks and gratitude to the members of the L'Esterre Quadrille Group, particularly to Sonnelle Allert, Cosmos Bristol, and Gus Adams. The New Tide Carolers, L'Esterre's Hosannah band, allowed me to be part of their competition experience during the Parang Festival of 1996, for which I am deeply grateful. I thank all of them and particularly Brian Lendore, Lionel Stiell, and Thora Stiell for this opportunity and for their friendship. I also thank Gaby MacFarlane, singer with Wind-

FIGURE O.2. Claude, Claudine, and Clearine Alexander (three of Canute Caliste's grand-children), July 1995, L'Esterre, Carriacou.

ward's Hosannah band, Splendiferous, for her kindness and assistance. Pastor Philip Mendes, his wife, Gloria, and the members of the music class of the Church of Christ, Hillsborough, generously gave of their friendship and good humor.

I thank Dennis F. Carter, Consul, St. George's, Grenada, and his staff for their assistance during our stays in Carriacou. The staff of the National Archives and Public Library in St. George's, Grenada, allowed me access to critical research materials, for which I am grateful. Finally, I offer my sincere thanks to those who helped me bring our son, Samuel Lawrence Randall, into this world: nurse-midwife Marguerite Blakey and Dr. Ronald Lendore, both of Belmont, Grenada, as well as Nurse Kathleen Leggard and the other nurse-midwives at the Hillsborough Clinic in Carriacou for their excellent ante-natal (pre-natal) and post-natal care.

The members of our extended families—the Millers, the Randalls, and the Epsteins—provided much support during the fieldwork phase of this project. I am forever grateful to my parents, Nathan Miller and the late Lillian B. Miller, for all their love, encouragement, and support along the way. My deepest thanks go to my husband, Tom Randall, for his tremendous musicianship—including his expertise and help with the music transcriptions—and his love and unwavering support. Finally, I thank our sons, Sam and Gabriel Randall, for their perky good natures and healthy perspectives on the balance between work and play.

CARRIACOU

STRING BAND SERENADE

1

⊚/⊚

INTRODUCING CARRIACOU
AND THE PARANG FESTIVAL

If you know what you did was wrong,
listen for your name right here in Parang.

The Ghetto Boys, 1996

I FIRST HEARD STRING BAND MUSIC from the small Caribbean island of
Carriacou entirely by chance, one day in 1988, as I was walking down Seventh
Avenue in New York City. From two tinny speakers mounted on the door
frame of a pawn shop, I heard what sounded like North American old-time
string band music over a bed of West African polyrhythms played on drums
and other percussion instruments. I literally staggered when I heard this propulsive, violin-based music. As a fiddler, public sector folklorist, and documentary maker, my ears were always open to finding musics and their makers
from New York City's diverse immigrant communities, particularly lesser-
known traditional and folk styles and especially those featuring a violin.

Inside the store, I asked the clerk, a man in his mid-twenties, what he
was playing over the sound system. He told me that it was just a cassette
from his home, nothing that I could buy, so I probably wouldn't be interested. This only sharpened my curiosity, and I asked where he was from. He
told me that he was from a small Caribbean island, probably not one I
would know, called Petit Martinique. Mistakenly associating Petit Martinique with the much larger Caribbean island of Martinique, I asked the
clerk if he also spoke French. He replied that he didn't speak French and
that Petit Martiniquans spoke English. We chatted a bit more about the
music, string bands in general, and the fact that he lived, along with other
immigrants from that part of the Caribbean, in Brooklyn. He was very kind
and gave me the phone number of a violinist from Petit Martinique who
also lived in Brooklyn. A few days later, I called this violinist, who was now

FIGURE 1.1 "Welcome To The Carriacou Parang Festival" banner, Hillsborough, Carriacou, December 1996.

a doctor with a busy practice, having received his medical degree since im-migrating to the United States. Like some U.S. immigrants who practiced a folk tradition in their native home, the doctor had neither the time nor the inclination to play string band music now. He told me that although he ap-preciated my interest, he couldn't help me and didn't know anybody else in the area who played this music. So I shelved my interest until 1994, when I began the doctoral program in ethnomusicology at Brown University and began again to search for this music. After several months, I was actually able to locate Petit Martinique, an island so small it virtually never appears on conventional maps of the world. I also located its larger sister island, Car-riacou, and it was only then that I discovered that the two islands were part of the tri-island nation of Grenada.

My husband, Tom Randall, and I first visited Carriacou in January 1995. So vital was its string band musical tradition that it took exactly one inquiry to start meeting musicians in both Carriacou and Petit Martinique. We were also urged by virtually everybody we met to visit Canute Caliste in the vil-lage of L'Esterre. A well-known folk artist whose paintings are collected by folk art aficionados worldwide, Mr. Caliste was the island's sole remaining quadrille violinist. We soon discovered that he and a handful of accompanying musicians played often for a small but active group of quadrille dancers. I was mesmerized by the overt grace and embedded humor of quadrille dance and its remarkable similarities to the music I played on the fiddle for New England contradances. I was driven to learn quadrille and string band musics and through them to explore the culture of Carriacou.

After this initial visit, I came to learn that this small island had intrigued researchers since the 1950s and had been the subject of several major anthropological, sociological, linguistic, and ethnomusicological studies (Pearse 1956a, 1956b; Smith 1962; Hill 1973, 1942, 1977, 1980; McDaniel 1986, 1992, 1998; Kephart 1985, 2000). Although there certainly remained similarities between the Carriacou I encountered and that of the earlier accounts, by 1995 it was apparent that this small society was in the midst of a major postcolonial transformation informed by a myriad of national and regional influences. After seven years of my own fieldwork and research, it would also become clear that the music I enjoyed so much and many of the complicated political, social, and cultural issues that attended it were neatly embodied in the Parang Festival, one of Carriacou's largest annual public events. Taking place over a full weekend prior to Christmas, the Parang Festival features music and song competitions and performances organized by an entirely volunteer, local community group called the Mount Royal Progressive Youth Movement. Originating as a means of preserving traditional culture in Carriacou, the Parang Festival by the mid-1990s consisted of two music competitions—a Friday night Hosannah band competition (a cappella carol singing) and a climactic Sunday evening string band competition. In addition to a non-competitive calypso concert held on Saturday night, performances of quadrille music and dance and other traditional genres warmed up the audience each evening as well.

This study examines societal transformation in contemporary Carriacou using the Parang Festival as its lens. Born during a period of enormous political and social upheaval—just prior to the 1979 Grenadian Socialist Revolution—the Parang Festival itself represents the evolution of Carriacouan traditional culture. Since 1977 Parang has served, in part, as a platform for criticism of Kayaks by Kayaks (the local term for Carriacouans) and thus reinforces local mores and social codes of behavior.[1] The event also offers Kayaks a public forum through which to articulate issues associated with local events and politics as well as the growing effects of globalism on this small society. Moving what were once community-based music, song, and dance genres to the stage as newly competitive performances, the Parang Festival transforms expressive genres that have, over the last forty years, been changing along with the society around them. The format of the event thus underscores certain realities of the life cycle of traditional culture, particularly as folk genres outlive their use value and are replaced by contemporary musics. The Parang Festival in part attempts to preserve and present folk traditions, including those being replaced by non-local, popular music and song styles from elsewhere in the English-speaking Caribbean.

This tension between the old and the new, the local and the regional, imbues the Parang Festival and contributes to an emergent postcolonial Kayak identity. Component parts of the festival articulate and assert Kayak cultural autonomy while also furthering an understanding of regional belonging and pan–West Indian solidarity. Moreover, how and what people choose to perform or, conversely, *not* to perform exposes changing understandings of heritage and self. How and why new or non-native musical expressions are integrated into traditional forms tells us much about the politics of aesthetics and the evolution of cultural identity in an increasingly global context.

INTRODUCING CARRIACOU

Located in the Lesser Antilles in the southern Caribbean, Carriacou is the largest of the Grenadine islands and lies 140 miles north of Venezuela. Carriacou and its smaller sister island, Petit Martinique, form two of the three islands of the nation-state of Grenada. Carriacou is approximately seven and a half miles long and three and a half miles wide; its estimated on-island population is 6,081 (OECS Report 2005), although the island population fluctuates due to a near-constant level of emigration and reverse-migration. Among Kayaks, it is commonly believed that the number of Carriacouans living abroad in Brooklyn, New York, England (communities in Huddersfield and West London), and throughout the English-speaking Caribbean equals or exceeds the number of those living in Carriacou itself.

All three islands were first inhabited by the Arawak people; sometime prior to 1492 the Arawaks were conquered by the invading Carib people, who presumably migrated north from South America. From 1651 to 1654 the Caribs were largely exterminated in nearby Grenada by the ruling French; the Carib population in Carriacou saw a similar fate during or just

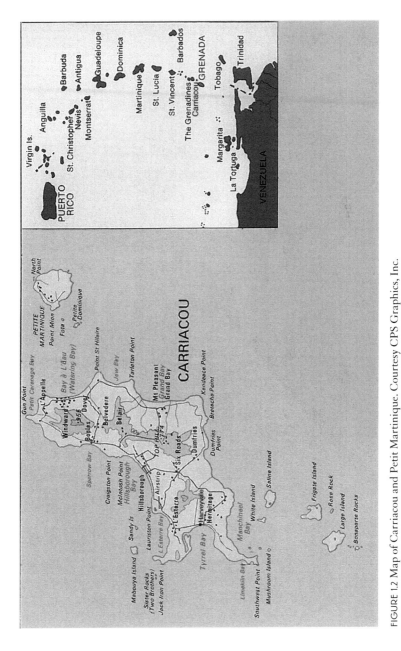

FIGURE 1.2 Map of Carriacou and Petit Martinique. Courtesy CPS Graphics, Inc.

after these years, although exactly what happened remains unknown. The legacy of this native population lives on in the name "Carriacou," which is probably Carib in origin.[2] Like Grenada, Carriacou and Petit Martinique bounced between English and French rule for nearly two centuries. Although the British gained control of the islands in 1784 through the Treaty of Versailles, the French influence remains strong and is reflected in place names, family names, and the last vestiges of *patois* mixed into the local English language.

By the mid- to late 1600s, enslaved Africans were brought to work on cotton plantations and, somewhat later, when Britain regained control of the islands in 1783, sugarcane plantations.[3] Today, the population of Carriacou is primarily of West African and Congolese descent. In general, Carriacouans are exquisitely aware of their African heritage, and many know their specific African lineage—Cromanti, Mandingo, Kongo, Igbo, and so on (Caliste, interview, 1995; David 1985: 25). In this regard, the population of Carriacou is largely unique in the former British Caribbean (Hill 1993: 10). In the northern villages of Dover and Windward, the population is largely descended from generations of intermarriage between the Afro-Caribbean population and the Scottish boat builders who settled in Carriacou toward the end of the eighteenth century. Much of this population is lighter skinned than elsewhere in Carriacou, a fact that may contribute to occasional racial tension in the context of some of the Parang competitions. Vestiges of Scottish culture also exist in the decorative carved wooden exterior trim (known as "fretwork") that adorns local homes, and in the reputation of Windward men as excellent boat builders, skills presumably handed down over the generations from their Scottish ancestors.

In 1833 the British Parliament passed the official act abolishing slavery in all of its possessions. At the time, Carriacou's total population was about 4,000 people, of whom 3,200 were enslaved. In 1838 emancipation was enacted in Grenada, Carriacou, and Petit Martinique. With this came the collapse of Carriacou's direct involvement with global economies and, like other dependency islands, Carriacou's economy reverted to subsistence agriculture. In the years following emancipation, Carriacou's population suffered from major economic instability as sugar prices fell and drought conditions and land erosion contributed to disastrous crop production. Estate owners abandoned Carriacou but retained their land, forcing the freed slaves to squat, pay rent, or enter into a sharecropping arrangement. By 1841 masses of ex-slaves left Carriacou, lured by the promise of work in Trinidad. Sugar production in Carriacou ended altogether in 1871; lime trees were planted and the cultivation of the lime became a minor crop.

Reports from visitors to Carriacou during these years paint an image of an impoverished society where the population went "hungry and thirsty" (Devas 1932). The period around 1886 has been described as "the darkness" by "older heads" (the local term for senior citizens), who recalled widespread famine as late as the 1930s. While this term might have referred, at least in part, to a memorable total solar eclipse in 1886, it also suggested the difficult living conditions, captured by Sydney Olivier in a travelogue from the era: "All the people were wretchedly poor. It is all owned by a few absentee proprietors in England and the people cannot get land of their own or rent any except by the year at exorbitant terms" (cited in Devas 1974: 174–75).

In 1901, half of the land in Carriacou remained uncultivated. Two years later the colonial government enacted land reforms, and by 1938 nearly two-thirds of the population was described by the Colonial Commission of Enquiry into Economic Conditions as "peasant agriculturists" who owned small parcels of land but remained largely impoverished. Scholars Donald Hill (1973, 1977) and M. G. Smith (1962) have demonstrated that the net result of this ongoing poverty in Carriacou has been a steady emigration from the island since emancipation. For example, the early years of the twentieth century saw extensive Kayak emigration, first to Panama to work on the canal, then in 1915 to Trinidad to search for work in that country's developing industry and oil fields. By the 1920s Carriacou's economy had worsened, a situation that was exacerbated in the early years of the Great Depression by declining overseas work opportunities. With emigration dwindling, the island's population swelled to an estimated 8,000 or 9,000 people, resulting in extremely crowded living conditions and a severe lack of food (D. Joseph, interview, 1997). Kervin Stiell was a young boy in Carriacou in the late 1930s and 1940s, and he remembers that even once plentiful local foodstuffs became rare: eating a newly fallen coconut on the way to school was a special treat to be carefully divided among the children who found it (personal communication, 1996).

By the 1940s cotton ceased to be the staple of the Carriacou economy; instead, cash remittances from Kayaks working abroad kept their families afloat. After World War II a steady stream of Carriacouans left the island in search of work opportunities in Aruba, Trinidad, and, by the early 1950s, the United States. Taking advantage of the North American postwar employment boom, Kayaks settled primarily in Brooklyn, where decently paid, union-protected jobs could be had. By the mid-1950s a similar stream of Carriacouans left for England to take advantage of postwar industrial jobs there as well. By the 1960s and 1970s, the island's already fragile economic infrastructure devolved into a largely cash economy that combined income from fishing, boat building, and subsistence agriculture with wage-labor remittances and barrels of goods regularly sent to island residents from Kayaks living abroad.

CONTEMPORARY CARRIACOU

In the early years of the twenty-first century, Carriacou's economy remains much the same, with the significant addition of a burgeoning construction industry that offers fairly regular employment to Kayak men. Fueled by the demand for new homes for older Kayaks who, upon retirement, return to Carriacou from New York City or England, construction has brought badly needed income to Carriacou since the early 1990s. Women are slowly entering the workforce in the service industry as well, but many remain at home, rearing their families and, with the help of their husbands, cultivating large gardens and tending livestock (cattle, pigs, sheep, and goats), all of which are raised for local consumption. Many Kayak men and women own small stores that sell food and alcoholic beverages, or rum shops that sell alcoholic beverages and soft drinks for on-site consumption. Both enterprises serve as social centers where local residents meet and chat. In addition, a significant source of income for the island comes from the trafficking of contraband (locally termed *bobol*) that moves from Trinidad and South America to St. Vincent and beyond. Household appliances are the main items smuggled; there are occasionally rumors of drugs as well, although most of these are unsubstantiated.

Church life is very important for many Kayaks, most of whom are Catholic, Anglican, Protestant, or one of several messianic sects. Most Carriacouans have a range of spiritual beliefs that combine seemingly disparate African-derived and Western religious practices. It is common, for example, for Kayaks to attend church in the morning and then return home to prepare for a Big Drum ceremony in the evening. Similarly, Kayaks might attend a boat launching ceremony at which chickens are sacrificed and the blood scattered for good luck, followed by prayers and hymns led by the local Catholic priest. These intricately intertwined belief systems are an integral component of the society and easily coexist in the minds of Kayaks; one night a neighbor in our village of L'Esterre paid me a casual visit and, in the course of conversation, warned me that I needed to accept Jesus Christ as my savior if I wanted to protect myself and my family from *obeah* (witchcraft) and *maljo* (the evil eye or a hex) (M. Frazier, personal communication, 1997).

Carriacou is home to a wealth of expressive folk traditions that play an important role in Kayak social and religious life. The range of traditional musics in Carriacou, for example, reflects the diversity of their old-world heritage: instrumental music, song, and dance largely derived from African cultures (Ibo, Moko, Congo, Temne, Mandinka, Chamba, and Cromanti [Kay 1987, McDaniel 1998]) joins creolized English and French musical and lyrical genres. Since the early years of the twentieth century, a Latin American influence—primarily from Venezuela, Trinidad, and Aruba—can be heard in local musics, and particularly in the string band music tradition. At the same time, regional and transnational influences are steadily altering traditional culture and arts in Carriacou. KYAK, the local Carriacou station, and several regional radio stations bring popular music from the Anglo-Caribbean, such as soca, calypso, raggamuffin (also known as ragga), and reggae, as well as North American R&B and rap. Providing an almost constant aural backdrop to Carriacou daily life, these popular musics are played loudly from rum shops and the minibuses that provide transport.

Unlike many of the nearby islands, tourism has not been heavily developed in Carriacou, although there are guest houses, a small resort, and some services and activities that cater to visitors. However, tourism still has an effect on the performance contexts, repertoire, and aesthetic decisions made by Kayak string band musicians and by members of the L'Esterre Quadrille Group. Ensembles adapt to the increased opportunities for paid work by altering the semiotics of their performances (in the case of quadrille) or by adapting their repertoire to suit an outsider's notion of "the Caribbean."

Some Kayak practitioners of traditional music and dance worry that fewer Carriacouans—particularly the younger generation but also older members of the community—are interested in learning and/or participating in such expressive arts as string band music or quadrille music and dance (Fortune, interview, 1997; C. Bristol, interview, 1997; MacFarlane, interview, 1997). Most attribute this disinterest to a change in the pattern of cultural consumption in Carriacou: a steady rise in the presence of the media—radio, recordings produced outside of Carriacou, and particularly the growing number of television sets on the island—coupled with the importation of North American cable network programming. Increasingly, the opportunities for performing ritual and traditional genres give way as culture becomes more of a passive activity and one born outside of Carriacou.

Nevertheless, rituals involving music, song, and dance remain important in Carriacou, particularly the Big Drum ceremony. This African-derived percussion, song, and dance genre is central to sacred and life-cycle events and is performed in the yards of people's home upon the appearance of a deceased ancestor in a "dream message." To appease the spirits or simply to make an offering for the benefit of the community, a performance of the Big Drum is organized, complete with a *saraca* (accompanying feast). Together with the accompanying Nation Dances, this musical tradition was created in the early 1700s by enslaved Africans in Carriacou who mixed, transformed, and recreated a new genre from their respective West African and Congolese dance and song repertoires. As such, Carriacou's Big Drum ceremony, largely unique throughout the African diaspora, reveals a history of an enslaved people and offers another connection to Carriacouans' ethnic past. While the Big Drum is primarily a community-based ceremony, two formal troupes also present performances on stages in Carriacou and off-island.[4]

Creolized or syncretic styles of traditional music combining European and African musical elements, such as string band music and quadrille music, enjoy varying levels of popularity and performance among Carriacouans. While these genres may, on rare occasion, take the place of a Big Drum ceremony, string band music and quadrille dance have traditionally provided music and entertainment for social events. A cappella choral groups known as Hosannah bands combine local Afro-Caribbean singing styles with Western Church-based hymns and carols. A fading British-derived folk song and sea chantey tradition is now largely restricted to the northern village of Windward.

Amid Carriacou's many social, religious, and community celebrations, three major annual events stand out in terms of anticipation, planning, and production by organizers and audience alike: Carnival, an island-wide celebration prior to Lent that takes place for one week in February; Regatta, a five-day event in August that features sailing and boating races and land

and water contests for all ages; and the Parang Festival, a Christmastime weekend event that combines music and song competitions and performances. All three events garner publicity and acclaim and, organizers hope, attract tourists to Carriacou as well as expatriate Kayaks. Only the Parang Festival, however, presents the traditional music, song, and dance of Carriacou primarily to and by Kayaks.

INTRODUCING CARRIACOU PARANG

A three-day event that takes place the weekend before Christmas, the Parang Festival and the surrounding excitement is palpable four or five weeks beforehand. With an annual estimated budget of just over EC$93,000 (Eastern Caribbean dollars), the Parang Festival features two music competitions and a Saturday evening calypso concert. The competitions pit bands from Carriacou's villages against each other, reflecting a longstanding social orientation of village loyalty and inter-village rivalry. In the preceding weeks, the Parang Committee—an arm of the organizing group, the Mount Royal Progressive Youth Movement—distributes hundreds of small yellow flags with "PARANG" in blue letters for attachment to the antennae of cars. A huge banner with the dates of the event goes up in the center of Carriacou's main village of Hillsborough. The Carriacou post office starts stamping outgoing mail with an oval cancellation mark that reads "Pay A Visit For Carriacou Parang Festival" with the event's dates. The Parang Committee organizes concerts and dance parties in various villages throughout Carriacou to whip up excitement and fundraise for the event. Radio station KYAK plays songs from past festivals for weeks prior to the upcoming Parang and broadcasts live the three evenings' events in their entirety.

Friday night of Parang features the Hosannah band competition, in which a cappella vocal groups perform two Christmas carols, one of their choosing (the "choice" piece) and one assigned by the Parang Committee (the "test" piece). Combining lovely multipart harmony singing with a highly melismatic vocal style, Hosannah singers, at least in the context of the Parang Festival stage, offer a somewhat staid physical presence but sing with conviction and joy. Derived from the now largely defunct custom of strolling Christmas carolers, the Hosannah band competition is a formalized and staged recontextualization of what was once a church- and community-based celebration of the holiday. As an opening act for Friday and Saturday evenings, the L'Esterre Quadrille Group and/or one of the two formal Big Drum dance groups prime the gathered audience.

Saturday evening of Parang features a noncompetitive calypso show with performances by local, national, and regional musicians. A popular form that emerged in the late nineteenth century, calypso today is enjoyed by young and old alike in Carriacou and throughout the Anglo-Caribbean. Calypso powerfully and directly critiques the social and political elite and has fomented controversy since its inception (Warner 1982: 141; see also Rohlehr 1990). Calypso songs deal variously with affairs of love and other social relationships, "comment[ing] . . . on people's problems with each other . . . [by] draw[ing] attention to a discrepancy between an ideal form of living and actual life" (Hill 1993: 2–3). Other calypsos are geared towards celebratory or seasonal themes. In 1996, for example, the Parang Committee booked the charismatic calypso king, Ajamu (Edson Mitchell) from Grenada, whose rocking song "In de Parang Band" and seasonal plea "Put Back de Christ in Christmas" dominated local, national, and regional radio stations for months prior to Christmas. Ajamu's presence at the Saturday evening calypso concert added an element of regionalism and major prestige to that year's Parang Festival.

But of primary interest to Kayaks during the Parang Festival is the Sunday evening string band competition, which always boasts the largest audiences of the three evenings. To perform this creolized Caribbean musical style, string bands in Carriacou variously include the violin, guitar, bass guitar, Venezuelan *cuatro* (small, four-stringed guitar-like instrument), four-stringed banjo, locally made three-stringed banjo, and mandolin, as well as a wide range of percussion instruments. Each band hails from a different Carriacou village, thus reinforcing a historic tradition of village rivalry. All competing Parang Festival bands perform an assigned Christmas carol (the "test" piece) and, in the second round, an original composition (the "choice" piece), which is referred to as either the *melée* or the *lavway* and which comprises the centerpiece of the Parang Festival.[5] An original composition written collaboratively by band members, a *lavway* can be hysterically funny, completely subversive, and downright embarrassing. It consists of eight or ten four-line verses alternated with a catchy, four-line chorus. Each verse of the *lavway* offers a different "story" or item of gossip from the community, often featuring the embarrassing behavior of various community members. With each "story" culminating in a calypso-like *picong* ("sting"), the *lavway* reinforces community values and expectations as well as the vagaries of human nature.

The Parang Festival begins with a somewhat low-key, almost reverent atmosphere wholly appropriate to Christmas carol singing. The audience is sparse and comprised largely of older people as well as friends and family of Hosannah band members. By the second night, however, the ambiance is heightened to a party mode (locally described as "jump up") and attracts a much larger and younger audience. By Sunday night, crowds fill the performance venue with a nearly Carnivalesque atmosphere.

PARANG TRADITIONS IN TRINIDAD AND CARRIACOU

In Carriacou, "parang" refers both to a style of music and to the Christmastime tradition of serenading by local musicians, as the founder of the Parang Festival, Bentley Thomas, notes: "We would say here 'Let's go paranging.' When you talk about 'let's go paranging,' you're talking about a few musicians, a bunch of merrymakers, during the period leading up to and during the Christmas season, playing music and going from house to house" (interview, 1999).

It is unclear how seasonal serenading arrived in Carriacou. From 1608 to at least 1793, Capuchin Franciscans settled in Carriacou and attempted to proselytize the native Carib population (Devas 1974: 37, 187). It is entirely possible that the Capuchin brothers introduced this Christmastime serenading to the earliest enslaved Africans there. The tradition also may have developed as part of an ongoing cultural exchange between Trinidad and Carriacou beginning in the early 1800s (see McDaniel 1986, Hill 1977).[6] Indeed, the word "parang" is derived from the long-standing holiday tradition of serenading families, friends, and patrons in Venezuela as well as in Trinidad's Hispanic communities (Taylor 1977; V. Martin 1982; Sealey and Malm 1982). That the term "parang" is of probable Hispano-Trinidadian and/or Venezuelan origin is also underscored by its Spanish derivation, *parran,* an abbreviation of *parranda,* meaning "spree" or "carousel" and used colloquially to refer to four or more musicians who go out at night singing with musical instruments.[7]

While serenading in Trinidad is no longer as widespread as it once was, the parang tradition there has always had social, religious, and cultural import. With its origins firmly rooted in Trinidad's Afro-Spanish population, parang serenading traditionally begins during the last week of November and ends on January 6, the *Dia de los Reyes* ("Day of the Kings [Magi]"). As in Carriacou, Trinidadian musicians serenade from house to house, eventually covering several neighboring villages. Musicians perform secular parang songs (*estribillos* and *sabana blancas*) and songs about the nativity and other religious themes (for example, *aguinaldos*); they also play for social and couples dances.[8] They might also perform a *guarapo,* an improvised song about the family and friends who are hosting them. After food and drink, and praises and blessings for the household, the musicians depart for the next house, often accompanied by those who were just serenaded.

In like manner, Carriacou string bands traditionally serenade throughout the villages for weeks or even months prior to Christmas. Their repertoire includes Christmas songs and secular songs but none of the other religious songs commonly associated with Trinidad parang musicians. As in Trinidad, "parang" in Carriacou refers to the activity as well as the song genre (and the aforementioned *lavway*).

Beginning in the late 1960s the aesthetic and functional aspects of Afro-Spanish parang in Trinidad changed as the media and the recording industry increasingly included traditional parang music in Christmas broadcasts of Anglo-American Christmas carols and songs. The first publicly staged performance of parang music was in 1967 as part of Trinidad's Best Village Competition, a program designed by Trinidad and Tobago's first prime minister, Eric Williams, to inspire newly independent Trinidad to reassess and revive its traditional music and culture. Within the next few years, a neotraditional parang style emerged as Trinidadian businessmen and radio programmers saw marketing and consumer potential in this music and began organizing parang competitions that attracted large audiences from outside the traditional parang region. The tradition was further institutionalized with the 1971 formation of the Trinidad and Tobago Parang Association and its subsequent reformation into the National Parang Association of Trinidad and Tobago, which today produces a Christmastime parang fiesta. According to Amelia Ingram, this annual event remains a "deeply embedded part of the national cultural calendar and has come to embody a national Christmas tradition, as participants have widened to all ethnicities/backgrounds" (Ingram, personal communication, 2005).

These presentations and competitions moved musicians from the yards and homes of their friends and neighbors to the stage. Along with this massive change in venue and performance context came stylistic changes in the music: the competition format privileged an emerging popular aesthetic over the older folk style. Instead of a relaxed, rolling rhythm, parang songs increasingly were played with "a hard driving, mechanical rhythm" (Sealey and Malm 1982: 36) with a faster tempo and less emphasis on lyrics and other adaptations. In addition, parang songs in Trinidad were traditionally improvised in the creolized Spanish spoken by Afro-Spanish Trinidadians; participants in the large Trinidadian parang competitions no longer improvise their lyrics, largely because most performers, like their new audiences, neither speak nor understand the language in which they are singing. Thus the folk emphasis on lyrics and personal improvisation is rendered irrelevant. Some scholars feel that the commercialization of Trinidadian parang music has served to reinvigorate the tradition and that the competition format is congruent with other aspects of Trinidadian music culture (Manuel 1995: 184). Others argue that this relatively new competitive format, one increasingly mediated by radio airplay, is a stark example of how governmental and corporate appropriation and institutionalization of this music has caused its demise in terms of community meaning and significance (Malm 1978: 43, Sealey and Malm 1982: 35–36).

Trinidad's annual Parang competition served, in part, as the model for local cultural expression for a small group of civic-minded Carriacouans, who established the Carriacou Parang Festival in 1977. For some, the Kayak use of the term "parang" is contentious. Elwyn McQuilkin, Cultural Officer at the Grenada Ministry of Culture and a judge for the Carriacou Parang Festival, feels that the Kayak use of the term is culturally inauthentic because it refers to the Trinidadian event. Its use in Carriacou, he believes, is "commercially" the right choice, in terms of "selling the show" (interview, 1997). Kayak string band musician Kenly Joseph disagrees, noting that what defines the notion of parang universally is string band music: "I think we could call it whatever we want to call it. And let's say if in Venezuela, [they] call theirs Parang, and you could have different Parang. Parang is like string band music. . . . Okay, Venezuelan is string band also. And once all is string, we can call our own Parang, just like them. We just have a different beat" (interview, 1997). Similarly, Carriacou string band musician Jerry McGillivary sees the Kayak use of the term "parang" as mirroring the Trinidadian but also specific to Carriacou, where it is often referred to by its other local moniker, *melée:* "You see, we have a tradition, just as Trinidad have a tradition. Right? Trinidad Parang and Carriacou Parang is two different thing. You see how we call it the *melée?* And look at what we calling *'melée'* in Carriacou. What they call it "Parang" in Trinidad" (interview, 1997).

The Parang Festivals in both Trinidad and Carriacou were born in the years immediately following each country's formal independence. Both festivals were informed by a growing nationalism and a self-conscious engagement with the notion of heritage—responses common to newly independent nations. Trinidad gained independence in 1962; the first staged competitions of parang music there took place in 1967 and coincided with an era of increasing political and social self-awareness, both in terms of national identity and of the value of local culture (Ingram, personal communication, 2005). Carriacou's Parang Festival similarly signaled a reassessment of its heritage and served as a strategy for preserving traditional Kayak culture. While the recontextualization of what were once community-based traditions as a staged competition is common to both places, the Carriacou Parang Festival, in contrast to the Trinidad Parang Festival, does not allow electric instruments and stresses folk authenticity over popular commercial aesthetics. Carriacou also privileges a discourse of social expectation and norms through its emphasis on original verses sung in the local English Creole. While the profits from Trinidad's Parang Festival go largely to the businessmen who organize and advertise the event, Carriacou's Parang Festival is produced by volunteers and serves as the major fundraiser for the island's largest charitable group, the Mount Royal Progressive Youth Movement. All proceeds are returned throughout the year to Kayaks in need, thus addressing a historically fragile economic infrastructure while reinforcing the traditional cultural notion of self-help by and for Carriacouans.

The Parang Festival and especially the string band competition offers Kayaks the opportunity to reinforce social mores and expectations while simultaneously affirming social belonging. The entire event allows for community participation concerning issues of cultural authenticity, particularly as Carriacou undergoes transformation generated by global processes of modernization. Moreover, the Parang Festival can be used to gauge an emergent postcolonial identity in Carriacou that is simultaneously informed by a growing sense of cultural autonomy and by a seemingly oppositional trend toward solidarity with the larger Caribbean community. I examine these issues in this study through a contextualization of the genesis of the

Parang Festival in terms of social and culture history as well as ethnographic methodologies. I focus initially on the years between 1950 and 1984, a period marked by widespread poverty and emigration, the end of British colonialism, and the attainment of independence from Britain in 1974, which was followed by the neo-colonial, post-independence government of the late prime minister Eric Gairy. More critical to the formation of the Parang Festival are the years just before Grenada's 1979 Socialist Revolution, the revolution itself, and the subsequent establishment of the People's Revolutionary Government under the late prime minister Maurice Bishop, which ended, four and a half years later, in bloodshed and the invasion by U.S. troops in 1983.

Drawing on contemporary ethnographic approaches, I also examine the component parts of the Parang Festival—string band music, Hosannah bands, and quadrille music and dance. I focus on these traditional musical expressions with respect to their transformed roles in the cultural and social lives of Carriacouans and to the changing social realities and political sensibilities that have informed their recontextualization from community-based forms of expression to staged genres and/or competitions. I argue that culture and identity on the island are shaped in some way by a distanced yet ongoing collective memory of enslavement and colonial subjugation, and I analyze the new meanings and significances that each of these musical forms holds for their practitioners and audience members today.

THEORETICAL UNDERPINNINGS: DOUBLE DEPENDENCY

Elements of Carriacou parang are reflective of a long history of poverty as well as this society's contemporary process of modernization. Historically, Carriacou's fragile economic foundation has tended to break down in the face of social upheaval, largely the result of its historically marginalized status as a dependency island of Grenada, which was itself a dependent colony of France and then Britain. This peculiar status as a dependency of a dependency—what I term a "double dependency"—typically results in economic neglect and political disempowerment. As a plantation economy, Carriacouan landowners once benefited from their place in global markets as Grenada's dependency: when demand for sugar and cotton overwhelmed Grenada's own production capacity, Carriacou's plantations reaped the benefits. With the collapse of slavery and in the years following emancipation, Carriacou, like other double dependencies, was severed from this global involvement.

In addition, economic and political resources tend to concentrate in the colonies closest to the ruling hegemony. In the years between emancipation and independence, Grenada reaped whatever benefits there were to be had from its colonial relationship to Britain, with little going to the outer islands in the way of infrastructural, technical, or economic support from the governing mainland. Because of this ongoing history of neglect, Carriacou's educational and health facilities and overall infrastructure today range from inadequate and underfunded to wholly absent. This economic fragility and failure to integrate into the global economy characterizes other double dependencies. In Tobago, for example, a historical dearth of linkages to the British ruling elite, combined with years of economic deprivation in the educational sectors, resulted in the lack of formation of a middle class (MacDonald 1986: 30). Other double dependencies have sought radical political change to ameliorate their economic dysfunction. The population of Anguilla, for example, rebelled in 1967 after 153 years of trade and fiscal policy discrimination by the metropole island of St. Kitts, choosing in 1971 to revert to the status of a British dependency rather than remain a dependency of St. Kitts and Nevis (Brisk 1969: 14–15).[9] Barbuda, a former slave-breeding colony, ceased to function as a contributor to the global economy after emancipation. All but ignored by Antigua (itself a former colony of Britain), Barbudans attempted a failed secession in 1969 (Henry, personal communication, 1997; see also Lazarus-Black 1994: 225 and Bissio 1988).

CYCLES OF GIVING AND FOLK INSTITUTIONS

To compensate for the neglect and poverty wrought by its double-dependency status, Carriacouans have generated a complex intra-island economy based on reciprocity, volunteerism, and cycles of giving. Gift-giving ranges from a simple present such as a *paw-paw* (papaya) or a bowl of *cerise* (tree cherries) to clothing or small appliances. In response to fluctuating levels of need over the years among Kayaks, this redistribution of resources also evolved into what Donald Hill (1977) terms "folk institutions," borrowing from Andrew Pearse's study of mid-nineteenth-century Trinidad (1956a). Folk institutions arise within the community around traditional forms and modes of communication, transmitting the values and aspirations of the people. With little support emanating from mainland Grenada, Carriacouans were forced to look to each other, and folk institutions such as informal cycles of giving provided a crucial support system.

Hill contrasts folk institutions with "metropolitan institutions," imposed colonial entities that were generally outside the control of Carriacouans such as the Church and the colonial Grenadian government. Overseeing the administrative infrastructure of Carriacou, among other things, such metropolitan institutions relied on the written record and other standardized modes of administration. Folk institutions, on the other hand, were maintained by local elders, who passed on knowledge orally and filtered cultural elements from metropolitan institutions as well as returning migrants for use in Kayak folk culture. Folk institutions such as the Mount Royal Progressive Youth Movement continue to operate on a volunteer basis, receiving little if any support from larger governmental institutions.[10]

INTRODUCING CULTURAL AMBIVALENCE

Years of colonial rule of Grenada and her dependencies resulted in the transmission of the European ruling elite's values and aesthetics to Carriacou's Afro-Caribbean population. This imposition, particularly given the gross disparities of power between the two populations, has had decidedly mixed results. On one hand, the organic processes of cultural syncretism over more than two centuries resulted in the growth of a unique and richly complex culture on Carriacou, whereby new, creative forms emerge from the collision of different cultures. The result, points out Michael Dash, is an ongoing process that is at once "dynamic and unpredictable" (Dash 1996: 47).

On the other hand, this imposition also resulted in cultural colonization. In pointing to some of the psychological repercussions of colonialism, Gordon K. Lewis notes that the colonized subject might respond to "ingrained prejudices of racial superiority" by assimilating them and ultimately accepting the low cultural status conferred by the colonizer's ideological system: "The whole system of colonial government and education has persuaded him that success in life depends upon his acceptance, not only in mind, but also in deeper, innermost spirit, of the metropolitan standards by which success is defined. This leads in turn to the psychopathology of rejection, which includes not only the rejection of native roots in culture and religion but, even more, the rejection of self; the colonized person learns to live a life of self-denigration and even at times self-hatred" (Lewis 1987: 133).

The imposition of elements of European culture and the unique connection that Carriacouans maintain with their African past have in specific instances resulted in what I term cultural ambivalence, the contemporary contestation of the meaning and significance of certain historic expressive modes. Carriacouans express this ambivalence largely toward some creolized genres, indicating a level of discomfort felt by some toward European-derived expressive arts. Cultural ambivalence is a direct result of syncretic processes and their subsequent formation (and re-formation) of identity. It is most evident during periods of major social, political, or economic upheaval—moments of societal fracture when identity must be renegotiated in the face of external forces.

Caribbean scholars have long drawn upon a general notion of ambivalence to explain a variety of cultural processes. Melville Herskovits used "socialized ambivalence" to refer to what he interpreted as incongruous European and African elements that generated discomfort among Haitian peasants, resulting in a "fundamental clash of custom within the culture" (Herskovits 1937: 295). Other scholars underscore a common thread of political domination, enslavement, and colonialism as an underlying cause of ambivalence in the Caribbean (see, for example, Austerlitz 1997, Bourguignon 1951, Fanon 1963, and Singham 1968) and among former colonial subjects in Ireland and among Irish Americans (Miller 1996). In recent years, the work of contemporary Caribbean and African American novelists has also seized upon this theme of ambivalence in clarifying complex issues of identity, family, and the notion of home (see, for example, Alvarez 1998, Danticat 1994, Kincaid 1990, and Marshall 1983).

With its recontextualized music and dance traditions, the Parang Festival also resonates with the now historic academic polemic of African cultural retention throughout the black Atlantic. While scholars in the mid-twentieth century disagreed about the degree or relevance of African cultural retention among African American diasporic communities,[11] a contemporary paradigm has emerged from this discourse that focuses less on the question of African cultural retention than on the processes of cultural creation and the need for historical evidence to shed light on the development of African American culture (Gates 1988, Levine 1977, Mintz and Price 1992, Price and Price 1980). Denis-Constant Martin (1991) notes that privileging heritage or filiation, whether African or European, denies that black Atlantic communities are capable of creating new and truly black cultures; what is instead important, he insists, is the process of cultural innovation. Building on this, Andrew Apter argues that the concept of cultural syncretism in the African diaspora must be amended to include both an understanding of the process of "the inventedness (and inventiveness) of New World African identities" as well as their "cultural and historical associations with West African peoples" (Apter 1991: 236). The appropriation of European-derived cultural forms by the enslaved and their descendants in the Americas is thus essentially cultural piracy, an act of "resistance waged through syncretic struggle" (Apter 1991: 253). At the same time, such appropriation serves to reproduce and perpetuate the dominant culture. For some, this results in feelings of profound ambivalence toward the appropriated material itself, while for others, such appropriation is accepted as part of "the African family" (Adams, interview, 1995).

REVOLUTION: THEORY AND PRACTICE

The 1979 Grenadian Socialist Revolution and subsequent four and a half years of governance under the People's Revolutionary Government (PRG) ushered in a period of massive political and social upheaval. Amid myriad political and economic challenges, the PRG, like other newly formed liberal nationalist and socialist states, deployed local cultural symbolism to legitimize a national initiative toward cultural decolonization, or the "attempt to shake off the values of the colonizer and to reclaim and revalorize the native heritage" (Henry 1983: 56, 118; see also Henry 1990). Kayaks thus were challenged to reconsider issues of heritage and identity through national cultural programs that underscored their African past. Other educational and cultural initiatives focused on the notion of regional, pan-Caribbean membership, an often articulated ideology by then prime minister Maurice Bishop (see, for example, Bishop 1979a). A variant of Du Bois's early-twentieth-century notion of pan-Africanism (Du Bois 1969), pan-Caribbeanism in Carriacou translated into staged presentations of music, art, poetry, and other expressive genres by artists from elsewhere in the Caribbean. Similarly, programs designed to underscore the connections between Africa and Afro-Caribbeans as well as competitions to better involve the masses were seen as strategies toward fomenting a new identity and reframing culture as a matter of political significance. The PRG similarly emphasized local solidarity for rebuilding Carriacou through the development of symbols of unity such as state- and locally organized work cooperatives—a politicized version of self-help, youth groups, and educational programs largely modeled after C. L. R. James's application of Marxist principles to the Black Power movement (James 1967). On an international level, Prime Minister Bishop and others worked toward a geopolitical application of pan-Caribbeanism through the signing of the Treaty of Basseterre in 1981, which resulted in the establishment of the Organization of Eastern Caribbean States (OECS).

The genesis of the Parang Festival can also be viewed in terms of Frantz Fanon's theory of liberation as the second moment of decolonization (Fanon 1963), particularly in tandem with Edward Said's extension of that notion. In contrast to nationalism and, as Said notes, as an alternative to nativism (for example, *négritude*), liberationist ideology develops after the attainment of national independence, at which point societies begin to look inward, critique themselves, and question extant class distinctions (Said 1994). At this point, the people are "called upon to fight against poverty, illiteracy, and underdevelopment" (Fanon 1963: 93–94)—in short, a move toward modernization. With its emphasis on the maintenance of local Kayak culture, the Carriacou Parang Festival offers a platform for the public critique and contestation of social mores while endeavoring to expand the Kayak sense of a greater Afro-Caribbean belonging. The Parang Festival thus minimizes the ideal of nationalism with Grenada, rather insisting on cultural autonomy and local identity while moving toward regional belonging and unity with other Caribbean peoples.

FIELDWORK, GENDER, PREGNANCY, AND CULTURAL DIFFERENCE

I conducted fieldwork in Carriacou between 1995 and 2001 through visits ranging in duration from three weeks to nearly one year. Like all fieldwork experiences, there were many delightful moments and outcomes, made possible, no doubt, by the fact that Carriacouans are very welcoming, not to mention full of good humor and warmth. Fieldwork was largely a pleasure, as was developing what I anticipate will be lifelong friendships with many Kayaks.

Nevertheless, fieldwork could also be challenging to the extreme. Becoming accustomed to realities such as "Kayak time" (events generally begin two hours later than advertised) was easy compared to the larger cultural differences and misunderstandings. On several occasions, for example, it was suggested (never to my face, in true Kayak fashion) that I was there to "tief" (steal from) local musicians. Coming from a ten-year background of cultural advocacy on behalf of immigrants and refugees in the United States, these moments of distrust were personally devastating. As a public sector folklorist in the United States, my relationship with traditional musicians was somewhat more equal; I could offer something in return, such as artist fees (most notably) as well as the prestige of a completed film/video or public radio documentary, the opportunity to perform in a concert setting, a completed CD recording, and so on. But fieldworkers in search of information for an academic dissertation have little to offer in return, apart from volunteering in various capacities within the community.

As a well-trained student of ethnomusicology, I arrived in Carriacou wholly subscribing to the concept of participant observation—that is, I would live as much as possible in the manner of the native Carriacouans. While we indeed lived in the community in a house that was typical of many Kayaks, it is also true that our income was derived from various research fellowships that covered our expenses. And while I accepted the exigencies of life in a so-called "third world" culture (electricity cutting out, fresh water cisterns running dry, and so on), I knew that these inconveniences were temporary because I would ultimately return to the United States. I also knew that if illness struck, we could fly home to advanced medical technology, in contrast to what is available to most Carriacouans. This became a horrible reality a few years after we returned from Carriacou, when we were notified of the death of our former neighbor in L'Esterre, a generous and kind woman slightly younger than me, whose illness had not received the requisite medical attention in time and whose death might have been prevented with adequate health care. I have to conclude then that the notion of participant observation is at best a fantasy given the very real disparities of wealth and power of the observed and the observer, not to mention the inherently temporary nature of fieldwork.

Still, participant observation does earn some semblance of validity when applied to learning and exchanging music in realistic performance contexts. While my fieldwork in Carriacou was often complicated by what seemed to be insurmountable cultural differences, what remained a constant was the pleasure of playing string band music in sessions with Kayak musicians, occasionally teaching an American dance tune to another violinist, and learning to play quadrille violin music with Canute Caliste. While it is simplistic to assert the existence of a universal understanding among musicians regarding aesthetic expectation and, in particular, social behavior during music gatherings, there are crucial moments when the music and the sense of a musical community and camaraderie take over. Cultural difference is eased, though not erased, via the sheer sonic and kinesthetic energy and joy of playing music together.

In learning the Kayak violin style—a beautiful improvisatory technique that subtly embeds rhythmic complexity within the context of melody—I sought out such masters as the late Norris George, Harrison Fleary, "Tailor" Coy, and Lawrence Chase, all of whom were as gracious as they were generous with their time. I also learned much about the propulsive polyrhythms of string band accompaniment through such guitarists, banjo players, and mandolinists as Godwin Moses, Jerry McGillivary, Desmond Dixon, Ronald Jones, Kenly (Rhyno) Joseph, Lionel Stiell, Enel James, the late Marxman Joseph, Anselm James, and Welcome Cummins. My husband and I frequently played alongside Carriacou's finest musicians in sessions at rum shops, parties, pre-wedding celebrations, *saracas* (feasts), and other community events. On Christmas and New Year's Day we went serenading from house to house with many of our friends—musicians, singers, and revelers from our village of L'Esterre. We often played music on our porch with local musicians who stopped by for a drink and a tune, and, in turn, we were invited to music sessions at the homes of musicians elsewhere on the island. Our reputation spread: we were eventually asked to perform as a duo for various community shows and events. Tom, who volunteered as a music teacher at Hillsborough Secondary School, was asked by the Church of Christ, also in the main village of Hillsborough, to teach congregants how to read music, which he happily did for five months.

As I completed this book, I was notified in late November 2005 of the death of my main teacher, Canute Caliste, a master of quadrille violin music and the last practitioner of this style in Carriacou. Mr. Caliste (affectionately known as "Mr. Canute" or "CC") and I had become great friends. I had the very good fortune to learn a substantial portion of his quadrille dance repertoire as well as other dance and listening tunes. Mr. Caliste's enthusiasm eventually put other residents at ease when I accompanied him and/or played next to him at social events. (Some might have viewed me initially with suspicion, perhaps as someone who might be trying to "tief" Mr. Caliste. He was also a well-known folk artist who made his living by painting beautiful images of Carriacou life and culture. Over the years, he was the victim of the occasional unscrupulous art collector, publisher, or tourist; his family and fellow villagers were therefore extremely protective of him.) My enthusiasm in turn stimulated some local, albeit passing, interest in playing the violin; I was asked to teach the basics of the instrument to two of Canute Caliste's grandchildren, though they apparently abandoned it. Apart from mourning the death of a great friend, I reluctantly acknowledge that his passing might very well spell the end of the quadrille music and dance tradition in Carriacou.

As a former public radio journalist and a longtime fan of the spoken word, my research relies largely on in-depth interviews and, more specifically, oral histories to best present ethnography and cultural history. I thus spent many happy hours doing high-quality tape-recorded interviews with musicians, singers, dancers, civic and political leaders, and business owners in Carriacou, Grenada, and neighboring islands such as Petit St. Vincent, one of the islands of St. Vincent. In Grenada's capital city, St. George's, I made use of the National Archives of Grenada and other sites that housed historic documents. The main portion of the National Archives is located in a single room of the main public library, and I spent hours there reading original newspapers from the early 1800s to the present. While I appreciate the easy access to such a wealth of historical documentation, I fear for the physical integrity of these materials and continue to hope that someday they will be preserved on microfiche. Other fieldwork methodologies included making audio recordings, taking still photographs, and shooting video footage of musical performances and social events. This latter component of my fieldwork was by far the most contentious, twice resulting in accusations that I would take music back to the United States and somehow profit from it. I was not able to iron out these misunderstandings, resulting in a handful of musicians who ultimately distanced themselves from me and my work. The reality of my best intentions notwithstanding, I have, over time, come to suspect that this attitude might have been less about me personally than about a painful legacy of ongoing cultural and economic exploitation of Kayaks, first by Europeans and, more recently, by North Americans.

Finally, the issue of gender was a constant source of interest and entrée as much as a basis of puzzlement or misunderstanding. String band music

is almost exclusively a male-dominated tradition; the two Kayak women
who participate in string bands do so mostly for the annual Parang Festival.
I know of only two other woman instrumentalists—a bass player in Carriacou and a *cuatro* player in Petit Martinique. As a lone white woman who
played the violin—the lead voice in a string band—and other instruments
well enough to participate in string band performances, I was, at the very
least, correctly perceived as an oddity, but I was nevertheless always made
welcome in music gatherings.

Gender, however, certainly did inform my fieldwork research, and my
results. When I was in Carriacou without my husband, I was immersed in
the men's world of music making, which is locally associated with revelry,
alcohol, and late nights, none of which are considered appropriate for
women. Nevertheless, the stuff of fieldwork was never easier: I was invited
to participate in regular music sessions, always offered rides to these events,
and largely included in this community. But I had blinders on: Kayak culture demands modesty on the part of men and women. Just as Carriacouans
frown on European and American women and men who walk about Hillsborough in bare feet and bathing suits, so, too, did I occasionally hear concerns about why I chose to play music in the evenings at social events. This
begs the question of whether academic fieldworkers are on some level ethi-
cally obligated to conform to the prevailing cultural standards (in my case,
essentially ending that particular path of research) to avoid the appearance
of disrespect of local values.

This might have changed somewhat when Tom and I settled in L'Esterre
in September 1996 for what would be nearly a year's stay. Because I was in
the company of my husband, my "problem" of late-night music sessions
seemed at first to be ameliorated. However, I was three-and-a-half-months
pregnant when we arrived, and as soon as I started to "show," I understood
there to be general criticism (again, never to my face) about the inappropri-
ateness of a pregnant woman being out late in a party atmosphere. There
seemed to be a fair degree of understandable suspicion as to why I was there
at all, as pregnant European or North American women rarely opt to
give birth in a country where medical facilities are less advanced than at
home. Indeed, a small number of pregnant Grenadian and Carriacouan
women—those who can afford to—travel to the United States so that their
babies are born with all the benefits of medical technology and, potentially,
American citizenship to boot.

Despite all of this, the fact of my pregnancy added an exceptionally complicated but delightful dimension to my fieldwork in Carriacou. For one thing, it opened up opportunities to forge wonderful and enduring friendships with many Kayak women. I was welcomed into the local women's culture, a community that I had sorely missed during earlier visits thanks to my almost exclusive involvement in the male world of string band music performance. And because I was pregnant, my fieldwork necessarily extended to other aspects of Carriacou culture. I was an avid participant observer in the field of ante-natal (pre-natal) care, as administered by the very capable Carriacouan nurse-midwives. I was invited to attend workshops for Kayak women on childcare and nutrition, at which I took careful notes. I documented Kayak and Grenadian folklore concerning pregnancy, labor, delivery, and infant care. And I routinely drank the various herbal teas recommended by my Grenadian midwife and by Kayak women (lemon grass tea, for example, is a tasty and excellent remedy for an upset stomach). Some advice was questionable too: I was urged, for example, to avoid vinegar, hot sauces, and spices such as cinnamon and ginger because ingestion of these, according to local lore, would blind the baby while in the womb. I was also privy to much practical advice about caring for a newborn during the Carriacou dry season (a terrible time to be born, it turns out, given the propensity of many Carriacou cisterns to run out of water before the advent of the rainy season).[12] Many other incidents, great and small, involving pregnancy and attitudes towards pregnant women and/or childbirth opened my eyes to new dimensions of the Kayak belief system. Through it all, I continued my fieldwork and research, and on March 15, 1997, I gave birth to our red-haired, blue-eyed son, Samuel Randall, in Richmond Hill, St. Georges, Grenada.

Sam's arrival into this world was unexpectedly hailed two months later, in early May 1997, when we attended one of Carriacou's largest *maroons* (a celebration that honors the ancestors) in the village of Limlair. Winston Fleary, a cultural activist and Big Drum musician and dancer, was about to lead a large procession from the graveyard at the top of the village to the crossroads where the Big Drum ceremony would take place. Having helped me in the past with my fieldwork and now seeing me as a spectator with Sam in my arms, Fleary, dressed in his ceremonial robes, approached me and took Sam, carrying him close to his chest as he led the procession through the village. At one point, a spectator from the crowd called out "Winston carry white man baby!" Fleary smiled. I smiled. Everything was exactly right: Sam's participation in the procession celebrated new life in the context of honoring the dead. It also offered a poignant reminder of a fundamental life-cycle connection shared by all cultures, but one that nevertheless must coexist with the complicating realities of cultural and racial difference.

ON LANGUAGE/ORGANIZATION

This study relies on interviews undertaken with many Carriacouans. Some Carriacouans speak only the local English Creole, a language that contains structural elements from English and French and vocabulary borrowed from these languages as well as African sources. (See Kephart 2000 for an in-depth study on Carriacou Creole.) Others speak a range of languages from the local Creole to a "Queen's" (or metropolitan) English. All interviews used herein are transcribed verbatim and reflect exactly the local grammar. For the sake of readability, these transcriptions do not indicate local variations and variants in pronunciation, for example "de" for "the." I also avoid the use of the convention [sic] in my transcriptions, because such notation implies an "error" in grammar. Local grammar is correct grammar, and if we are to understand Carriacouan culture, it must be on—indeed, in—its own terms.

I begin this study with a social and political history of the era during which Carriacou's Parang Festival was born, specifically the genesis of the People's Revolutionary Government (PRG) and its mixed successes in organizing Carriacouans. In chapter 2, I analyze the politically generated programs in Carriacou from this era, those that promoted a cultural decolonization of the people through a foregrounding of African-derived arts and a similar but smaller revival of creolized cultural forms such as quadrille dance and string band music.

The remainder of this study is structured around Parang weekend, examining in turn each of the component parts of the festival.[13] Because the L'Esterre Quadrille Group often performs at the beginning of one of the Parang evenings, chapter 3 offers a history and contemporary ethnography of quadrille music and dance and introduces the notion of cultural ambivalence. I argue that the professionalization of quadrille in Carriacou in part serves to negotiate the conflicted perceptions of and ambivalent feelings toward the genre among Kayaks. For many, quadrille is a beacon of Kayak identity despite its associations with enslavement and colonialism. Because of this, I argue that collective memory in tandem with the processes of creolization can give rise to new and unique cultural forms, and that this is a creative and empowering (if often messy) process.

Chapter 4 is a study of the Friday night Hosannah band competition and the dynamics generated by inter-village rivalry, fueled in some instances by racial difference among Carriacouans. I also examine the influences that over the years have moved Hosannah singing from its community-based roots toward an increasingly homogenized Church choral aesthetic. Germane to this discussion was my role as the outsider who coached one of the competing Hosannah bands and the conflicts inherent in working directly with the musicians and singers who were the subjects of my study.

In chapter 5, I introduce Carriacou string bands—the music, performance contexts, performance practice, and significance to performers as well as the increasingly diverse audiences. The most visible performance context for string band players is the climactic Sunday evening string band competition of the Parang Festival, which is then the subject of chapter 6. As the event that has come to define the Parang Festival, this competition, through the *lavways* performed by each band, consistently reflects the contemporary values and local mores of Carriacou culture and offers a snapshot of this society's concerns. While some aspects of the performances privilege local aesthetics and articulate the primacy of cultural autonomy, others borrow from regional musical signifiers—gestures that insist on some Carriacouan connection and affiliation with the greater Afro-Caribbean community, hearkening back to the years of the PRG. In the final chapter I look at the overarching issues brought into relief by the Parang Festival, including the maintenance of traditional social values in Carriacou society, the negotiation of cultural identity in the face of modernization, and the increasingly outward focus of Kayaks toward a regional, Afro-Caribbean belonging.

2

⊚⊚

"FORWARD EVER, BACKWARD NEVER!"

The People's Revolutionary Government
and the Makings of the Parang Festival

ON OCTOBER 25, 1983, by order of President Ronald Reagan, six thousand U.S. Marines and Green Berets invaded Grenada under "Operation Urgent Fury." Coming six days after the assassination of the Grenadian prime minister, Maurice Bishop, and four of his cabinet members in a military-backed coup, the invasion brought an abrupt end to four and a half years of Grenada's socialist government. Given its close ties to Cuba, Grenada was perceived to be a threat to U.S. security. The military action was ultimately sold to the American public largely on the basis of the need to rescue American medical students in the capital city of St. George's. During a White House briefing on the day of the invasion, President Reagan outlined his additional concerns: "to protect innocent lives, including up to 1,000 Americans . . . to forestall further chaos. And third, to assist in the restoration of conditions of law and order . . . where a brutal group of leftist thugs violently seized power" (Ronald Reagan, as cited in Payne et al. 1984: 154).

Some scholars describe the 1979 coup and Grenada's subsequent experiment in socialism as too short-lived to qualify as a Marxist success (P. Henry 1990: 80), while others argue that these years were "a heroic effort in social and economic reconstruction and, at times, transformation" (Lewis 1987: 26). Tony Thorndike asserts that Grenada's revolutionary government developed into a paternalistic socialism with an "authoritarian and undemocratic core where dissent could, and was, met with severe punishment," conditions that ultimately failed to garner widespread public support (Thorndike 1990: 47). Still other scholars note that Bishop's administration ultimately moved away from a hardline socialist ideology toward a more grassroots democracy and economic cooperativism (see, for example, Lewis 1987, Sunshine 1985). Whatever their political direction, successes, or failures, Bishop and his administration, the People's Revolutionary Government (PRG), sought to move Grenada into a larger cooperative social and economic relationship with other Caribbean states in the name of regional unity and solidarity. At the same time, the PRG aimed to provide the nation with progressive social change from within, encouraging popular participation and dialogue as well as cultural programs that would prove critical to the development of a collective postcolonial identity.

This impetus to societal self-knowledge was particularly effective in Carriacou. Many of the PRG cultural programs helped to undo years of colonial oppression and loosen the mindset of dependency instilled by European hegemony. By highlighting expressive arts that spoke to Carriacouans' African heritage as well as syncretic genres that developed in Carriacou over two centuries as uniquely Kayak, the PRG programs began the process of forming a postcolonial identity. Through its inter-Caribbean cultural initiatives, in turn, such as foregrounding Creole language programs, writing and poetry workshops, and events that featured visiting artists from Africa and other parts of the Caribbean, the PRG helped create a sense of regional and global belonging and unity.

One of the projects in Carriacou that emerged two years before the Socialist Revolution and expanded during the early years of the PRG was the Christmastime music festival and competition called the Parang Festival. Its organizers initially sought to stem the massive migration away from the island, address local poverty through self-help, and revive a flagging Kayak musical tradition. Founded in 1977, the Parang Festival emerged during an era when revolutionary and anti-neocolonialist ideologies permeated the country. In many ways, Parang was a local response to daunting social and economic pressures that was fueled by a sense of community empowerment and the possibility of massive social change, a possibility that ultimately resulted in revolution.

A group of committed Kayak activists, Parang Festival organizing committee members have repeatedly asserted that their organization always was and still is nonpolitical in its approach and nature (W. Collins, interview, 1997; J. Collins, interview, 1997; Thomas, interview, 1999). Yet this era of unprecedented progressive ideological thought and political upheaval nevertheless left its mark, and the infrastructure and organizational strategies of the Parang Festival committee and of the PRG are remarkably similar, particularly those designed to garner and solidify popular support. While some of the PRG's structure served as a model for the Parang Festival's organizing committee, many of the PRG's cultural and educational initiatives were successful in Carriacou precisely because they paralleled extant social institutions and hierarchies—signifying systems that were already familiar to Kayak culture.

Because the Parang Festival was and remains primarily a local initiative designed to foster the community-based tradition of self-help and inter-reliance among Kayaks, it brings into sharp relief Carriacou's troubled history as a dependency of Grenada, which itself was, for years, a dependency of England. This complicated postcolonial relationship of the double dependency society (Carriacou) to the metropole (Grenada) in part stimulated the Parang Festival's genesis and continues to inform its structure, aesthetics, and approach as a source of cultural representation and expression for Kayaks.

"AH CAN'T STAY NO MORE IN CARRIACOU": GRENADIAN INDEPENDENCE AND THE FOUNDING OF THE PARANG FESTIVAL

The history of Carriacou's Parang Festival begins in 1974, the year that Grenada gained independence from England. As a dependency (or "Ward Island") of Grenada, Carriacou had, at this point, experienced some twenty-eight years of economic neglect under the neocolonial government of Prime Minister Sir Eric Gairy. Gairy emerged in 1951 as the charismatic leader of the populist movement, an agitator who hailed from Grenada's black working class and opposed the white power elite and brown middle class. He ruled alongside the British colonial administrators—often in conflict—until 1974; as head of a newly independent state, Gairy's near-totalitarian style of governing worsened, as did conditions throughout the nation. By the end of his regime, Gairy's administration had, among other things, repressed oppositional media, limited trade union activity, and harassed, brutalized, and occasionally murdered those who opposed him via the "Mongoose Gang." Gairy's neglect of the economy and tendency to raid the public treasury ("squandermania") sent the nation's historically shaky economy into a tailspin.

During his leadership, Gairy all but ignored Carriacou and Petit Martinique; indeed, by 1970 Carriacou was referred to as "The Forgotten Island" or "The House of Exile." Carriacou had electricity only in parts of two villages, Hillsborough and Windward; its roads were unsafe and often unusable;

health care was wholly inadequate. Its sister island, Petit Martinique, had no electricity, health care facilities, or paved roads. Both islands suffered from high unemployment, bleak educational opportunities, and, for many, poverty so intense that children and adults often went hungry (D. Joseph, interview, 1997; Alexander, personal communication, 1995; K. Stiell, personal communication, 1996). This severe economic climate stepped up Carriacou's historically more or less constant exodus of its people, first to Trinidad and Aruba, later to England, Canada, and the United States. The need to emigrate during these years was captured in the 1970 calypso "England Ah Want To Go!" by Carriacouan calypsonian The Mighty Scraper:

> *Two years now, ah waiting*
> *Ah get ah letter, me voucher coming—*
> *Man ah felt so glad!*
> *Ah send for two grips in Trinidad,*
> *When ah hear the blows—*
> *Me voucher turned in Barbados.*
>
> *(Chorus) England, ah want to go*
> *Send me voucher*
> *Send me passport*
> *Tell me what to do*
> *Ah can't stay no more in Carriacou*
>
> *Man ah felt so bad*
> *So very sad,*
> *Everybody leaving*
> *Imagine how ah feeling.*
> *Who going Canada*
> *Also America*
> *But ah can't understand*
> *Why me voucher won't come this time,*
> *'cause I really want to see our Queen,*
> *Her Majesty.*

In an effort to stem emigration, rejuvenate the villages, and offer activities for the young people, approximately sixteen island youth groups were formed through community initiative in the years around independence

FIGURE 2.1 Hillsborough Center, January 1979. Photo by Raymond Joiner, used with kind permission.

(E. Stiell, interview, 1997). One of these was the Mount Royal Cricket Club. Founded by Bentley Thomas and composed of volunteers, the members of this club saw as their main objective the development of their village of La Resource (now called Mount Royal). They began by creating a "stronger and better organized" cricket team to raise the standards of the game (Mount Royal Progressive Youth Movement 1991). Shortly thereafter, they changed their name to the Mount Royal Sports Club to reflect their growing interest in Carriacou's sports in general. Concerned that older Carriacouan cultural expressions such as string band serenading and *lavway* singing were falling into disuse, the Mount Royal Sports Club expanded its vision in an effort to preserve and revitalize these traditions. The club produced Carriacou's first official Parang Festival in December 1977. The event was one night only, featured just a few bands, and suffered from birth pains, remembers string band musician Harrison Fleary:

> The Parang competition . . . was introduced as a means of getting people to sort of keep . . . doing a sort of street music, like. Which was an integral part of Christmas celebration. And that was sort of dying

FIGURE 2.2 Road to L'Esterre, Carriacou, January 1997.

out. With the older folks going and the young people didn't seem to take interest in that. They prefer to perhaps listen to the straight calypso or the reggae music.

One would have thought that [the first Parang competition] was just a few guys who just used to be sitting in the rum shops and thing and making up little rhymes when people have to pass so and things like that. And they just went and did that on stage and there wasn't much to it really. Some of them could hardly play more than a banjo anyway. Had some more buckets and percussion. And that was the form of Parang. (Interview, 1995)

The organizers of Carriacou's Parang Festival took as their inspiration Trinidad's parang tradition, which itself had been recontextualized from an informal local artistic practice to a competitive, staged performance (G. Collins, interview, 1997). Since string band serenading had been for generations a Christmas custom in Carriacou, the organizers believed that despite differences of language and culture, the essential meaning and aesthetic of Trinidadian parang would be valid in Carriacou: "The music would be a little bit different. Like in Venezuela, they play the Spanish music in the Parang. In Trinidad, is more Spanish [language] as well. But in Carriacou, we English and we sing English songs. But [it] mean the same thing to us" (G. Collins, interview, 1997).

Most Carriacouan Parang Festival participants agree. For example, Kenly Joseph, the leader of the Ghetto Boys, one of Carriacou's most active string bands, acknowledges that parang originated in Venezuela and Trinidad but notes that the term refers generally to string band music, whether it is played in Venezuela, Trinidad, or Carriacou. In his view, each Parang Festival is unique and authentic to its culture (K. Joseph, interview, 1997). Such a construction of authenticity diminishes the importance of origin and, more usefully, privileges the Parang festival as a statement of Kayak cultural identity.

"NOT JUST ANOTHER SOCIETY, BUT A JUST SOCIETY": THE NEW JEWEL MOVEMENT AND THE GRENADIAN REVOLUTION

On March 13, 1979, the New Jewel Movement (NJM), a political party that had formed some six years earlier, overthrew Gairy's government in a bloodless coup.[1] A young, British-educated lawyer named Maurice Bishop was installed as prime minister and the government's name was changed to the People's Revolutionary Government (PRG). With regard to the dependency (or "Ward") islands of Carriacou and Petit Martinique, the PRG enacted the strategy articulated in the NJM's 1973 manifesto, which declared: "We propose that the people of Carriacou and Petite [sic] Martinique will run these islands in their own assemblies" (Searle 1982: 13–14). To this end, the PRG began by changing the status of Carriacou and Petit Martinique from dependency islands to "Sister Islands," attempting to establish the two as "equal partners [with mainland Grenada] in the revolutionary and development process" (Aberdeen 1986: 65).

The Grenadian Revolution turned the nation upside down.[2] Emigration of both skilled and unskilled laborers continued unabated because some civilians feared life under socialism (C. Bristol, interview, 1997) and some felt political pressure (Joefield-Napier 1990: 99).[3] The PRG inherited—and was unable to solve—Grenada's extensive and long-entrenched economic problems, now exacerbated by a devastating reduction of international aid from the United States. Compounding this was the refusal of high-ranking U.S. government officials to meet with Prime Minister Bishop, due to

Grenada's newly installed socialist government and its ties to Cuba. In his famous "nobody's backyard" speech, broadcast by Radio Free Grenada on April
13, 1979, Bishop deplored the drastic reduction in American aid to Grenada:

> We feel forced to ask whether the paltry sum of a few $5,000 is all that
> the wealthiest country in the world can offer to a poor but proud
> people who are fighting for democracy, dignity, and self-respect based
> on real and independent economic development. . . .
>   Grenada is a sovereign and independent country, although a tiny
> speck on the world map, and we expect all countries to strictly respect
> our independence just as we will respect theirs. No country has the
> right to tell us what to do or how to run our country or who to be
> friendly with. . . . We are not in anybody's backyard, and we are defi-
> nitely not for sale. (Bishop 1979a)

Adding to the economic woes of the tri-island state, tourism, then as now
an important source of revenue, took a nosedive during the Bishop admin-
istration and would need nearly a decade to make a comeback after the
American invasion (M. Bullen, interview, 1997; Nimrod, interview, 1997;
Starbird 1979). With their naturally protected bays and beautiful harbors,
Grenada and Carriacou have long been considered prime islands world-
wide at which luxury yachts often dropped anchor. According to Hazen
Richardson, the owner of Petit St. Vincent, an exclusive resort island next to
Petit Martinique, the revolution and four and a half years of the PRG
"frightened yachtsmen away" (Richardson, interview, 1996).

Other aspects of the revolution and the installation of the PRG were up-
setting for many Carriacouans. Educator and dancer Cosmos Bristol recalled anxiety surrounding the shift of local power to newly established
militias, the public display of and training with arms, and the militia's treatment of civilians:

> Immediately after the revolution, the government set up a militia in
> Carriacou. And I was one of the first peoples to . . . own a gun in Car-
> riacou, under PRG. . . . But at the time, what we thought was that we
> were being armed so that Gairy wouldn't return. 'Cause the kind of
> experiences we had under Gairy was one everybody hate to recall.
>   There was two instances when the man in charge of the militia

here pull his gun on me. . . . Every time they come up with something that didn't make sense, I tell them plainly this doesn't sound reasonable, you know. They get mad. . . . They sent people from Grenada to train us in the cleaning, well, servicing of the weapons and give us a couple of practice sessions. But as you know I am school teacher and I . . . told them I couldn't do any training on Saturdays. Saturdays is my day off. And Sundays is my day off, worship and rest. And so the guy insisted that we would have to train on Sunday and he started talking about if there was no God and we shouldn't think about that. So I just hand him his weapon and I quit. And that was one of the times when he crack up on me.

Mr. Bristol's experiences point to a local resistance by Carriacouans toward the PRG's inflexible Marxist perspective on the role of organized religion and the Church in daily life. This anti-religion platform only alienated Carriacouans who, for centuries, had embraced both Christianity and various West African religious practices. In this regard, the PRG missed an opportunity to frame progressive cultural policy in the signifying system— organized religion—that was both familiar and accessible to the masses (Henry 1990: 70–71). Despite the PRG's stance on religion, most Carriacouans, PRG supporters or not, continued to worship as they always had.

In spite of the problems that besieged the new administration and the ensuing challenges that Carriacouans confronted, there was widespread popular support for the PRG throughout Grenada, Carriacou, and Petit Martinique. Many celebrated the liberation of their country from Gairy's neocolonial government and embraced the new ideology with optimism. For them, Bishop and his party offered hope, as recalled by teacher and musician Lionel Stiell, who joined the People's Revolutionary Army in Carriacou:

> LS: The revolution [was] to be a popular one. People believe in themselves and believe that they could help the country to rise and so on. That aspect of it was good because to make any contribution to your country, you got to believe in your country.
>
> RSM: People in Carriacou felt that way?
>
> LS: Yes, a lot of people. . . . I was supportive of the government because they were doing a lot that the other governments didn't

do . . . But a lot of people benefited from the revolution. . . . I benefited because I was in the army and had that experience. Learned
how to handle a gun. Started teaching at the time [and] . . . overall the
programs that they had meant to benefit the poor people.

This optimism swelled as Carriacouans saw improvements in the infrastructure of their island as well as gains in health services, local economic
initiatives, education, job opportunities, and other social services. To this
day, the slogan of the Grenadian Revolution—"Forward Ever, Backward
Never!"—is maintained on murals and billboards throughout Carriacou
and Grenada.

"PEOPLE'S POWER" AND "SELF-HELP"

Among the various political, economic, and social initiatives identified by
the PRG, "people's power" was among the most important, and three strategies were undertaken toward its implementation: mass organizations (including the militia), the village-based structure of participatory democracy,
and a new sense of industrial democracy, the last created largely through the
repeal of anti-worker ordinances (Thorndike 1990: 33).[4] Of these institutions, the village-based structure of participatory democracy cohered best
with extant Carriacouan social structure and norms. Grenada was divided
into seven parish councils, one of which was the island of Carriacou.
Chaired by a central committee member, parish council meetings offered a
platform for locals to discuss policy and question the PRG leadership and
civil servants. Coordination of the PRG with mass organizations such as the
militia or trade union branches, on the other hand, was organized through
another entity, the Village Coordinating Bureaus (VCBs). In time, the
VCBs (rather than the parish councils) would become the main link between the people and the party, and therefore the government (Thorndike
1985: 89). It is not surprising that village-level organization prevailed over
parish councils or, in the case of Carriacou, an island-wide council. Carriacou society was and is deeply rooted in the village (in many instances consisting of a cluster of extended families). One's village serves as a source of
basic identity, and Kayaks are famous for their allegiance to their villages.
Exploiting this reality, the PRG made its political aims and cultural initiatives more easily integrated into daily life.

Entities such as the youth general meetings, women's parish councils, farmers' zonal councils, trade unions, and student groups were established to organize the masses. Open to all residents, they were intended to engender communal decision-making and introduce issues with ministers of cabinet or other public officials, including Prime Minister Bishop. Such communal initiatives were, as Gordon Lewis (1987: 33) notes, one of the lasting achievements of the revolution, instilling a sense of direct involvement among the people. Many Carriacouans, including Lionel Stiell, remember this as a time when disparate sectors of society worked together for change and shared a sense of empowerment:

> The Ministers had [a] pay drop, first thing. And they started working among the people. . . . They actually took the tools. . . . They give the people confidence in themselves and all the projects that were going on, it was a lot of self help programs. They supplied the material and the labor was free.
>
> And the people believe in that. That's the only time I've seen people believe in themselves and in what they do. . . . It was a certain awakening for the people. Just like they found their identity with the war and a lot of things. The politics, people were understanding more what it was like. People were coming out.

Mobilizing the population for the task of national reconstruction was tremendously successful, contributing to a local sense of empowerment while providing inexpensive solutions to historical problems of infrastructure, as noted by Lyle Bullen, who served as the Secretary for Carriacou and Petit Martinique Affairs (1979–81): "We had a lot of voluntary work on weekends, clean sidewalks, dig drains and cut bushes, build community centers. All these things were voluntary. Government was able to save money and put it into productive use. This is what confounded a lot of critics— they couldn't understand how the PRG did so much in such a short period of time. But this is because we were able to capitalize on the nationalistic spirit of the people" (interview, 1997).

Along with People's Power, the PRG put into place the notion of "self-help," which was also congruent with Carriacou's existing social structure. Work cooperatives were established under the auspices of the National Cooperative Development Agency (NACDA) to stimulate the local economy, including fishing cooperatives, house repair programs, and other labor programs. Through cooperative work efforts, new roads were cut and old roads repaved, electricity was brought for the first time to Petit Martinique and to most of Carriacou, and houses were refurbished or entirely rebuilt. In addition, new jetties were built, medical and health facilities were improved or newly constructed, a public transportation system was launched, and schools were refurbished (Aberdeen 1986: 35).

"Self-help" describes what Kayaks had been doing for centuries as a direct result of Carriacou's status as a double dependency. Continuous neglect by Grenadian-based colonial and neocolonial governmental administrations resulted in the concentration of most goods and services in the metropole alone. With little assistance from the central government, Kayaks developed a strong system of inter-reliance, one that remains in place today. Self-help in Carriacou thus ranges from regular giving of gifts of food to collaborative work on large-scale community projects. Indeed, the PRG's concept of self-help is akin to the notion of the Carriacou "folk institution," in which community members create an entity that returns services and assistance to them, a centuries-old practice of collaborative endeavor and giving (see Hill 1977).[5] Self-help—the very essence of folk institutions—was thus a deeply engrained concept that was easily engaged by the PRG.

The Bishop administration attempted to extend the concept of self-help to a statewide level in the name of national unity and economic growth. To this end, the PRG instituted cultural programs that would link the three islands, thus forging a new and unprecedented model of economic equity between the dependency islands and mainland Grenada. Calling for state-sponsored competitive events to rebuild the tourism industry, Prime Minister Bishop directed the Grenadian Ministry of Culture to develop a "cultural month," beginning with the Carriacou Regatta in early August, followed by the Caribbean Netball Championship in Grenada, the Caribbean Calypso King Competition in Grenada, and the climactic two day Grenada Carnival in mid- to late August. In a 1982 interview, the prime minister expressed hope that initiatives such as this would begin to resolve the centuries-old disparity of wealth and access to resources between Grenada and its sister islands: "We think that this is a key way of guaranteeing that all three islands of the nation are dealt with simultaneously and therefore share the benefits of tourism" (Bishop 1982: 24). The PRG's redistribution of wealth between the smaller islands and mainland Grenada was largely if not totally without precedent throughout the history of Carriacou–Grenada relations. Coupled with the promise of infrastructural improvements and an optimistic approach to the future, these initiatives garnered popular support for the PRG among Carriacouans.

"EACH ONE TEACH ONE:" THE PRG AND CULTURAL REVITALIZATION

Equally profound were the short- and long-term effects of the Grenadian Revolution and PRG years on cultural production. One of the PRG's most visible accomplishments was the successful revival of interest in and cultivation of traditional arts and culture throughout the tri-island state, and particularly in Carriacou. Along with programs in poetry and creative writing, the PRG's initiatives helped affirm the importance of Big Drum, French *patois* (an older creolized language that was all but replaced by Grenadian English Creole by the mid-twentieth century), and quadrille dance by bringing these programs into the schools as well as sponsoring community performances and other events featuring visiting artists from Africa and elsewhere in the Caribbean. In an interview from June 4, 1982, Prime Minister Bishop elaborated on the PRG's policy of support for the cultural activities in Carriacou: "In terms of the entire nation, Carriacou is by far the most vibrant parish culturally. . . . We are concerned that the tradition of the Big Drum and the tremendous cultural creativity and activity of the Carriacou masses continue and flourish. We would like to develop programmes with the people to ensure that we exploit that potential to the fullest and guarantee that the remarkable cultural vibrancy and dynamism remains" (Bishop 1982: 24).

One of the most visible and universal elements of traditional culture that the PRG focused on was the establishment of various programs advocating the incorporation of the local English language—Grenadian Creole—into educational and public institutions. Until the revolution, Grenadian Creole had been relegated to only domestic and social use. It was reintroduced as an important component of the PRG's literacy campaign under the auspices of the new Centre for Popular Education (CPE). Teachers were encouraged to use Grenadian Creole in the classroom and were trained to do so in the PRG's newly established National In-Service Teacher Education Program (NISTEP). Far from excluding what American linguist Ron Kephart terms

"Metropolitan English" (the variety of English generally considered "standard" in England, the United States, and Canada), the PRG instead recognized that the nation was essentially bilingual. Kephart himself was invited by the Grenada Ministry of Education in 1982 to find solutions to the educational problems posed by the coexistence of Creole English and Metropolitan English (Kephart 1985, 2000). The aim here was to further decolonize the relationship between the two languages, allowing both to inform emergent processes of postcolonial communication and identity formation (see P. Henry 1990).[6]

This validation of local language also extended to the French *patois* that had once flourished on the island but increasingly was spoken only by the "older heads" (senior citizens). Through the CPE, seniors were taught basic literacy skills by younger Carriacouans. Many of these seniors were asked in turn to volunteer their services to in-school programs designed to teach and reinforce traditional language and culture to young Carriacouans. Eslyn ("Tateen") Stiell (born 1923) of L'Esterre was asked by the CPE to teach French *patois* and Big Drum dance to the students at the L'Esterre Rosary School:

> A woman from Harveyvale come to me and ask me if I could help.... They call her Miss Raymond from Harveyvale. She Alexis.[7] ... Well she tell me what they about to do. And I say, well alright. During the Revolution ... they used to give me ten dollar. They call it "self help," so. So helping yourself, helping the children to speak *patois*. When they say self-help, they not paying you. You helping.... So at one o'clock I would go to the school and teach the children how to speak *patois* and how to dance the Big Drum. After they kill Bishop and t'ing, all that stop. (Interview, 1997)

Teaching *patois,* like promoting Grenadian Creole, benefited students and teachers as well as the school system, particularly when the teachers attended mandatory training programs administered through NISTEP:

> When teachers from all the schools were made to gather for training, [we] went through the communities and enlisted people, [those who] speak *patois,* do quadrille dance, do Big Drum dance, and they would go into schools and on that day the schools were really immersed in

those activities. This killed two birds with one stone: teachers got training and we had substitute teachers from the community with a skill. . . . These were people who had the time to go and do these things. Or on some occasions, people get time off from jobs. The government did a whole lot of groundwork in various villages spelling out the importance of a program and trying to get people involved. (L. Bullen, interview, 1997)

While teaching *patois* certainly encouraged the preservation of a dying language, few if any young Carriacouans speak it today. However, the program did bring attention to and affirmation of the skills and wisdom of the older generation of Carriacouans and directly involved them in programs aimed at social change. Perhaps most importantly, educational programs such as these administered by the CPE offered Carriacouans a model that systematically refuted the colonial concept of a limited and usually prohibitively expensive education. Instead, by offering education to all, particularly with a system that privileged Afro-Caribbean culture and language over their colonial counterparts, these initiatives helped to decolonize various cultural attitudes and assumptions.

While the PRG validated Creole forms such as English Creole, its main concern for national cultural revitalization was the foregrounding of African-derived expressive genres. Generated in response to the Black Power Movement, which reverberated throughout the African diaspora in the late 1960s and 1970s, this refocusing of national identity was the brainchild of young Grenadian professionals and intellectuals who had been educated in Britain and the United States, such as Maurice Bishop, then a law school student in England, and his future political deputy, Bernard Coard, also in England as a doctoral student in economics at Sussex University. For both Bishop and Coard, and for many of their West Indian colleagues, living abroad brought with it a political awakening. Student protest movements, exposure to racism and the plight of West Indian communities in Britain, and the anti-colonialism sweeping the third world informed what would become the basis for the PRG (Heine 1990b). Bishop's thinking about colonialism and race relations itself was shaped by the writings of Frantz Fanon, Malcolm X, and Nkrumah (Ghana's first post-independent head of state), while much of the New Jewel Movement's political ideology was predicated on Guyanese historian/activist Walter Rodney's notion of black power, "a movement and an ideology springing from the reality of oppression of black peoples by whites within the imperialist world as a whole" (Rodney 1969: 28). Calling for black control of the state, Rodney argues that the people must build a viable system of socialism to stimulate social, economic, and political self-reliance. In building such a state, the Bishop administration put into place programs that would encourage social self-reliance through a rejection of the colonial mentality imposed by British rule and through the celebration of cultural expressions from Africa and throughout the black Atlantic.

To this end, Carriacouans enjoyed events that refocused Kayak identity from an imposed British image of the colonial self to one that foregrounded African and Afro-Caribbean cultural heritage, as Cosmos Bristol remembers: "It was a rich development of culture. . . . A number of performers [and] artists were brought in from the African continent, from Cuba, from other Caribbean islands. . . . We had a number of Vincentian poets, a number of Guyanese coming in and performing. We had a cultural activity on a regular basis; maybe every month or every two months, we had a big outdoor activity where culture is concerned" (interview, 1997).

By looking toward membership in the greater Caribbean region, the PRG's Ministry of Culture established programs that would apply the notion of pan-Africanism to pan-Caribbeanism, that is, reach out to other West Indian cultures through a shared understanding of African heritage, among other things. Cultural and civic leaders in Carriacou made this connection to Africa and other parts of the Caribbean by reframing the significance of local belief systems and ceremonies such as the African-derived Big Drum: "You understood you have a natural rhythm for the Big Drum dance because of your natural link with Africa. . . . They say peoples' culture comes deep from within, gives them a sense of identity. This was needed at the time because we had to endure a *lot of* damage done by colonialism. . . . Big Drum link us back with Mother Africa and it's important to know about these things because it gives you a sense of identity, of belonging, like an extended family" (L. Bullen, interview, 1997).

In a 1982 essay, Kayak educator and dancer Christine David demonstrates a similar ideology from a related perspective. A strong proponent of Big Drum and other African-derived traditions, David affirms the existence of a cultural hierarchy in Carriacou that valorizes African artistic expressions over creole forms: "We have dances [in Carriacou] too, which have come through our history, like the Lancers' Quadrille, which is called 'the Old People Dance,' and which the people dance for sheer enjoyment. In that way it is very different from the Big Drum, which is important to the people's security, as they feel they must be in contact with their ancestors" (David 1982: 89).

The PRG's integration of the Black Power Movement into social and artistic initiatives in Carriacou was in no small part a politicization of cultural identity. In a 1982 speech, Prime Minister Bishop called for a new understanding of the very notion of culture as, in addition to the arts, "all of our shared habits, all of our collective responses to our common situation" (Bishop 1982: 204). Cultural initiatives were seen to do the work of raising political consciousness. For example, Document 11727 of the *Grenada Documents,* a collection of 35,000 pounds of documents recovered from Grenada by the U.S. Central Intelligence Agency after the October 1983 invasion, notes the following on the subject of traditional dance: "The main purpose of this type of activity is to transform and utilize the very strong cultural undercurrent to elaborate on and reinforce the program and policies of the Revolution (Document 11727, "Draft 1983–1985 Plan for Culture," April 20, 1982, as cited in Dujmovic 1988). Similarly, the party's official view of steel band ("pan") music in the same document is less concerned with aesthetics than with its surrounding political ideology: "Pan is a child of struggle born of the dialectical tensions between an inherently oppressive system [superstructure] and an oppressed people's need [to] liberate their creativity." Hardline rhetoric notwithstanding, what the PRG actually achieved here was a first-time national institutionalization of African and Afro-Caribbean performance and artistic expression.

Some scholars argue that the psychological dependence resulting from years of colonial rule "doomed" movements such as Black Power "to failure" (Thorndike 1985: 3); others note that this search for roots "eroded much of the old anglophilism . . . and helped the new and younger generation to slough off the old feelings of ethnocultural inferiority" (Lewis 1985: 135). In Carriacou, the application of ideologies from the Black Power Movement cannot be interpreted as an entire failure: while success was manifest mostly among the younger generation, aspects of Black Power served older Kayaks as well, precisely because the movement reiterated and underscored an already integrated and unusually strong understanding of Carriacouan African heritage. For along with the socio-spiritual significance of the African-derived Big Drum ceremony, many Kayaks possess a concrete knowledge of their African forebears. Such a renaissance of interest in and celebration of African and African-derived expressive arts helped Carriacouans begin to abandon centuries of foreign cultural domination. The simple pleasure of attending these events, either as a participant or a spectator, offered opportunities for affirmative expression. Nowhere was this more evident than among Carriacouan youth, who stood to benefit the most from this revitalization of cultural identity and the attendant consciousness of local and regional autonomy.

"YOUTH IN ACTION:" THE NATIONAL YOUTH MOVEMENT

Twasn't easy to get a job. It's never easy to get a job really. . . . At
the time, you had to get involved in something. There was
nothing else really. . . . So it was utilizing that time factor . . . you
stay home and do your parents' work, that's about it. Because [of]
the organization from [earlier] youth groups, you had an idea
of say, how people organize to work together. OK? Then
during the revolution they had the same sort of groups being
formed. Parish groups, village groups, youth groups.
Nobody thought it was political groups.

(L. Stiell, interview, 1997)

At the time of the revolution, the problems confronted by Kayak youth revolved more around unemployment than around a lack of sports or cultural opportunities. Offering the younger generation something to do after decades of few, if any, options drove the PRG's initiative to create youth groups. For young adults, employment brought the most satisfaction, as George Nelson, a resident of the village Six Roads, writes in his essay "Weself As One People": "Young people wasn't organized at all, we used to idle around the place and there was much more thieves around at that time. Now with the employment, the youths much freer" (Nelson 1982: 73).

The PRG put into place local cooperative work programs for youth and young adults almost immediately after the revolution. In addition to new initiatives (for example, quarry work to collect the gravel for work crews to improve Carriacou's roads), programs were also established to help existing industries re-form as local work cooperatives. For example, the Mount Pleasant Fishing Cooperative in Carriacou was established with the support of the National Cooperative Development Agency (NACDA), which sponsored the cooperative's fishing boats (Callender 1982: 61–62).[8] Young adults and youth also found work with the House Repair Programme, whose Carriacou parish coordinator was Bentley Thomas, the founder of the Parang Festival and a founding member of the Mount Royal Progressive Youth Movement. He notes that in addition to mending homes and helping "to keep alive the spirit of the community and communal work," this state-sponsored program served as an outlet for Carriacou young people, who worked alongside seasoned local carpenters and masons to repair homes (Thomas 1982: 118).

In 1978 the PRG established the National Youth Organization (NYO), an institution that stressed physical fitness, national pride, and political awareness.[9] A highly politicized "anti-imperialist organization," the NYO focused on teaching youth "how imperialism as a system of exploitation is responsible for high unemployment, how it prevents them from having adequate facilities for sport and culture, how it is responsible for the poverty of our nation" (from the Grenada Documents 1979, as cited in Thorndike 1990). Because community-based institutions that focused on youth, sports, and culture were already familiar to Carriacouans, the initiatives of the NYO were relatively easy to put into place and quickly attracted large groups of participants. Some scholars view this involvement as an attempt by the PRG to indoctrinate the youth with political propaganda, a crucial tactic in the "totalitarian" transformation of society (see Dujmovic 1988: 59). However, the results of these programs did not necessarily reflect their initial intentions. In the case of the voluntary NYO, these "political groups" for youth were perceived as nothing more than useful entities for enriching the quality of life in Carriacou (L. Stiell, interview, 1997) by addressing the problems wrought by persistent poverty, migration, and several decades of cultural stagnation, as noted by Cosmos Bristol:

> The Department of Culture was given a mandate to enhance the cultural heritage of our people under the Bishop government. [Traditional culture such as quadrille and Big Drum] was activated or perhaps I better say regenerated . . . [it was] given a boost. Well, of course, if the Department of Culture didn't give it that kind of kick, it could

have died. . . . A lot of our [quadrille] dancers left for the US and if the little stimulus wasn't pushed, it could have gone.

And it also gave a lot of credit to writers, so you had a number of young people writing poems and the poems being put in the press. . . . Well, everybody liked it 'cause it was just a lot of fun and you had somewhere to go, you had something to do. (Interview, 1997)

Given its initial successes, the PRG saw as its next task the expansion of the NYO's membership, and by mid-1981 the NYO nationwide exceeded eight thousand people in some one hundred different groups. Less than two years later, however, membership fell to half that as the NYO was besieged with administrative and ideological controversy, erratic educational campaigns, and funding woes, compounded by youth anger over the detention without trial of young Rastafarians and "lumpen elements" (Thorndike 1990: 39). These and other problems led to the NYO's overall decline in influence and membership throughout the tri-island state and particularly in Carriacou.

The reasons for the NYO's initial success in Carriacou also allowed for its precipitous decline, as its presence in Carriacou was neither novel nor particularly innovative. Indeed, village residents had routinely organized non-political youth-based sports and/or cultural clubs for years prior to the revolution to give young people something productive to do with their spare time. The NYO was simply another opportunity to do the same thing. Lionel Stiell remembers the positive atmosphere around these groups:

The focus was to help in the community, to get youth involved and to build morale, building leaders really. Making [them] more aware of what they can do. . . . Everything reflected what your culture was like. The African music, we did a lot of African dances. The plays reflected things like *saraca,* the *maroon* [sacrifice/feast], those sorts of things. . . . I think that is one of the main focuses of starting the group. It was like taking your everyday habits of eating, drinking, how you walk, how you play, and putting (them) in plays and dances form to showcase it to the people. Make them aware of the importance of it. (Interview, 1997)

Certain PRG programs were ultimately successful because their agendas were in many ways congruent with the existing social norms and expectations of Kayaks. But that success was not due solely to this happy convergence of political ideology with social familiarity. Indeed, while the environment was ripe for change, the PRG put into place programs that institutionalized extant artistic expression, reconfiguring what had once been locally produced, community-based programs.[10] Rather than serve as a means toward primarily radical political indoctrination, it was precisely this state-sponsored institutionalization of culture that created something of a cultural renaissance among Carriacouans, affirmed a rethinking of heritage and culture, and, perhaps most significantly, fueled the beginnings of a new postcolonial identity.

THE MOUNT ROYAL PROGRESSIVE
YOUTH MOVEMENT AND THE PRG

By 1979, the Mount Royal Sports Club was quickly becoming an important community entity and vital youth group in Carriacou. A few months after the revolution, members changed its name to the Mount Royal Progressive Youth Movement (MRPYM), to reflect both the revolutionary ideology that permeated the nation and the group's support of Prime Minister Bishop's commitment to youth (W. Collins, interview, 1997). Although the MRPYM was established as and remains an apolitical entity, the group welcomed the help offered by the PRG, given the dearth of support from the preceding Gairy administration. According to Godson "Jango" Collins, one of the group's earliest members, support came in the forms of financial assistance and encouragement: "[The PRG] give encouragement but no, there wasn't that close contact between . . . the group and the government. . . . Because an important part of our operation or function was to be non-political. But it is true that they always give the encouragement, like they show their appreciation for the things that we do. I think they, the first government, that start lending that kind of support. Like when we had Parang . . . two of the ministries, the relevant ministries, would give financial support and . . . give support with personnel and stuff like that. In that regard, we had very nice neat cooperation" (interview, 1997).

Some of the infrastructure and ideological bases of the Mount Royal Progressive Youth Movement paralleled those of the PRG. For example, the PRG's Central Committee saw self-criticism as an "essential ingredient in the class struggle," as is recorded in the minutes from an April 1981 meeting (Ledeen and Romerstein 1984). Paralleling this, the MRPYM built into its infrastructure an official "critic" whose role was to critique the contributions of the membership and the presentation of discourse during meetings. Godson "Jango" Collins has served in almost every post in the MRPYM since 1974; of all the positions, he enjoyed most the post of "critic," a sort of built-in oversight officer: "The critic has the responsibility to criticize during discussion.... For instance, one member might come up with an idea, but even though the idea might be good, but sometime his approach is bad, the critic have the responsibility to criticize his approach, or whatever, his introduction and try to put it right. And if ... anybody—even the chairman, president or whatever—is going on with [something] the critic think is unbecoming to the session ... 'tis the critic responsibility to get down on it" (interview, 1997).

The behavior of MRPYM members was also regularly monitored and, if necessary, criticized by their colleagues:

> During the early years of the group ... when [it] come to discipline and behavior, it used to be like a correction home to members. If a member of the group is out there and misbehaving, somebody report it to a group meeting, that member come to group meeting, we discuss the idea with the member and he be punished for bad behavior and stuff like that. And during those times that member would take the punishment to do something or to stay away from meeting, ban them or suspend them from meeting for two meeting days or a month or something like that. And whatever the punishment is meant to be, that member out, take the punishment and return to the group as a member with an excuse, apologizing for having behaved whatever way. The entire community looked at the group as a symbol of correction, of discipline and good living, respect and stuff like that. (G. Collins, interview, 1997)

Like the MRPYM, the PRG was also set up to critique itself at every step, a process that may have contributed to its notorious bureaucratic inefficiency. Yet the value placed by those in power on the freedom of everybody to critique those in authority (at least in theory) and the social control learned through the direct criticism of peers departed radically from the repressive Gairy administration. Criticism of those in political authority under Gairy risked retribution in the form of arrest, or worse, whereas the revolution brought with it a level of freedom of speech never before experienced by an entire generation of Kayaks, as noted in a 1982 essay by Catherine Mapp: "For me since the Revolution, the freedom to *talk* is the most important thing. Before, people couldn't complain openly about what was happening, but now everybody is talking out and giving their opinions and ideas. They can criticize or condemn those things they don't like about the Government programmes or about the ways in which they are inefficient, and they can also give suggestion and contribution for their improvement" (Mapp 1982: 110).

Interestingly, the open critique had been anathema to Carriacou society in general. Carriacouans tend not to criticize directly, opting instead to air grievances via third parties. The revolutionary atmosphere of inward examination and public criticism was, for some, a liberating departure from a longstanding social norm. Nowhere was this manifested more than during the climactic string band competition of the Parang Festival during these years when bands performed their *lavway*, a song style that publicly criticizes the behaviors of individuals throughout all sectors of Carriacou society. Once a community-based genre of derisive singing, the elevation of the *lavway* to an island-wide public forum signaled a basic transformation in social mores as a direct result of progressive political change.

The MRPYM expanded their work to include other Carriacou villages in addition to Mount Royal. In keeping with the spirit of the times, founder Bentley Thomas notes, the scope of the MRPYM's assistance broadened from sports and cultural events to an extensive system of charitable giving: "We were and are a very progressive organization, forward looking. . . . [We] went as far as taking on the responsibilities of community work, that is other villages throughout Carriacou and Petit Martinique as a whole. Up to now, people see us as the local government. When there is a problem among the sick, less fortunate, they come to us" (interview, 1999). So established was the MRPYM that by October 1983 both the group and its main project, the Parang Festival, were able to survive the trauma of Grenada's military coup, the subsequent assassination of Prime Minister Bishop, four of his cabinet members, and untold numbers of civilians, and ultimately the invasion of Grenada and Carriacou by American troops.

THE INVASION AND ITS AFTERMATH

Eight days after the October 23, 1983, invasion of Grenada, three hundred American troops landed in Carriacou in a bloodless and ultimately fruitless search to find Cubans. (The four Cubans in Carriacou—two doctors, a dentist, and a teacher—had been evacuated before the invasion.) This absurd show of American military strength included one company of 150 marines in twenty helicopters and another 150 marines in thirteen amphibious vehicles, as well as airborne units that landed on what was then a dirt runway (*New York Times,* November 2, 1983). Encountering no resistance, the troops were led by local Carriacouans to a cache of ammunitions and weapons. Carriacouans reacted with stress and "wonderment" at this show of military power, noted ethnomusicologist Angela Lorna McDaniel, who had been in Carriacou just over one month when the invasion took place:

> The United States military invasion was to me and to Carriacouans a horrible experience as is war in any form—a debilitating knowledge. . . . Even though there were virtually no armed conflicts on Carriacou, accidents like the killing of a teenager and the maiming of a child who discharged a stray grenade do take place when arms are deployed. . . . The fear aroused at the sight and sound of helicopters on daily patrol, amphibious "Amtrak" tanks that could hardly find passage through the tiny main town street, ominous coast guard vessels that cruised silently around the island, jolted the gentle society. Musical performances ceased during the weeks of crisis, but the belief systems and spiritual values that undergirded the culture patterns found verbal expression. (McDaniel 1986: v)

After the invasion, Grenadians, Carriacouans, and Petit Martiniquans were so emotionally worn and tired of politics that all they wished for was an extended period of "national calm" and reflection. A caretaker government was appointed by the governor general following the invasion, and it remained in power for over a year. General elections were then held in November 1984, and Carriacouan Herbert Augustus Blaize was elected prime minister of Grenada. A leader of the newly created New National Party, Blaize had briefly served as premier of the Associated State of Grenada in 1967, before his government was replaced with that of Sir Eric Gairy. Blaize's election as prime minister was regarded by the U.S. government and President Ronald Reagan as an "achievement of historic importance" and praised as "the first time a country which was ruled by a Marxist Leninist regime had been returned to the democratic fold" (*Trinidad Guardian,*

December 5, 1984, as cited in Ryan 1990: 282). Carriacouans, who cast 90 percent of their votes in favor of Blaize, were clearly heartened by the election of a Kayak as prime minister of the country.

With Blaize serving until 1989, the MRPYM continued to receive limited but annual support for the Parang Festival at the level received earlier from the PRG. The festival was growing in both its artistic ambition and its numbers of participants and audience members, and by 1985 the competitions were large enough to warrant the presentation of trophies. For these as well as for some financial support, the MRPYM made a direct but modest request to Prime Minister Blaize: "The challenge trophy. Yeah, when [the Parang Festival] was big enough . . . the idea come about to have a trophy included. We decided, well, we need bigger people, you know, to help. And we approached government for financial support. And [Blaize] came without no hesitation, he provided the trophy" (G. Collins, interview, 1997).

THE MOUNT ROYAL PROGRESSIVE YOUTH MOVEMENT TODAY

As an egalitarian, democratic institution, the MRPYM has a body of "Executive Members" headed by a chairman who also chairs the Parang Committee. Under the chairman is the deputy chairman, public relations officer, secretary, critic, assistant secretary, and treasurer. A "news reporter" reports at meetings on the local, regional, and international news of the day and records the news in the organization's news book. To solicit and raise funds, the MRPYM organizes events such as local dances, cultural presentations, and the largest fundraiser of all, the Parang Festival. In addition to these sources and other individual contributions, the MRPYM receives grants from national entities for various projects. In 1996, for example, the Grenadian Government (via the Ministry of Culture) gave EC$5,000 to support the Parang Festival that year; fundraising groups in England and the United States each raised EC$1,000 to support it; local businesses donated between EC$250 and $400 each; and so on. Because the MRPYM is so successful at fundraising outside of the immediate community, and because it serves as a conduit for these funds between local, national, and international sources, it can be seen as having evolved from a Carriacou folk institution to a hybrid entity, an organization with elements of both folk and metropolitan institutions. Carriacouans generally view the MRPYM as a benevolent association whose agenda aims to contribute to the overall good of Carriacou and Petit Martinique.[11] Restaurant owner/singer Glenna Bullen, for example, agrees to be one of the judges at the Hosannah band competition at the Parang Festival every year precisely to support the MRPYM's efforts: "I [do] it more for the Mount Royal Progressive Youth, to give them the support they needed because they are the hardest working community group on Carriacou" (interview, 1997).

This reputation is derived from the MRPYM's ongoing commitment to returning its profits to the community through supporting a wide range of charitable programs (W. Collins, interview, 1997; Mount Royal Progressive Youth Movement 1991). These include refurbishing or building houses to upgrade the living conditions of low-income families throughout Carriacou; giving financial support to those in need; creating annual scholarships for needy students; financially supporting the improvement of education, including preschool, in Carriacou; and sponsoring national charitable drives. In 1996, with the help of a grant of EC $50,000 from the National Lottery of Grenada, the MRPYM undertook the primary responsibility of renovating the Tennis Courts, where the Parang Festival, Carnival performances, and most public and civic presentations take place.

While most Kayaks and others readily acknowledge the vast contributions made by the MRPYM to Carriacou, the group is also criticized for a myriad of reasons, both petty and more significant. The group is quick to return the criticism, and the weeks before the Parang Festival are filled with accusations and counteraccusations between the MRPYM and other island institutions. In 1996, for example, the local radio station, KYAK, was accused by MRPYM of not giving the upcoming Parang Festival the publicity and promotion expected by the committee. Parang Chairman Wallace Collins alleged that the management of KYAK was embittered because the Parang Committee chose to have a Grenadian produce their radio publicity spots rather than a producer at KYAK itself. The animosity between the MRPYM and the radio station grew to such a heated pitch that Collins soundly criticized KYAK for their lack of cooperation during his formal welcome speech from the stage on both Friday and Saturday evenings of the 1996 festival.[12]

These conflicts have the potential to grow in magnitude so as to eventually involve local government. Senator Elvin Nimrod, Minister of Carriacou and Petit Martinique Affairs, related an example from 1996 when his office called a meeting between the MRPYM/Parang Committee, the Car-

riacou Carnival Development Committee, and the Carriacou Regatta Committee to discuss how to further cultural activities on Carriacou with an eye
toward expanding tourism. Instead, he wound up mediating an argument
between the three groups regarding the renovation of the Tennis Courts.
Senator Nimrod notes that such infighting between cultural groups in Carriacou only serves to stymie Carriacou's economic growth: "We cannot
move forward in terms of enhancing our culture when we fighting over
petty things. Because when a person comes here, they're not particularly interested in who the president of this, or who the president of that. They
want to know what Carriacou has to offer in terms of culture. . . . And I
think that is our biggest task before us now. Because once we get the people
in that mindset, to acknowledge that there is a national interest at stake
here, not parochial interest. Until we do that, we would have problems. And
to me I see that as a task" (interview, 1997).

Infighting between community-based groups in Carriacou has historical
roots in village rivalries dating back to the days of the plantations. The
MRPYM's failure to comply with a directive issued from a metropolitan institution—in this case, the senior local governmental office, the Ministry of
Carriacou and Petit Martinique Affairs—can be read partly as a legacy of
the self-reliance developed by folk institutions in response to historical governmental neglect. It also can be understood as a natural result of the
MRPYM's increasing influence in Carriacou and the group's recognition of
their powerful status. Yet Carriacou's local government at the time was also
growing stronger, with greater visibility and a louder voice in Grenada's
parliament. On December 31, 1996, Prime Minister Keith Mitchell upgraded the position of Parliamentary Secretary for Carriacou and Petit
Martinique to a ministry post, so that Carriacou's representative is now also
a cabinet member with a voice in the national decision-making process. As
Carriacou's local government consolidates its power both locally and nationally, it is quite possible that such folk institutions as the MRYPM will
come into conflict more often with governmental agencies.

CONCLUSION: LOOKING INWARD, REACHING OUT

Decolonization is always a violent phenomenon. At whatever
level we study it—relationships between individuals, new
names for sports clubs . . . decolonization is quite simply the

replacing of a certain "species" of men by another "species" of men. Without any period of transition, there is a total, complete, and absolute substitution."

(Frantz Fanon, *The Wretched of the Earth* [1963: 35]).

As Grenada and its dependencies, Carriacou and Petit Martinique, moved from the status of a British colony to an independent state, the rejection of Gairy's neocolonial government—an administration that, in Fanon's terms, indeed replaced "one species of men by another"—was fueled in no small part by a growing nationalism. In postcolonial nation-states such "conventional nationalism," as Edward Said (1994: 224) notes, is "insufficient and crucial, but only the first step." What is needed, according to both Fanon and Said, is a strong new post-nationalist theme of liberation framed as a political transitional period; only after this can a measure of postcolonial freedom be attained. In short, if nationalism is the first stage of decolonization, then liberation marks the second. The 1979 Grenadian Revolution and the installation of the PRG formed the crucial period of political transition, an era cut short by the military coup, Bishop's assassination, and the invasion of Grenada by American armed forces. While the political and economic repercussions of the PRG became largely insignificant after 1983, the four and a half years of this quasi-socialist government did bring considerable social change, some of it transitory, some of it lasting.

Liberationism in Fanon's sense results in the rejection of the cultural models imposed from outside the subject community by the colonial and neocolonial ruling elite. Fanon's "second moment of decolonization" is thus marked by the need to refocus inwardly, specifically on the self and the community. The PRG's efforts toward cultural revitalization sent precisely this message to Kayaks: it was time to shed the colonial and neocolonial perspective of looking toward a ruling culture in an effort to define oneself. In a 1979 speech to the National Education Conference, Prime Minister Bishop articulated this with reference to the legacy of colonialism on education:

As a colonial people . . . it has been our practice to look outward, outward away from the needs of our country and the problems facing our people, and outward instead to the needs, to the problems, to the solutions that the metropolitan masters wish to impose on us.

> Perhaps the worst crime that colonialism left our country . . . is
> the education system. This was so because the way in which that sys-
> tem developed, the way in which that system was used, was to teach
> our people an attitude of self-hate, to get us to abandon our history, our
> culture, our values. To get us to accept the principles of white superi-
> ority, to destroy our confidence, to stifle our creativity, to perpetuate
> in our society class privilege and class difference. (Bishop 1979b)

The PRG confronted these issues head-on. Carriacouans traditionally had
maintained a personal relationship with their African past, specifically
through the knowledge of their African lineage and their participation in
the Big Drum ceremony. Via initiatives designed to raise consciousness and
further the cultural decolonization of the masses, Bishop and the PRG politicized this relationship and knowledge while simultaneously institutionaliz-
ing the performance of African and African-diasporic expressive arts.

Ironically, this inward reassessment of heritage ultimately helped inform an emergent understanding of Carriacou as part of a greater Afro-
Caribbean collective culture, a notion underscored by the 1981 formation of
the Organization of Eastern Caribbean States (OECS). With the signing of
the Treaty of Basseterre, Maurice Bishop and six other leaders of eastern
Caribbean countries pledged to "promote co-operation among the Member
States . . . to promote unity and solidarity . . . and to defend their sovereignty,
territorial integrity and independence" (Treaty of Basseterre, OECS). While
the treaty stresses cooperation in political and economic relations among members states, it also includes "Scientific, Technical and Cultural co-operation"
among its extensive list of fields to benefit from collaboration as well. In
helping to create an institution that today continues to assist eastern
Caribbean nations as they navigate contemporary economic and political
concerns, Bishop and the PRG reinforced their vision of cultural autonomy
framed by regional belonging and cooperation.

Liberationism also resulted in a nearly regular process of group critique
as a mode of evaluation, communication, and self discovery. In creating an
increasingly open atmosphere, Carriacouans, in turn, were allowed the lib-
erty of public criticism, a measure of expressive freedom that would become
the capstone of the MRPYM's Parang Festival. Initially established to address the need to preserve traditional music and song, the Parang Festival,
in the spirit of the times, also offered a public forum whereby people could

speak out, a process that no doubt also contributed to psychological decolonization and helped to shed, as Jay Mandle (1985) notes, some of the "small island" mentality.

The Parang Festival embodies many of the values inculcated by the PRG: the ongoing need to organize locally while acting nationally and regionally, the recognition of traditional culture as a postcolonial source of identity for Carriacouans, and the positive reassessment of heritage and identity, particularly in the face of ongoing social and political change. The MRPYM bears out many of the practical applications of the PRG's initiatives and strategies toward social change through self-help and cooperative work in the interest of bettering the lives of Carriacouans. In this regard, community self-reliance is realized through annual profit from the Parang Festival, and that money today constitutes one of Carriacou's main sources for charitable and community giving. The MRPYM and the Parang Festival are thus based on a historical accumulation of folk traditions from both local and regional sources; on elements of what was a revolutionary ideology gleaned from a crucial period in Carriacou's political past; and on the need of a small, postcolonial society to regain its expressive voice.

3

@/@

CULTURAL AMBIVALENCE

The Case of Carriacou Quadrille

We playing this violin here, the bass [drum] . . . and
tambourine and the steel [triangle]. Got four pieces
and playing like that, that is fire!

—Canute Caliste, 1995

EACH OF THE THREE EVENINGS OF the Parang Festival opens with a series of lengthy speeches by festival organizers and local and national dignitaries, who alternately celebrate and critique the meaning of the festival and
the process of mounting it each year. The mood changes abruptly when
members of one of Carriacou's formally organized traditional music and
dance troupes take to the stage. The lineup varies from evening to evening
but generally includes one of two Big Drum ensembles or the L'Esterre
Quadrille Group. Perhaps more important, these "warm-up" performances
serve as a public recognition of the ongoing—but changing—significance
of traditional Kayak expressive culture in Carriacou today, one deeply informed by cultural memory.

A 1996 performance by the L'Esterre Quadrille Group begins with the
seating on stage of four of the few remaining quadrille musicians in Carriacou: Canute Caliste, then an eighty-three-year old master violinist; seventy-
year-old Sonnelle Allert, an exceptional tambourine player; Enel James (in
his late forties) on the "bass" (a large, double-sided drum); and, on triangle or
"steel," Curtis Joseph, the youngest member of the group at age thirty-eight.
The musicians begin to play and eight quadrille dancers move onto the stage.
Evoking cheers and whistles from the audience, the dancers wear splashy,
colorful costumes that convey an image of tropical Caribbean energy.

Like most public quadrille performances, this one begins with a ritualistic "wetting of the ring" or libation for the ancestors, an African practice

FIGURE 3.1. Canute Caliste (violin), Enel James (partially hidden, bass drum), and Sonnelle Allert (tambourine) playing at a quadrille dance, Harveyvale, Carriacou, February 1997.

common to many diasporic cultures. The performers dance in a circle, sprinkling the ground with water, rum, and other beverages and thereby inviting the ancestral spirits to join the ceremony. The eight quadrille dancers then take their places as opposing couples forming a square. With a confidence born of familiarity and practice, they begin the first of six quadrille figures, performing choreographies reminiscent of or identical to English country dance and American square- or contradancing. The violinist plays tunes that are similarly reminiscent of English and French dance music; indeed, the tune commonly played for the first figure of the quadrille is almost identical to one found in the repertoires of American contradance and English country dance musicians (Woolf, personal communication, 1999). These links are not surprising, as North American square- or contradancing and Caribbean quadrille dancing are legacies of a shared European colonial heritage. Yet quadrille music and dance simultaneously resonate with African movement and sound: the three percussion instruments provide a steady polyrhythmic underpinning to the European-derived violin melodies, and the dancers infuse the choreography with a graceful inner body movement, adding a unique kinesthetic fluidity. The emphasis on musical syncopation and a rhythmic, gentle hip sway are both commonly found in many Caribbean

FIGURE 3.2 Quadrille dancing, L'Esterre, Carriacou, January 1995. Left to right: Canute Caliste (violin), Enel James (bass drum), Unida Edmunds, Sonnelle Allert, unknown male dancer, Bernice Lendore.

dances derived from Africa, specifically those of the Kongo people (Averill 1997: 32–33).[1] In this manner, Carriacou quadrille both sonically and visually links Kayak African ancestry with the historical legacy of European colonialism.

Until the 1960s, monthly quadrille dances in Carriacou served as a basis for community social events; today, quadrille is rarely participatory and its performance is largely limited to one extended group of practitioners, the L'Esterre Quadrille Group. Those who know how to dance the quadrille today are aging: the dancers in Carriacou are between thirty-five and sixty years old. Thus the tradition has not been actively passed on to the younger generation of Kayaks. More critically, there are only a few musicians who are able to play quadrille tunes.

Because of its European origins and link with slavery and then colonial rule, quadrille music and dance today have an uncertain meaning and role in contemporary Carriacouan cultural memory. On one hand, quadrille carries traumatic association with an enslaved and colonized past. Partly as a result, quadrille is a dying tradition. On the other hand, quadrille contin-

ues to enjoy a fair amount of visibility: the L'Esterre Quadrille Group is invited to perform onstage at every major Carriacou public event, in occasional
performances on mainland Grenada, and at the rare community social or
ritual event. Perhaps more significantly, Kayak audiences continue to enjoy
quadrille performances. Many audience members have told me that quadrille
is fun to watch and deserves support because it remains a part of the Carriacouan cultural heritage. Quadrille thus is neither fully embraced nor completely rejected; the result, then, is a collective ambivalence conditioned by
a remembered past of powerlessness and disenfranchisement.

To be sure, global processes of modernism are also important factors in
the replacement of this older folk form with newer, mass-mediated genres
such as soca, reggae, and calypso musics, particularly for the younger generation. What is critical here, however, is that Carriacou's other prominent
traditional music and dance genre, Big Drum, has not suffered the same
lack of interest and remains vital and significant to Kayaks of all ages.
An African-derived ceremony that is both sacred and social, Big Drum
music, song, and dance contains few European influences; indeed, the genre
is perceived by Carriacouans as a direct and important spiritual link to their
Kayak ancestors and to an African past (see Pearse 1956a, Hill 1977,
McDaniel 1998). In contrast to Big Drum, extant creolized styles of Carriacouan traditional music—those combining European and African elements such as sea chanteys, quadrille, and so on—are increasingly falling
into disuse.

The outcome of the contemporary Kayak association of quadrille with
historical European oppression can be characterized as cultural ambivalence, wherein members of a society are conflicted over some component expression of their cultural identity. Because cultural ambivalence signifies a
rupture within the historical understanding of community and self, its presence typically signals a loss of some local traditions and holds serious rami-
fications for a small (and typically disenfranchised) population, especially
given the powerfully homogenizing effects of global cultural forms.

Academic discourse on the subject of ambivalence in the Caribbean
dates back to Melville Herskovits's (1937) briefly mentioned notion of
"socialized ambivalence" in his book *Life in a Haitian Valley*: "Socialized
ambivalence ... describes this tendency to manifest those rapid shifts in attitude toward people and situations that characterize the responses of the
Haitian peasant to such a marked degree that the same man will hold in

high regard a person, an institution, an experience, or even an object that has personal significance to him, and simultaneously manifest great disdain and even hatred for it" (Herskovits 1937: 295).[2]

While both forms of ambivalence are to various degrees rooted in cultural syncretism and the formation of identity, cultural ambivalence is a contestation of the ongoing significance of cultural expressions that have played a historical and continuous role in the society. Cultural ambivalence typically emerges during a period of social upheaval via conflicting representations and diverse perceptions of identity that reflect, in part, Erika Bourguignon's model of syncretism and ambivalence in Haiti. Here, societal ambivalence is "characteristic of people on whom new pressures constantly impinge," and, she argues, it can disrupt the process of self-identification (Bourguignon 1951: 172–76). Underscoring Bourguignon's notion of ambivalence as a response to societal pressure, Lois Wilcken (1998: 165) argues that ambivalence toward staged Haitian folklore in Haiti and among Haitians in New York City as representative of Haitian identity "waxes in the absence of a strongly critical discourse on race and class." Bourguignon's argument that societal ambivalence interferes with identity formation is more problematic. Paul Austerlitz, for example, demonstrates that Dominican merengue music has endured as a beacon of Dominican identity precisely "for its very success in articulating the contradictory forces at play in Dominican life, including race, class, and ethnic discomfort" (Austerlitz 1997: 8–10).

Earlier studies of Caribbean quadrille music and dance focus not on cultural ambivalence but on performance practice, representation, and quadrille as an expression—sometimes parodic—of class difference. Jocelyne Guilbault, for example, demonstrates that *kwadril* performers in St. Lucia used this music and dance as a "means of representation (surrogate) rather than a means of identification (portrayal of who they are)," a strategy that had the potential to place the disempowered closer to those in power (the European plantocracy) (Guilbault 1984: 151; 1985). Thus appropriated from what was once white and Creole "high society," the dancing of the *kwadril* by St. Lucians today continues to heighten the prestige of every participant. Class tension is also manifest in the historical performance of quadrille in Trinidad: Gordon Rohlehr (1990) notes that by the 1880s, quadrille was elevated to one of Trinidad's "national" dances and over time was appropriated by the lower classes to parody the pretensions of those in power. In Cuba

and Puerto Rico, Peter Manuel (1994) argues that by the late nineteenth century creolized dance genres including *danza* and *contradanza (habanera)* served
as explicit beacons of national identity and expressed anticolonialist senti-
ment in both places.

OFF THE STAGE: A QUADRILLE DANCE EVENING IN HARVEYVALE

Largely limited today to staged performances, quadrille dances occur only
infrequently at local social events such as weddings, gravestone raising ceremonies, and so on. One such occasion is an evening quadrille dance that takes
place in the village of Harveyvale in early February 1997, an annual event
sponsored by a Mrs. Lizzie Joseph to honor her deceased husband, Mark
Joseph. Mrs. Joseph has invited members of the L'Esterre Quadrille Group
to attend the celebration and perform a quadrille at her store. Mrs. Joseph's
large wooden-floored store is packed with invited guests, ranging from elderly women who sit on chairs around the room's periphery, chatting and
sipping beverages, to middle-aged and younger men and women as well as
a handful of children who, for the most part, remain by their parents' or
grandparents' sides.

The four musicians sit on a small wooden stage against the back wall.
Unlike formal concert performances, there is no sound system; some of the
instruments can be heard, others cannot. The musicians this evening include Canute Caliste on violin, Enel James on bass (drum), Sonnelle Allert
on tambourine, and Marxman Joseph on *cuatro* (a small, guitarlike instrument originally from Venezuela) as a replacement for the triangle player. To
begin the evening, the band plays incidental music for listening and dancing, including improvisatory "break-aways," waltzes, polkas, old calypsos,
and faster syncopated waltzes (locally referred to as *cacians*).[3] After an hour,
Mrs. Joseph approaches the musicians, indicating that it is time to begin.

Because this quadrille evening is held to honor the late Mr. Joseph, its attendant rituals deeply reflect long-held spiritual beliefs. Foremost in this regard is the strong sense of the power of the ancestors and the need to offer,
as a sign of respect, a ceremony that, among other things, ensures safety
from their disfavor (Pearse 1956b). Such a socio-ritualistic need would more
commonly be fulfilled via a Big Drum ceremony, which, according to Lorna
McDaniel, "expresses [Carriacouans'] relationship with the past and their
adoration of another world" (1998: 17). However, in the villages where

FIGURE 3.3 Playing for a quadrille dance, Harveyvale, Carriacou, February 1997. Left to right: Sonnelle Allert (tambourine), Canute Caliste (violin), Enel James (bass drum), Marxman Joseph (*cuatro*).

quadrille was especially popular (L'Esterre, Windward, Belmont, and others), a quadrille dance might be substituted, particularly if the deceased was a quadrille dancer or musician, as was Mr. Joseph.

Like the Big Drum ceremony, Mrs. Joseph's quadrille evening begins with a ritualistic "wetting of the ring" or libation for the ancestors.[4] Two tea towels are crossed on the floor in front of the musicians and, as violinist Canute Caliste begins a medium-tempo quadrille tune, Mrs. Joseph and her family dance, outlining a circle of space (locally known as "the ring") immediately in front of the musicians. The eldest living male relative sprinkles rum on the floor and Mrs. Joseph follows him, tossing rice. A female relative spills water, and another male relative sprinkles Coca-Cola. Beginning with Mrs. Joseph, each family member then takes the towels, holding one in each hand, and gently waves them as they dance toward the north, south, east, and west—a ritual reminiscent of the Kongo cosmogram representing the cardinal corners of the world (Thompson 1984: 108). At the conclusion of their short dances, each family member replaces the towels in a crossed formation on the floor. Mrs. Joseph then dances once more; when she is finished, she touches Canute Caliste's knee to signal the end of the dance. She places bottled beverages (water, soft drinks, rum, and so on) in front of the musicians. The crossed towels symbolize the intersection between the living and dead, while the wetting of the ground acts as an invitation to the ancestral spirits to join the ceremony, as noted by quadrille dancer Cosmos Bristol:

> It is customary, if it is stone feast or it is just *saraca* over a dream or something like that, a lot of things is thrown on the ground for the people who have gone before us. . . . That our foreparents seem to be hungry or thirsty or something like that . . . it is done in a kind of ceremonial form where three or four or five members of the family carry . . . rum and water, usually the person carrying the water goes first because what they tend to think is that this is not in any kind of anger or any mood like that. We want peace. We need love, we want unity and that sort of thing. So you throw the cold water first and then the Jack Iron [very strong local rum] and any other drink . . . whiskey, Bacardi, brandy, soft drink, juice, whatever follow. (interview, 1997)

After a short pause, the musicians begin a faster quadrille tune in duple time. The quickened tempo announces the arrival of the ancestral spirits (Caliste 1995; see also Hill 1977: 363). Mrs. Joseph and another female family member pick up the towels and dance briefly together, concluding with a "wheel" (swing), where one woman holds the other about the waist as they spin around each other. This European-derived move in the midst of an otherwise wholly African ritual marks the end of the dance. To great applause, the towels are removed and the actual quadrille dance begins.

QUADRILLE DANCE

Historically, there have existed three distinct types of quadrille in Carriacou: Albert, Lancers, and English quadrille. Until the 1930s, Lancers quadrille was quite popular in people's homes (David 1985: 27; Hill 1977; W. Fleary, personal communication, 1997). While no longer danced in Carriacou today, Lancers quadrille is still performed by a group of older individuals in the Grenadian village of Grenville, accompanied by a modified string band led by a tenor saxophonist.[5] The Albert quadrille also once offered alternative choreographies and tunes to the more popular English quadrille in Carriacou.[6] Occasionally, violinist Canute Caliste mixes an Albert quadrille tune into an English quadrille; the choreography remains the same among the dancers, however, because the Albert quadrille figures have been, for the most part, forgotten.

Danced by four men and four women in opposing couples forming a square, the English quadrille consists of six separate dance figures, each of which is accompanied by a specific violin melody. The male in the "head" couple (the dancers with their backs to the musicians) calls out the dance moves—choreographies that are related to some North American social dance styles: promenades (in which each couple marches or dances around the square in a stylized promenade hold); balancing, where the members of each couple dance facing each other without touching; forward and back, in which either the couple or an individual dances forward to the center of the square and back again; chaining, in which the individual dancers wind their way around each other and progress around the square until they are back "home"; the "right through, no balance," also known as the *paisadé* step, in which dancers weave in and out, forming the *huit* or figure eight; and other choreographies.[7]

As the dancers complete the figure, the male of the head couple notifies the band to end the music by touching the violinist's knee. After a brief pause, the musicians begin another tune to coincide with the next figure, and the dancers start anew. In years past, when quadrille was danced strictly for social gatherings, an evening might have included an English quadrille, followed by a few waltzes and polkas, followed by an Albert quadrille. As with the quadrille held at Mrs. Joseph's, the few remaining social quadrille dance events feature only the six figures that constitute a "set," followed by polkas, waltzes, and *cacians*. A staged quadrille performance, on the other hand, typically features only three figures of the English quadrille, given the time limits typically imposed by the producers of the event.

The first four figures of the Carriacou English quadrille remain the same from performance to performance. The fifth figure is typically upbeat, and the sixth figure takes the form of either a waltz quadrille, a *cacian,* or the "heel and toe" polka (also known locally as the "Magica Polka"). Perhaps because quadrille only infrequently benefits from an influx of younger practitioners, the L'Esterre Quadrille Group tends to perform the quadrilles with few adaptations or changes. This was not always the case, however, as can be seen in the evolution of the fourth and fifth figures, of which the lat-

ter is the improvisatory "break-away." Both figures feature non-European
choreography inspired by the legendary late quadrille dancer Mano Joseph
of L'Esterre (D. Joseph, personal communication, 1996). Dating back to the
1940s and 1950s, his innovations include an up-tempo gyrating move
whereby dancers "wind" lower and lower to the ground, and a "shaking"
move that directs dancers to shake or shimmy their torsos in place for eight
measures. Most famous, however, for audience and dancers alike is Mr.
Joseph's famous head-scratching choreography, whereby the dance caller
instructs the ladies to "scratch you partner head" as they dance in place.
Mano Joseph's penchant for humorous and playful moves is well remembered by his son-in-law, musician and dancer Sonnelle Allert, who is also
known for putting an "act" into his dancing: "Lot of people admire him, you
know, because he make a lot of joke in the dance. So he tell you, 'Keep
standing and shaking, just keep standing and shake!' Then he tell you,
when you wheel [swing your partner], you go to this other partner, he'll tell
you, stand up and keep scratching heads, you know. . . . That's his way in
those dances, so we get that from him. . . . You know, it going back a bundle
of years and we keep doing that" (interview, 1997).

Like its counterparts in Western Europe and the United States, Carria-

FIGURE 3.4 Quadrille dancing, L'Esterre, Carriacou, August 1995.

cou quadrille choreography is organized around symmetry; that is, for every individual movement, there is a countermove and for every larger choreographed pattern, there is a counterpattern. For example, the head and "tail" couples (the couple facing the "head" couple) dance a series of steps with each other; when the entire sequence is finished, the "side" couples repeat the sequence. This type of symmetric movement is the rule throughout each of the figures and points to a European origin in its kinesthetic linearity.

QUADRILLE MUSIC

In contrast, quadrille music is more cyclic, both in form and content, and thus reflective of its Central and West African influences. Although the music has a discrete beginning when the violin starts the tune, the other instruments rarely begin with the violinist and enter, instead, in a staggered manner, a performance practice that is also typical of West and Central African musics (Chernoff 1979: 47; see also Thompson 1966: 93–94 and transcription 1). Similarly, the dancers often finish the figure before the violinist has finished the tune, hence the need for the head dancer to notify the violinist that the figure is ending.[8] Finally, the percussion instruments rarely end with the violinist during an actual dance performance; more typical would be a staggered ending much like the beginning.

Carriacou quadrille music is led by the violinist, who is accompanied by a "bass" (a large drum held on one's lap and played with a stick in one hand and a soft-headed mallet in the other); a triangle or "steel" (whose player typically alternates open notes with dampened ones by closing the hand around the top of the triangle); and a tambourine with jingles. Like dance music from Western Europe, Carriacouan quadrille tunes are instrumental (as opposed to vocal) and organized into two eight-bar phrases with internal melodic repetition. Most tunes are in major keys, although Canute Caliste (and Carriacou string band violinists as well) renders specific pitches slightly sharper or flatter than those heard most often in North American or English fiddling. This tendency to use microtonal intervals is reminiscent of African tonalities, which greatly differ from the tempered pitches of Western musics.

The melodies of the tunes are largely in a 6/8 meter as well as the occasional march in 2/4. However, quadrille music is strongly and inherently polyrhythmic and consists of African-derived stratified rhythms, including especially the juxtaposition of duple and triple time. In transcription 1, the polyrhythmic nature of quadrille music arises from the moderately fast triplet feel (four groups of three per measure) of the violin's melody against the steady duple meter of the percussion instruments, where the bass (drum) reinforces the triangle's meter by playing a syncopated line in duple time. The melody is phrased like an English or Irish jig (which is also in a fast triple meter and typically notated in 6/8, 9/8, or 12/8 time).

FIGURE 3.5 Transcription 1: Carriacou quadrille, figure 1.

FIGURE 3.5 *(Continued)*

Like much of the music from Central and West Africa, the bass drum and the triangle are "time-keeping" instruments, providing the pulse or, in Chernoff's words, the "heartbeat" of the music (1979: 43). The next sonic layer, provided by the tambourine, is played mostly in duple time in an improvisatory, even explosive manner, acting, in effect, like the master drummer in an African percussion ensemble. By what is locally known as "beating" (hitting the tambourine head with the hand) or "ringing" (running the hand over the jingles), the tambourine player serves an important function in the ensemble as he sonically marks the eight-bar melodic phrases by ringing at the end of the last bar and into the first bar of the next phrase. Because the tambourine plays here with a markedly duple feel against the violin's triplets, their interaction creates a hemiola effect, again reminiscent of the interplay of instruments in many African musics.

Canute Caliste also often creates another layer of polyrhythms and syncopation by tying or slurring the last eighth note of a six-beat phrase (which, in some instances, falls in the middle of the 12/8 measure) over the bar line to the first eighth note of the next measure. Most impressively, Mr. Caliste often creates polyrhythms through variation and improvisation. Transcription 2 is Mr. Caliste's rendition of a tune in duple time. After playing through the tune once, he then plays a melodic variation using quarter-note triplets (six even notes per measure [see measures 19–24]) over the next five bars. Establishing triple meter (albeit temporarily), this variation creates a propulsive interlocking polyrhythm with the other instrumentalists, particularly the bass drum player. Mr. Caliste repeats this rhythmic figure several times throughout the course of the dance, in different parts of the tune and for different lengths of time.

Improvisation and variation are trademarks of Mr. Caliste's playing style, as they are for players of string band music as well. Rarely will a Kayak violinist play a tune the same way twice. However, while Mr. Caliste does improvise within the framework of the tune, he nevertheless limits his tune choices to a small repertoire when performing with the dancers. Specific tunes match specific figures of the quadrille and in this regard remain relatively static. Coupled with the fact that the most recent dance choreographies date back to at least the 1950s (Allert, interview, 1997; Adams, interview, 1995; Caliste, interview, 1995), it is clear that the Carriacou quadrille tradition—both the music and dance—is conservative overall. And because there are so

FIGURE 3.6 Quadrille musicians, L'Esterre, Carriacou, January 1995. Left to right: Gavis
Caliste (tambourine), Canute Caliste (violin), Enel James (bass drum).

few quadrille musicians remaining on Carriacou (six of them in 2001), the ensemble varies little from performance to performance.[9]

Like other violinists in Carriacou, Mr. Caliste holds his bow about two
inches above the frog (base). Rather than placing his fingers perpendicular
to the wood of the bow, he slants them toward its tip, so that his palm nearly
covers the frog. This grip, combined with his preference for tightening the
bow until the tension of the horsehair is extremely high, allows him to play
with great pressure on the strings, resulting in a louder volume.[10] Mr. Caliste also tends to slide into notes and uses only his first three fingers, whereas
most violinists and fiddlers elsewhere use all four fingers.

Mr. Caliste, like many of his musical peers, learned to play the violin and
acquired his repertoire of quadrille tunes through an oral tradition of listening and imitating. As he told me, "Quadrille is a great, great t'ing . . . Since
I was nine years old, I played. . . . Just seen something, then I do it. I got in
a lot of teaching [learning] where got people in dream and teach me one
in dreams" (interview, 1995). That Mr. Caliste learned the quadrille via
dreams underscores a significant psychosocial phenomenon in Carriacouan
culture. The power and importance of dreams extends throughout the

Kayak cosmology in the form of "dream messages," in which an ancestor appears and instructs the dreamer to hold a *saraca* and a Big Drum ceremony for the community in order to appease the spirit of the ancestor (McDaniel 1998, Pearse 1956b). On a purely musical level, it is common for musicians worldwide to dream about tunes and, upon awakening, attempt to reconstruct the music.[11]

FIGURE 3.7 Transcription 2: Carriacou quadrille tune.

FIGURE 3.7 *(Continued)*

DANCING THE QUADRILLE

Back at Mrs. Joseph's home store in Harveyvale, the quadrille evening is stymied after the ring-wetting ceremony, for only three of the requisite eight members of the L'Esterre Quadrille Group are present. The problem is to find five people who are familiar with the choreographies. Time passes.

On stage, the musicians continue to play, while the audience members chat and buy drinks from the beverage counter. Finally, Mrs. Samerson, the wife of the president of the L'Esterre Quadrille Group and its dance caller, Mr. Joy Samerson, agrees to dance as the head lady. L'Esterre Quadrille Group members Cosmos Bristol and Alicia Caliste (one of Canute Caliste's twenty-three children) form a side couple. Both dancers in the tail couple are L'Esterre residents and experienced dancers but not members of the group. The other side couple includes the son of Mrs. Joseph and a family friend, neither of whom is particularly experienced at quadrille dancing, but both of whom make up for their errors with an abundance of enthusiasm and good humor.

The dancers take their places as the music for the first figure begins. Mr. Samerson calls out the choreographies, and the dancers move through the dance. The less-experienced side couple relies on the gentle nudging and additional instruction offered by the other dancers. Spirits are high, however, and Mr. Caliste begins the next quadrille tune. The second figure opens with a "wheel," whereby couples swing their partner in a ballroom hold. The woman in the tail couple and the head man go "forward and back" while the other dancers dance the four-beat "step-step-step-lift" footwork in place. All the couples wheel again, the less-experienced couple a beat or two behind.

The audience is full of excitement, applause, and commentary in the form of praise and critique after each figure. After only two more figures, however, Bristol ends the quadrille portion of the evening due to the inexperienced dancers and the resulting uneven dancing. With great warmth and humor, the dancers shake hands, and the more experienced dancers congratulate Mrs. Joseph's son and his dance partner on a job well done. Cosmos Bristol later tells me that ideally all eight of the dancers would have been members of the quadrille group; after they had danced, members of the family and community would then be invited to participate too.

The musicians start a set of lively polkas, waltzes, cacians, and breakaways, and the dance floor immediately fills up with couples.[12] As things heat up, seventy-year-old Sonnelle Allert puts down his tambourine, jumps off the stage, and, with fantastic grace and energy, begins to polka with a woman friend. Dancing continues for an hour or more, and the evening eventually breaks up. Despite the disorganization and absenteeism of the L'Esterre Quadrille Group itself, the dance is deemed a great success.

Carriacou quadrille arose from three disparate cultural sources that have merged to create a thoroughly creolized music and dance tradition. The dance form itself is clearly European, as is the lead instrument and the overall symmetry of the choreography. The West and Central African influences appear in the use and roles of the three percussion instruments, the rhythmic patterns and hemiola effects created between the violin and the percussion instruments, the polyrhythmic music itself, and the dancers' mid-body dance movement. Finally, there is the distinctly Carriacouan component: newer choreographies, footwork and additional body movement improvised by Kayaks over the years, and an idiosyncratic musical elaboration that borrows equally from European- and African-derived aesthetics. Moreover, quadrille is essentially Carriacouan thanks to its overall creolized performance aesthetic specific to Kayak culture, born out of years of ritual and social use and, like quadrille forms elsewhere in the Americas, "modified and adapted to local cultural circumstances" (Szwed and Marks 1988: 29).

Carriacou quadrille continues to hold both spiritual and social meaning for older Carriacouans. However, the select group of them who can actually dance the quadrille is dwindling, unlike the number of people able to share in the largely participatory Big Drum ceremony. Because of this, the quadrille tradition is in danger of collapsing for lack of participants, despite its regular performance in island events, great and small. In order to better appreciate the changing aesthetics and significance of the role of quadrille in contemporary Carriacou, an understanding of quadrille's past is helpful, for the history of quadrille is the history of Carriacou—a legacy of enslavement, colonial rule, and changing postcolonial identities.

HISTORY AND GENESIS OF THE QUADRILLE

Quadrille dance originated in the late eighteenth century in France, quickly became the rage of the Paris elite, and remained one of the most popular ballroom dances in Europe throughout the first half of the nineteenth century.[13] The quadrille was introduced in London in 1815. By the time Queen Victoria came to the throne, the quadrille was firmly established there as the foremost ceremonial court dance (Richardson 1960: 61). By 1821 its popularity had spread to Berlin and Vienna, peaking perhaps by 1840. Quadrille's popularity during these years cannot be underestimated: in his dance manual *Analysis of the London Ball-Room* (1825), Thomas Tegg waxes eloquent about the introduction of quadrille in England: "Quadrilles are of novel introduction in this country, and we are indebted to the French for their revival, for they approximate so nearly to the dance termed the Cotillion that design or invention cannot with justice be applied. They are danced in sets of eight . . . [which are] best calculated for displaying the true spirit and the elegant graceful evolutions of this mode of dancing" (Tegg 1825: 92).

The classic nineteenth-century quadrille consisted of five or more distinct parts or figures. Unlike the individual choreographies of Carriacou quadrille, which are simply referred to as "Figure One," "Figure Two," and so on, each figure of the early–nineteenth-century quadrille had a name that did not change, although the accompanying music might. Many of these quadrilles were elegantly transcribed (and described) using ornate drawings and graphics by dance masters of the era such as Tegg or Vincent Masi (see Tegg 1825; Masi 18[??]). These published collections also included transcriptions of quadrille music, notated for various combinations of violin, flute, piano, and other string and woodwind instruments. Tempo markings indicate that the music was played at a moderately fast tempo appropriate for social dancing. The music consisted of melodies of eight or sixteen bars to a section, with repeated sections. Tunes were most often in 4/4 or 2/4 time, though some were in 6/8 and even 9/8.

European quadrille tunes were often adapted from popular songs or stage works, including operetta and opera. The Strausses in Vienna, Musard in France, and Jullien in England were among the prominent quadrille composers during the early to mid-1800s. Borrowed from a variety of elite and popular forms, quadrille music necessarily had to be altered to suit the length of the accompanying dance figures. Quadrilles eventually became less of an elite pursuit, and, like many expressive genres, moved into the culture of the European lower classes. At this point quadrilles moved across the Atlantic to the United States and were adopted into the repertories of both white and black social dance orchestras there during the first half of the nineteenth century.

Because Britain and France were key imperialist world powers during these centuries, quadrille and its variants spread prolifically throughout English and French colonies worldwide. Although quadrille eventually gave way to other social dances in the mother countries, its legacy remains in a number of former British and French colonies, especially throughout the

Caribbean (see Austerlitz 1997; Averill 1997; Guilbault 1984; Manuel 1994; Rohlehr 1990; Yih 1995).[14] In Carriacou, the music and dance of the European ruling elite was appropriated, combined with extant African musical and kinesthetic elements, and, as in the other former colonies, emerged as an important social and performative expression for slaves and their offspring.

HISTORY OF QUADRILLE MUSIC AND
DANCE IN GRENADA AND CARRIACOU

It is unclear how exactly quadrille music and dance arrived in Carriacou during the late eighteenth century.[15] The era was marked by several changes in ownership of the three islands of Grenada, Carriacou, and Petit Martinique, from Britain beginning in 1763, to France in 1779, to Britain again in 1783. The French presence in Carriacou, however, remained strong, so it is conceivable that the quadrille, as danced by French landowners and planters, was at this time assimilated into slave culture. A similar argument can be made for the possible contribution of British landowners, however, particularly on Carriacou, where at least half of the plantations by the end of the eighteenth century were British owned. Local lore also attributes the emergence of quadrille in Carriacou in part to the arrival of Scottish boat builders who, toward the end of the eighteenth century, settled in the villages of Windward and Dover (Briget Rao, unpublished local history of Windward, 1997; Bristol, interview, 1997; Allert, interview, 1997).[16] After generations of intermarriage, the population in this northern part of Carriacou is largely of mixed race; quadrille, however, is no longer danced in these villages.[17]

Whatever its origins, in the nineteenth century the elite populations of Grenada and Carriacou enjoyed quadrille and its cousin, English country dance. Frequent notices in nineteenth-century newspapers published in St. George's attest to the performance of quadrille dance, such as this account from 1828 in the *Grenada Free Press and Public Gazette:* "On Monday evening, the 24th instant, a subscription ball was given at BAKER'S. . . . Dancing commenced at nine o'clock, and was carried on with great spirit till one, when the party retired to the supper room. . . . The pleasures of the table did not, however, long restrain the eager party from returning to the fascinating *quadrille* and lively *country-dance,* which were kept to an *early* hour, when the company broke up; and, we firmly believe, that every individual felt the pain of parting" (1828: 496).

Similar notices attest to the performance of quadrille music and related instrumental dance genres throughout the 1800s as well. The regular importation of violins, flutes, concertinas, guitars, and other European musical instruments and accessories to Grenada and Carriacou is documented via the cargo lists of vessels and ships arriving in St. George's as well as in Hillsborough, Carriacou, and suggests an ongoing demand by the populace for portable instruments. An article from the *St. George's Chronicle and Gazette* dated April 14, 1857, details the importance placed by the European landowners in Grenada on music education, particularly the cultivation of young quadrille and ballroom musicians:

> A friend conversing with us a few days since on the subject of "Education" observed that numerous instances of *"native talent"* had fallen under his personal observation in this Colony . . . amongst other parties whom he had named, he instanced the two sons of Mr. Watson, boys of 8 and 12 years of age, whose performance on the violin he described as something extraordinary. We consequently sought an opportunity of hearing these children perform, and we must do our friend the justice to say—that he had in no way romanced in his commendation on their natural Musical Genius. The elder played as well as most performers of mature age—whilst the younger *infant* . . . played innumerable airs—quadrilles, waltzes, polkas, &c.—with a firmness of fingering, a command of his bow, and a power of execution, which were wonderful in a child of his tender years. We have no doubt that with proper *education* these talented children will, at a future time, become distinguished Musicians.

How exactly quadrille music and dance moved from the exclusive dominion of the plantocracy to the communities of enslaved Africans in Carriacou is unclear.[18] Scholars note that slaves often performed personal and mundane tasks, ranging from hard labor to caring for the children of the plantocracy (Goveia 1959, as cited in Mintz 1974: 81), and were similarly asked to play music for their owner's dances (see Southern 1977, Szwed and Marks 1988; for a poignant, first-person account, see Berlin et al. 1998: 161). Because quadrille music was, in general, disseminated among the white population largely through printed notation, slave musicians were either taught to read music or, more likely, learned though the oral tradition, that is, via imitation and listening to the playing of musically literate quadrille musicians. Enslaved Afro-Caribbeans presumably learned the dance also from watching and imitating. In addition, it is possible that some choreographies were learned from the aforementioned dance manuals, which offered detailed sketches of each dance; these manuals were widely disseminated throughout Europe and the English colonies (see Tegg 1825 and Masi 18[??]).

Published travelogues in the years leading up to emancipation attest to the assimilation and adaptation of quadrille and related dances into slave cultures. An 1832 issue of the *Grenada Free Press and Public Gazette,* written in the anti-emancipation rhetoric that was common to Caribbean and British newspapers during these years, compares the quadrille dancing of allegedly content slaves to that of the English peasantry:

REPLY TO THE QUERIES PUT BY THE COMMITTEE APPOINTED TO CORRESPOND WITH SIR WILLIAM STRUTH, AS DELEGATE FROM THE ISLAND OF ST. VINCENT, TO GIVE EVIDENCE BEFORE THE COMMITTEE OF LORDS AND COMMONS, By the Reverend Thomas Alexander Brown, of Grand Sable Estate September 23rd, 1832.

1st—What is the number of Negroes on your Estate at Grand Sable? An[swer] 683 . . .

Dances and entertainments are given all over the island at Christmas . . . On these occasions, they spend the greater part of day and night in dancing, with their usual characteristic ardour and agility, displaying such an easy graceful movement, and marking with so much precision the time and tune, that their performance would often do credit to the more practised elegante; and is very favorably contrasted with the rude earnestness and clumsy movement of the English peasant, who, neglecting or ignorant of the airy movement "on the light fantastic toe," confines his skill to the incessant thumping of his heel, in or out of tune, or an awkward swing, endangering his neighbours' shins by his ungraceful pirouette.

Such newspaper accounts, coupled with church records, a handful of slave ledgers, and census records from the slave-trade era (see Brinkley 1978), represent the few extant written sources about the lives of the enslaved in Carriacou. Here, I rely on Henry Louis Gates Jr.'s (1988) methodology, which suggests that in order to construct a historical narrative of the

African diaspora, scholars must reassemble the extant cultural fragments to read a textual past, an act that relies in part on fact and in part on speculation (see also McDaniel 1986, 1998). In Carriacou these fragments might include oral histories, songs descriptive of the era, contemporary beliefs, and material culture, all of which provide evidence of an enslaved past that remains deeply ingrained in the collective cultural memory.

CLASS, SOCIAL HIERARCHY, AND DANCE PERFORMANCE

Some contemporary practitioners of Carriacou quadrille believe that their enslaved ancestors learned to dance quadrille thanks to the good graces of the plantation owners, contributing to what many Kayaks view as Carriacou's historically classless society.[19] Today, most Kayaks acknowledge the existence of occupational classes in Carriacou and recognize that some Kayaks have more assets than others. In fact there is significant social pressure on those who accumulate wealth and do not share it with the rest of the community (Hill 1977: 338). That a basic acceptance of classlessness exists in Carriacou underscores the notion that income does not define social status; that is, nobody is socially above anybody else, despite differences in income level. Indeed, one of the most common expressions among Kayaks is "We is one family," a figurative concept that in fact derives from the literal reality that most people in Carriacou are related by blood or marriage, however distantly.[20] Cosmos Bristol articulates this understanding of historic classlessness in relation to quadrille dance, framed by family lore handed down from his great-grandmother:

> Carriacou had never been a class society . . . it was never defined clearly by any demarcation and that is why . . . it was so easy for [the people of L'Esterre] to get quadrille. 'Cause one would recognize that if there was a prestigious dance in any society, as the lower class citizen, perhaps you would never ever get a chance to even witness the dance, far less to be able to be dancing the dance. [Laughs]
>
> What I'm saying here is because there was no class system in our culture, if a slave was close enough to the master to adopt the dance, he was given a chance to dance. . . . They were not considered by their masters as this group of people who were so low in status. (Interview, 1997)

The belief that one's ancestors were better treated than slaves elsewhere is shared among descendants of enslaved Africans throughout the black Atlantic.[21] In Carriacou, it is at odds with other evidence, largely that from the oral tradition. For example, a Big Drum nation song ("Bongo") sung in the nearly extinct local French *patois* and written in the days of slavery relates the story of a husband and wife who were separated, sold individually, and sent, without their children, to Trinidad and to Haiti, respectively:

Pléwé mwê Lidé, Pléwé Maiwaz, oh
Hélé mwê, Lidé, hélé oh, Maiwaz
Hélé pu nu alé.

Weep for me, Lidé, weep, Maiwaz.
Lament for me, Lidé, lament, Maiwaz.
Lament for our going.

Dimâsh pwoshî bâtma-la-vol-a Haishi
Vâdi ya bâtmâ-la-vol-a kité, oh, Maiwaz.

Sunday next, the schooner sails for Haiti
Friday the schooner leaves, Maiwaz.

Sa ki kôtâ mwê, kôsolé yish mwê ba mwê
Sa ki kôtâ mwê, kôsolé Zabette ba mwê
Sa ki émê mwê, kôsolé Walter ba mwê

Whoever loves me, console my children for me
Whoever loves me, console Zabette for me
Whoever loves me, console Walter for me. (Pearse 1956b: 4)[22]

The Code Noir of 1685, which was later reinforced by the Grenadian Acts of 1825, prohibited the separation of enslaved children from their parents and the separate sale of married slaves (Brizan 1984: 104). Despite these enactments, at least some slave owners in Carriacou resorted to these practices—acts that were quite possibly more the norm than the exception.

Scholars in Carriacou similarly have found collective memories, folklore, and oral histories depicting the horror of slavery. An informant named Adam told Donald Hill, "We are a race of African ascendancy down here because they were selling those people in those days in Africa as animals. . . . In those days a white man in Harvey Vale was beating them so much. They used to put a woman that [have] belly big, dig a hole, and put a woman leg down, belly inside the hold and they beat them until they make child. This white man . . . die in Harvey Vale. The day he die a cannon go on hill cause he was too bad" (Hill 1977: 206). Lorna McDaniel (1986, 1998) has uncovered similar beliefs on the part of older Carriacouans of the extreme cruelty endured by their enslaved ancestors, conditions that, she argues, engendered a collective mythology of the slaves' figurative return to Africa by wing. This recurrent trope of cruelty has persisted over almost two centuries as a collective memory, passed down through the oral lore of Carriacouans.

My research in Carriacou identifies both historic and contemporary attitudes about the enslavement of Kayak ancestors. Carriacouans, for example, generally acknowledge that the steady decline in agriculture on the island over the past eighty years is largely due to its ongoing association with slavery (Hill 1977: 238). Senator Elvin G. Nimrod, Minister of Carriacou and Petit Martinique Affairs, agrees: "People have now come to believe, that well, I've heard it said [farming] is too reminiscent of slavery to be doing cotton and lime and these types of things. I think to take the attitude that to go back to the soil is reminiscent of slavery [is] a demeaning position" (interview, 1997).

Similarly, tourism in Carriacou has yet to be developed, despite many Kayaks' belief that this industry would benefit the island's economic future. In addition to factors stemming from an underdeveloped island infrastructure, other concerns may also be impeding tourism's growth, as Senator Nimrod observes: "And then you also have to deal with your own citizens and the attitudes towards tourists. Because if you have a populace who has a negative attitude toward certain foreigners and that could have a problem" (interview, 1997).

Given that most tourists in Carriacou are white North Americans and Europeans, it is possible that this reluctance to embrace tourism is rooted, on some level, in a collective memory of enslavement and colonial repression. In 1997, for example, I noticed a popular tee-shirt worn primarily by young Kayak men that said something to the effect that (the wearer) of this tee-shirt doesn't like white folks because they made (his) ancestors work for hundreds of years without pay. Such a postcolonial framing of history underscores the bitterness engendered by slavery more than 150 years after emancipation.

Among Kayaks today, there exists a wide range of perceptions as to the conditions endured by their enslaved ancestors. These perspectives on an enslaved and colonized past give rise to a contemporary cultural ambivalence, whereby members of a society are conflicted over some part of their cultural identity. Beginning in the 1960s, such a collective ambivalence arose surrounding the significance of Carriacou quadrille as a marker of Kayak identity. At the same time the island's population underwent a series of intense political, economic, and social upheavals—events that would force Kayaks to reconsider their political and social identity, as well as various expressions of their traditional culture.

EMIGRATION, INDEPENDENCE, AND REVOLUTION

Carriacou quadrille began to wane in the mid-1950s, eventually surrendering its familiar and important place in the community. Until 1955, "older heads," for example, recall attending social and ritual quadrilles at gravestone-raising ceremonies, "fishermen's birthdays" (ritual picnics to give thanks to the sea), celebrations in memory of a deceased member of the community, weddings, christenings, and "forty night" ceremonies, which take place forty nights after a community member's death (Adams, interview, 1995; see also Smith 1962).[23] In 1953, M. G. Smith conducted fieldwork in Carriacou, observing that "old time 'bouquet'" or "company" dances were the most popular form of secular dance in Carriacou, joining Lancers, reels, and "nineteenth-century dance patterns" (Smith 1962: 10). Bouquet dances acquainted people from different villages and provided an arena for socializing and marriage. Kayak musician and dancer Sonnell Allert (born 1928) specifically recalls that quadrilles, waltzes, and "heel and toe" were danced at these events: "Now there is people from [the villages of] Windward, Top Hill, Mt. Royal, they has a bouquet dance. . . . You make a dance in your home. . . . Then, [the hosting couple] has a bouquet, they come out with it at 12 o'clock in the night. And when they come from the room . . . they [throw] the bouquet. So then you know, when the dance finish, you have to decide what time you make your dance in you home, you who the bouquet falled on. Like if you get married and you fling your flowers."[24]

Bouquet dances continued into the 1960s until a combination of factors led to their demise. Most significantly, the rate of immigration of Carriacouans to England increased to staggering levels in the early to mid-1950s.

Furthermore, the long-lasting devastation of Hurricane Janet in 1955 significantly altered many aspects of Carriacouan society, first by leveling all but twelve houses island-wide (McIntosh 1955). By the early 1960s, changing British immigration laws made it easier for Kayak women and children to also emigrate. Donald Hill (1977: 227) writes that these changes in demographics were so extensive, that the upheaval "mark[ed] a new era in the island's history comparable with the abolition of slavery." With young adults steadily leaving Carriacou, the bouquet dances died out by the late 1960s for lack of participants.

Carriacou in the late 1960s and 1970s was changing in other ways as well. Taking their cue from the Civil Rights and Black Power Movements in the United States, younger Carriacouans began to look to Africa as an affirmation of heritage and identity. Young people presented concerts of African music and dance, including an annual, island-wide "Black Arts Festival" (L. Stiell, interview, 1997) and dramatic presentations depicting local Kayak African-based traditions such as the *maroon* (village celebration) and *saraca* (feast). Similarly, the more overtly African-based components of Carriacou culture took on greater meaning. According to businessman/politician Lyle Bullen, the Big Drum dance ceremony, for example, became a means to articulate through performance the prevailing black nationalist discourse. The Big Drum then took on a deeper cultural significance:

> You understood that you were brought from Africa as slaves. You understand that you were barred from certain things because you were slaves, such as [personal freedom], universal suffrage, owning land. You understood though that back in Africa, that you were master of your own fate, before your life was interrupted. . . . So forming that link and by using the language of the Big Drum transports you back to Africa and the richness that was Africa and the mother land. And the independence that you had. And it fires you up with that sort of a business to recapture what you had lost. (Interview, 1997)

Amidst this shift of focus to things African, it is not surprising that quadrille lost favor, right up through Grenada's independence from Britain in 1974. Paget Henry notes that as a black culture moves toward decolonization, blackness is revalorized while whiteness is devalued, both "attempts to undo and reject the process of cultural colonization" (P. Henry 1983: 108).

While quadrille was not completely rejected during this era, it did not enjoy a renaissance in interest as did African and African-derived cultural expressions. Winston Fleary sums up the collective opinion of many Carriacouans regarding the demise of quadrille: "They view[ed] it as a white man's dance, the white man's thing."

The years leading up to and immediately following independence were marked by a steady decline in the overall quality of life, a crumbling island infrastructure, and high unemployment, leaving young Carriacouans little choice but to emigrate (Hill 1977: 225–27; Searle 1982; Brizan 1984: 295). Carriacou's infrastructure deteriorated even further during the neocolonial government of Prime Minister Sir Eric Gairy, engendering growing opposition to Gairy and increasing discontent with the quality of life. Younger Carriacouans—those who stayed on the island—increasingly rejected folk traditions in general and turned toward more modern sounds from combo bands. With electricity coming to Carriacou in the 1970s (and reaching all parts of the island only in the early 1980s), these combo bands were truly modern by Carriacou standards. They featured electric guitars, bass, and sometimes organ, and they played the popular calypsos of the day, as well as Jamaican reggae, both of which were appealing in their open critique of authority. Young Carriacou musicians were also attracted to Trinidadian steel band music in the late 1960s and 1970s. Along with modern combos providing music for social occasions and dances, there was less demand for quadrille dances among the younger generation.

Despite these trends, quadrille was given new life in the village of L'Esterre. Up until the late 1950s, the Catholic Church had played an important part in promoting quadrille in the primarily Catholic villages of L'Esterre and Windward, as well as on Carriacou's sister island, Petit Martinique. After some years of decline, the Catholic Church in L'Esterre again began promoting quadrille in the late 1960s in its local elementary school, the L'Esterre Roman Catholic (RC) School.[25] Taught by the school's principal, quadrille violinist Andrew Benjamin, students during these years remember music and arts competitions among the Carriacou schools and that L'Esterre RC School often won with its quadrille demonstrations. Quadrille performances thus became a local badge of achievement and prestige: according to Cosmos Bristol, only the oldest students who excelled academically—those who passed an entrance exam to Class Six—were eligible to learn quadrille: "You had to attain Class Six of the school to be selected for dance. So every year a new group of students would get into the Class Six, except for instance, if some people fail the exam.... So if you should leave school early you would miss out on the dance" (C. Bristol, interview, 1997). [26]

The older residents of L'Esterre, concerned about the possibility of quadrille's demise, reinforced the church's encouragement. Musician Jerry McGillivary remembers being urged, as a youngster in L'Esterre, to learn quadrille: "Mrs. Samerson taught me.... I was never interested but then once she tell me, 'Jerry, come on, you have to do it.' Because I was musical. I could not dance quadrille and then, first night I do it. And it was perfect. And then I continue" (interview, 1997).

Lastly, this quadrille revival was fueled in no small part by national cultural initiatives put into place in the years following the Grenadian Revolution, when Prime Minister Bishop's administration actively encouraged the revitalization and performance of *all* local cultural expressions, including Carriacouan quadrille. Thus reinvigorated, quadrille music and dance took on something of a new life, becoming not only a proud emblem of the village of L'Esterre but also paralleling the gradual cultural transformation of Carriacouan society from a neocolonial mentality to a postcolonial identity.

QUADRILLE MOVES TO THE STAGE

In the decades since independence, Carriacouans have been forced to reconsider their role in an increasingly global economy. Tourism remains a largely undeveloped industry there, relative to the rest of the region—according to Mario Bullen, director of the Grenada Board of Tourism, the number of tourists who visit Carriacou is but a fraction of the already relatively small number who travel to Grenada (M. Bullen, interview, 1997). [27] Nevertheless, Carriacou Big Drum musicians, dancers, and singers, as well as quadrille and string band players, occasionally have opportunities to perform for small tourist audiences. The L'Esterre Quadrille Group was formed in 1995 to professionalize the musicians and dancers so that when the group is asked to perform at public functions, they are rehearsed, they have appropriate costumes, and the musicians' instruments are in good repair, as Gus Adams observes: "I think the idea came into their minds that instead of approaching individual people to dance ... why not form a group as the [L'Esterre] Folk Group used to be before. With the quadrille as part of it. So when any approach is made, the approach would be made as a group and not as individual members to dance" (interview, 1995).

A contemporary version of a social club or a folk institution, the L'Esterre Quadrille Group is community-based and strictly voluntary, and it has a formal infrastructure, including a president, a treasurer, and other officers.[28] The group has no established fee schedule for quadrille performances; indeed, they generally accept whatever the sponsoring entity might offer. In some instances, such as performances in Grenada, the sponsors pay for transportation, overnight accommodations and food, and a small honorarium to cover costumes and expenses. When they receive a fee, group members put it toward expenses and instrument maintenance. Community performances such as a *saraca* seldom pay at all, and the performers' compensation is simply food and drink.

Members of the L'Esterre Quadrille Group in part see their mission as one of preservation through presentation, and they often mention the need to promote quadrille music and dance because it is part of Carriacouan traditional culture. Gus Adams, like most, fears with good reason that quadrille will die out if younger Kayaks do not learn to play the music or learn the dance choreographies:

> Even after maybe I'm dead and gone, quadrille should remain. People should be able to see what the quadrille dance is all about. Because it's a unique dance, like the Big Drum. . . . If some young person does not at this stage learn to play the violin, in the next few years . . . after CC's [Canute Caliste] dead and gone, we'll wonder what quadrille used to be like. The other reason is if a lot of young people now doesn't take on quadrille as part of the cultural arts, it would die again because when we might be too old to dance or when we dead and gone, then what happens? (Interview, 1995)

QUADRILLE PERFORMANCE AS AN ELITE INSTITUTION

Formal performances make up the majority of the L'Esterre Quadrille Group's activities and include annual appearances at Culture Night during Regatta, at the Parang Festival, during Carnival, at concerts sponsored by various arts and civic groups in Grenada, and at Caribbean music and dance festivals. Unlike the occasional social or ritual quadrilles, where the dancers and musicians dress in regular clothes and shoes, the staged performances present the performers in one of two sets of costumes. When performing outside of Carriacou, the ensemble wears a "collar and tie" costume of formal black pants, white button-down shirts, black ties, and black shoes for the men, and elegant European-style ballroom dresses and white pumps for the women.[29] In performances for Kayak audiences, the men wear black pants and either white or colorful Caribbean print shirts, and the women wear long skirts made from the same colorful print material, white blouses, and black, low-heeled sandals (or dance barefoot).

The choice of costuming, like other aspects of the semiotics of formal quadrille performance, suggests the cultural ambivalence toward quadrille's role in defining Carriacouan identity. When the L'Esterre Quadrille Group performs in formal garb, they communicate an aesthetic of upper-class European elegance and wealth. While some people dressed in their "Sunday best" for bouquet dances years ago, the group members now specifically speak of the "collar and tie" as *costumes*—that is, clothing specific to quadrille performances that is not worn at other times.[30] Dancer Cosmos Bristol observes that costumes are selected based on the audience (local Carriacouan versus national Grenadian) and the occasion (informal versus formal). The prestige factor of the event, according to Bristol, is significant, as is the group's desire to present quadrille dance to audiences as a recreation of a different era and culture, that is, a European golden age: "At the big performances on stage, one has to be gentlemen. . . . The dance is a highly prestigious dance and of course you want to show the high standard that is part of the thing, you know? Whereas at the *saraca,* you can be yourself, you can free up a little, and you can really wheel around and stuff like that. . . . We [are] depicting the quadrille dance as [it] was. . . . Way back when it was brought here or probably as it was done in England and France in the . . . eighteenth century" (interview, 1997).

The L'Esterre Quadrille Group's off-island performances typically take place in Grenada, and this particular need to impress is partially rooted in the dynamic between Carriacouans and Grenadians. As a double-dependency island, Carriacou historically has had a somewhat turbulent relationship with the Grenadian national government and has long been viewed by Grenadians as a backwater. By formalizing the quadrille performance, the unspoken intent of the quadrille group is to elevate the "respectability" of this folk art genre, especially for Grenadian and other non-Kayak audiences. "Collar and tie" performances also contribute an air of historical authenticity, as Winston Fleary points out: "[The collar and tie is] essentially correct because it shows what the history of the thing is. It is related to Europe and that is how they dress. . . . We should respect people's culture and don't water it down. So Europe has what is good and . . . it should be expressed as theirs. [Quadrille] is something that we learned. This is theirs. This is Europe's" (interview, 1997). Fleary's primary interest is the Big Drum ceremony, and he is largely concerned with authenticity regarding Kayak African heritage. His view of quadrille as belonging to the "Other" is extreme; only some of the quadrille musicians, dancers, and audience members I've spoken with would concur. Others point out that quadrille has been an integral part of their specifically Kayak history, life, and identity. And, while quadrille was once strictly European, it is no longer; it is a creolized form that has been appropriated and personalized by Kayaks both musically and kinesthetically for nearly two centuries.[31]

The association of quadrille with elitism coheres on an aesthetic level with the pretense of wearing Euro-elite costumes for some performances. This emphasis on dress arises from the fact that quadrille was initially learned by house slaves rather than field slaves, a hierarchy common to slave cultures throughout the Americas, as noted by Winston Fleary: "There's a slavocracy and there's a plantocracy. . . . Inside slaves . . . ought to be proper, ought to be cultured, as it were. . . . Gotta be able to speak right, act right. . . . But the field slaves, ordinary, everyday, down to earth, into nature thing. They're the slavocracy. The plantocracy is the owners of plantations or the overseers. And they had servants and these servants belonged to them. So we really associate [these house slaves], yes, with the plantocracy" (interview, 1997).

That the house slaves danced quadrille alongside their owners contributed to the hierarchy within enslaved culture on Carriacou, one that persists in cultural memory today. For many, there is the sense that the practice of quadrille continues to be selective to the point of being exclusive and exclusionary, as L'Esterre teacher and musician Lionel Stiell explains:

If you know the history of the quadrille in L'Esterre, you would see that sometimes it's a select few who really dance. . . . All the people been dancing years, but they haven't been showing it out or teaching other people to do it. . . . Few people really dance the quadrille, though. I think they should teach a lot more people, you know. Have classes and maybe [teach] the schoolchildren. . . . People tend to keep things closed up, facilitate few so that they could say "I could dance the quadrille you know." (Interview, 1997)

Stiell's comments are underscored by quadrille's recent transmission history—that is, only the best students at L'Esterre RC School were allowed to learn it. Compounding this sense of privilege is the reality that the establishment of the L'Esterre Quadrille Group further limits participation by other residents who might know how to dance the quadrille. Because quadrille in Carriacou no longer fulfills an essential social or recreation need, the only opportunity to dance it is at the increasingly rare local event, such as a wedding or *saraca,* that involves families who enjoy quadrille dance. Both these performance contexts, however, remain the purview of the L'Esterre Quadrille Group.

QUADRILLE PERFORMANCE AS AN EXPRESSION OF REGIONALISM

At other times the members of the L'Esterre Quadrille Group perform wearing a more local, Caribbean-styled costume sewn by the women dancers: "It was thought that we should revolutionize the quadrille and make it a little more Caribbean, add a little more Caribbean flavor to it. And the whole concept of a Caribbean flavor is one that is based on color. And so the females had very floral skirts of which the men's shirts were made. So we had floral shirts. Matching the skirts of the females. We had black pants and the females would have had white tops" (C. Bristol, interview, 1996). Aside from being more comfortable to dance in than the "collar and tie," these outfits suggest an appreciation of the fact that quadrille has, on some level, been internalized by performers and audience as essentially Carriacouan, as opposed to European. This level of acceptance of quadrille as Carriacouan is underscored by Donald Hill's research from 1970, in which he noted that as a quintessentially creolized form, quadrille had become so much a part of the Kayak cultural landscape that it was sometimes referred to as "African quadrille," and it routinely included propitiations to the ancestors (Hill 1993: 150). Dancer Gus Adams confirms this level of acceptance: "A lot of people still appreciate quadrille because it has gone through the *African family* for years after it was handed down to us as part of the English thing. So a lot of people appreciate quadrille; they like to see quadrille" (Adams, interview, 1995; emphasis added).

FIGURE 3.8, 3.9 The L'Esterre Quadrille Group performing at the Carriacou Carnival held in the Tennis Courts, Hillsborough, Carriacou, February 1997.

The colorful and matching Caribbean costumes serve other semiotic purposes. They indicate the L'Esterre Quadrille Group's desire to be perceived by other Carriacouans as a professional dance troupe, thus elevating quadrille from the social event it once was to an art and performance form. In doing so, the collective memory associating quadrille with slavery, years of colonial rule, and attendant cultural ambivalence is supplanted by a prestigious contemporary aesthetic of public performance. Secondly, the quadrille group's pan-Caribbean costuming and the relaxed nature of the local performance of quadrille serves to locate quadrille as not only specifically Carriacouan, but also offers a postcolonial interpretation of Carriacou as part of a greater, pan-Caribbean culture.

Such a dual sense of belonging suggests a contemporary application of Du Bois's concept of double consciousness, whereby the African American "ever feels his twoness" (Du Bois 1969: 45). In Carriacou, this changing sense of identity is informed by the pervasive influences of regional and transnational cultures and economies (see Gilroy 1993: 126–27). Thus, practitioners of quadrille—as well as some of their audiences—express a dual understanding of identity via quadrille: on one hand, a powerful assertion of cultural autonomy and on the other, a decidedly postcolonial statement of belonging to the greater Caribbean region.

THE PROGRESS OF CULTURAL IDENTITY:
COLLECTIVE MEMORY/AMBIVALENCE

Many Carriacouans are cognizant of their specific African lineage— Cromanti, Mandingo, Kongo, Igbo, and so on (Canute Caliste, interview, 1995; David 1985: 25)—a sense of identity underscored in the performance practice of Big Drum Nation Dances.[32] This primarily sacred repertory of nine distinct dance types is representative of the specific West African origins of Carriacouans, in contrast to the two other genres that complete the Big Drum ceremony: the largely secular Creole dances and the so-called Frivolous dances, such as those that are borrowed and imported (McDaniel 1998: 18). Unlike many diasporic cultures, where African expressive traditions such as the Big Drum did not thrive, Kayaks already have a rare and unique connection to their ethnic past. It is against this knowledge of ancestral identity that Kayaks measure the meaning and significance of quadrille in their present-day lives. At one extreme is the ongoing association of quadrille with its European origins, the concomitant collective memory of colonialism and enslavement, and the historic contradiction of quadrille's perceived elitism in an otherwise classless society. For some, this results in a rejection of quadrille as it is perceived to largely belong to Europe. Such perceptions underscore the ambivalence surrounding quadrille in Carriacou.

The notion of cultural ambivalence parallels but more importantly counterbalances recent discourse on collective cultural trauma and identity formation. Cultural trauma, according to Ron Eyerman, refers to a "dramatic loss of identity and meaning, a tear in the social fabric, affecting a group of people that has achieved some degree of cohesion" (Eyerman 2004: 61; see also Eyerman 2001). Both models—cultural ambivalence and cultural trauma—are responses to historical displacement and disempowerment, when "members of a collectivity feel they have been subjected to a horrendous event that leaves indelible marks upon their group consciousness, marking their memories forever and changing their future identity in fundamental and irrevocable ways" (Alexander 2004: 1). Both address the repercussions of a historical reality on a collective consciousness, rather than on the individual. And neither theory requires direct experience with the trauma itself; indeed, collective memory is often distanced over generations, as underscored by Cathy Caruth's argument that traumatic memory moves beyond the unconscious and becomes more of a symptom of history (Caruth 1995: 5). That cultural trauma can be embodied through performance, Neil Smelser notes, reflects a society's ability to convert the trauma into something positive, resulting in subsequent generations engaging in "compulsive examining and reexamining . . . reinterpreting, reevaluating, and battling over symbolic significance" (Smelser 2004: 54).

However, the notion of cultural trauma is troubling inasmuch as it treats the process of identity formation as largely or entirely a reaction to a particular history or event. It tends to pathologize the population in question by assuming some type of disordered psychic or behavioral state from which all future identities emerge, and it thereby overlooks the ongoing role of agency, both collective and individual, in cultural production. Agency—in this case, aesthetic choice—informs artistic innovation and is thus critically important, especially in creolized societies where processes of cultural piracy, appropriation, and resignification often serve as powerful sources of local identity and empowerment.

Cultural ambivalence, on the other hand, though also in part an outcome of collective and distanced memories of a traumatic past, arises from the vitally important historical syncretic processes that foreground collective and individual innovation as key factors in cultural production. In Carriacou, for example, quadrille has been clearly adapted over nearly two hundred years via innovative performance practices and the integration of new choreographies to reflect a legitimate cultural expression that is, at heart, Kayak. As a theory, cultural ambivalence, then, argues for a progressive understanding of identity formation—that is, for the critical role of aesthetic choice and agency in the context of what is oftentimes the limiting frame of heritage.

In this regard, quadrille merits consideration in terms of Denis-Constant Martin's argument for a change of emphasis from filiation or heritage to an evaluation of the place and role of innovation in the creation of Afro-American culture (Martin 1991). There are many Kayaks, particularly the "older heads," who fully accept quadrille as an integral component of their culture despite its origins, given its longevity, its creolized adaptations, and its social importance. For them, Carriacou quadrille is not European quadrille; it is a wholly hybridized form that, like other creolized cultural products, "favors reversals, contradictions, and recombinations, and calls into question the idea of sacred origins and pure beginnings" (Dash 1996: 52). Thus, quadrille can be viewed as an adaptation or even a subversion of an expressive art once belonging to those in complete power. In this sense, quadrille served as a tool for the enslaved to help them make sense of their new world and, ultimately, has evolved into an Afro-Caribbean expression with a social and aesthetic relevance—albeit a changing one—over generations.

I believe, however, that the majority of Carriacouans—quadrille practitioners and others—fall somewhere between the extremes of rejection or acceptance and are at best conflicted when it comes to quadrille, a state of mind articulated by Paul Ricoeur as a "dialectic of distanciation and appropriation" (Ricoeur 1976: 43–44). On one hand, the historic embrace of quadrille can be viewed as an act of cultural piracy or, as Andrew Apter argues, of "resistance waged through syncretic struggle" (Apter 1991: 253). For this reason, many Carriacouans continue to support quadrille precisely because its appropriation represents a sort of cultural victory. At the same time, as Apter argues, the act of appropriation also serves to reproduce and perpetuate the dominant culture, which in this case causes the pervasive Kayak cultural ambivalence toward quadrille.

If Carriacou quadrille is to survive into the twenty-first century, it is this contradiction in the cultural memory that somehow must be negotiated and resolved. Its future is at best uncertain given the 2005 death of Carriacou's sole remaining quadrille violinist, Canute Caliste. Up to this point, while there was a continuing interest in watching quadrille performances, the genre did not hold enough prestige or reward to stimulate many young Carriacouans to learn it. Ultimately, whether a Kayak violinist chooses to learn the quadrille repertoire (from tape recordings of Canute Caliste) and, indeed, whether there is room for quadrille at all, with its historical significance and stigma, will depend on how Carriacouans negotiate the forces of modernity that inform and transform a developing postcolonial identity.

4

FRIDAY NIGHT

The Hosannah Band Competition

REGGAE CHRISTMAS CAROLS emanate from a L'Esterre rum shop as I walk toward the Roman Catholic Church in mid-November. As Christmas approaches, preparations for the holiday increase to a frenzied level, with socializing, church concerts, shows, and family and community parties. It is a hot day, but I am cooled almost immediately as I enter the Church, thanks to several fans and the fact that the building is constructed in the round, a style that allows for cross-ventilation. This type of architecture encourages maximum audience interaction, as congregants are able to see more of each other during services. It is a welcoming building; tonight, it is the site of one of the first rehearsals of the New Tide Carolers Hosannah Band of L'Esterre. And I have been invited to attend.

In an effort to revive interest in what had been a dying a cappella vocal tradition, the Parang Committee instituted a Friday night Hosannah band competition in 1989. Derived from a long-time community tradition of strolling groups of mostly women singers who serenaded from house to house in the weeks leading up to Christmas, the Hosannah band competition illustrates how authenticity is negotiated in the face of a recontextualized performance practice. Here, the Parang Committee attempted to revive and preserve a traditional Kayak Christian expressive form that had fallen prey to contemporary aesthetics and lifestyle. In transforming what had been a community activity into a staged event, the Hosannah band competition pits eight-member vocal ensembles from various villages against each other, bringing to the fore old village rivalries and sometimes resulting in bruised feelings and discontent. The competition is thus not without its critics and is often a site of great contention centering on issues of cultural authenticity. Part of the conflict was generated early on by the Parang Committee itself, when officers from Grenada's Ministry of Culture were invited to develop judging criteria and serve as judges for the competition—initiatives that ultimately privilege a more polished and modern church choir sound over the local Carriacou Hosannah singing aesthetic. Accusations from various bands regarding judging biases and favoritism thus abound, fueled also by the intense village rivalry, which is on some level rooted in racial and class tensions.

The Hosannah band competition itself poses an inherent contradiction: while the Parang Committee sought to revive and preserve a traditional (but dying) style of *local* expressive culture, most of the Hosannah bands that participate now require assistance in order to adapt their choral singing style to the contemporary musical aesthetic demanded by the judging criteria. Thus, Hosannah bands have recently sought the assistance of an outsider—in some instances, a representative or culture officer from the Ministry of Culture in Grenada, or a retired American music teacher who regularly spent time in Carriacou. These coaches helped the groups with arrangements, taught the singers their parts, and prepared them for the competition. In 1996, I was asked to assist the Hosannah bands from both L'Esterre and Windward—ensembles that historically had an intense rivalry. My experience in this regard sheds light not only on the vagaries of fieldwork but also on competing notions of authenticity, particularly in relation to the process of aesthetic change given the ongoing forces of globalization. The effect of non-Kayak involvement on local performance aesthetics, combined with the event's emphasis on competition, begs bigger questions as well concerning the manipulation of culture as it is increasingly institutionalized.

THE HOSANNAH BAND TRADITION

For as long as the oldest Carriacouans can remember, each village had one or two Hosannah bands—groups of carolers who strolled from house to house through their village and neighboring villages beginning as early as late October. Some believe that the earliest Hosannah bands were made up of emancipated slaves seeking an alternate singing style to the Christmas carols performed by their former owners (W. Fleary, interview, 1997). The word Hosannah is derived from the Biblical expression "Hosannah in the highest!" from the Gospel of Luke in the New Testament, and many Carriacouans refer to the practice as "go Hosannah" or "go Hosannahing." Singing Christmas carols, hymns, and seasonal songs, Hosannah bands were typically a cappella and sang in a style that privileged melody and harmony parts.

Women of all ages have traditionally made up Hosannah bands, but Hosannahing also provided an opportunity for the youth of Carriacou to stay up late and join in the fun, as Cosmos Bristol remembers: "For most young people, that was the only time they got a chance to stay out late. Parents— and grandparents who were acting parents anyway—were so strict about kids being out there late at night that one would look forward to . . . the advent of November. . . . However, it was a weapon too. Because if you didn't behave, if you didn't perform, you would not go" (C. Bristol, interview, 1997).

In the months leading up to Christmas, the women of each village Hosannah band sewed matching outfits—white blouses and maroon skirts—and carried a large banner displaying the name of the band's home village and one other word such as "Joy," "Peace," and so on. Beginning in the early evening, Hosannah singers would often carol late into the night:

> You'd be awakened by this just beautiful singing . . . it was always very late. I don't know why. You would always be awakened maybe about two or three in the morning. . . . And it wasn't people just dressed anyhow. They would have their uniforms: their white gloves, their maroon skirts. You know, really nicely dressed and you'd have a beautiful blend of voices. (G. Bullen, interview, 1997)
>
> You want to go quietly and sing for them and wake them up. . . . Because it's nice! I used to enjoy just lying in my bed and hearing beautiful singing when you sleeping and . . . just wake you up. So you think that people get a nice feeling of Christmas. (MacFarlane, interview, 1997)

In some instances, the lateness of the hour meant that some did not get up out of their beds to greet the carolers: "At that time of the night . . . most of them, they sleeping and a little bit sleepy. So they would just hand you the money by the window and go back and light off" (MacFarlane, interview, 1997). Others, though, rose from their beds and opened the door to the carolers. These individuals were rewarded with two or three songs drawn from the band's broad repertory, which would include an array of Anglo Christmas carols and Christian religious hymns. The Hosannah bands also performed what are locally referred to as "sankeys," or upbeat gospel hymns.[1] While most sankeys were learned from inexpensive hymnals, several local residents, particularly those from the village of Mount Royal, also composed sankey-like hymns, many of which have remained popular among Carriacouans (W. Fleary, interview, 1997).[2] Carols, hymns, and sankeys were sung in a local Carriacouan style: a thick, full vocal tone with little or no vibrato, a highly melismatic delivery, and variable vocal arrangements, depending on the voices in each group. Singing in unison or in two- or three-part harmony, participants would pick out the harmonies by ear: "You kind of adapt . . . from ear, you know. Just listening. And you can sing whatever part and it just blended in really beautifully. . . . It wasn't really trained groups but they really made beautiful music" (G. Bullen, interview, 1997).

The local aesthetic governing harmony singing featured a melody carried by the soprano, accompanied by a harmony alto line and either a second (lower) alto line sung by women or a tenor line if men were involved. Alternatively, the melody line could be sandwiched between what is locally referred to as an "alto" line sung a third above the melody, and a lower harmony sung by a low alto. Another combination of parts features the soprano melody, a high harmony sung by altos, and another melody line sung an octave below the sopranos by those women who could reach the low notes, or by any available men—a preferred arrangement because it emphasizes the melody (B. Lendore, interview, 1996; T. Stiell, personal communication, 1997; C. Bristol, interview, 1997).

As the serenading Hosannah bands completed their second song at a given house, a member would step forward to introduce the group and make the first of two "speeches" or "toasts" to greet the homeowners and offer wishes for good health and prosperity. An improvised verbal art form common throughout Africa and the African diaspora, these toasts are, for many Hosannah singers, the high point of the experience. Today, toasts are typically newly written rather than improvised, or they are derived from Kayak oral tradition, such as this one remembered by teacher and musician Brian Lendore: "I hung my jawbone on a fence, / I did not teach my jawbone sense. / My jawbone walked, my jawbone talked, / My jawbone eat with knife and fork" (interview, 1996).[3]

Some toasts are pastiches constructed from excerpts of English poetry, children's rhymes, and florid "Queen's English," or they are excerpts from the Anglican Book of Common Prayer. Their tone underscores the seriousness of the occasion—carolers bringing blessings to the house—while also maintaining an atmosphere of levity. At the 1996 Parang Festival, Briget Rao of the Hosannah band Splendiferous recited the following:

The moon is bright and the stars give the light,
Until matches glitter in the night.
Behind the curtains I can see,
Your beady eyes looking at me!
So awake, awake, good people all!
Awake and hear Splendiferous call.
For when Mary had a little lamb,
its fleece was white as snow,
the boy stood on the burning deck[4]
and didn't know where to go.
King George sailed from port to port
and never reached England 'til the Christmas morning,
Christmas? The time of food and plenty!
Christmas? The time for all and sundry!

Other toasts make use of a traditional Carriacouan trope of travel and arrival (for example, walking from village to village):

Ladies and gentlemen,
we have traveled many miles across this land,
to proclaim the gospel stories in songs we love to sing!
So around this Christmas time,
we take time out to say,
a merry, merry Christmas to you,
in a very special Parang way! (Bernice Lendore, 1996)

After the toast, Hosannah bands were typically given a small amount of money. (If the caroling took place on Christmas day, the singers were offered food and drink in lieu of money.) The money was pooled and put toward the purchase of materials to make new outfits, split between members of the group, or donated to a community institution (Brian Lendore, interview, 1996). Another example of the ongoing tradition of mutual aid in Carriacou, the giving of money to Hosannah groups underscored community members' support of the bands and/or a local church or charitable institution. One or two songs later, the Hosannah band ended their presentation at the home with a final toast, such as this one recited by the late "Boy" Stiell, as recalled by his widow, Eslyn "Tateen" Stiell: "Master and Mistress, I'm going to bid you good bye. Happy where we meet, happy where you pass, until we meet again." (E. Stiell, interview, 1997). Final toasts also spoke of departure, including this one recited by Briget Rao in 1996:

> *Our song is done, we must be gone,*
> *We can stay no longer here.*
> *God bless you all, both great and small.*
> *And send you a joyful New Year!*
> *May a cup always runneth over,*
> *May goodness and merry follow you,*
> *all the days of your life.*
> *And make all generations rise up and call you,*
> *Blessed!*

Alternately, the final toast could be a narrative, such as this one recited by Cosmos Bristol in 1996: "Monseignors, Ladies and Gentlemen: my quarrelsome, miserable, but charming grandmother didn't let me out last night. That's why I did not find you at your luxurious residence. Tonight, I camouflaged. Jump through the window. That's why I'm here. But my toes got bite, my nose not right! Thorns hurt my back. I can scarcely walk. A broom stick lash me in my head! Thank God I en' dead! Now I'm getting cold feet. Because I've just given you a Christmas spirit. Thank you!"

With the final toast, the Hosannah band would move on to the next home and then to neighboring villages, serenading sleeping Kayaks along the way. Groups from the villages of Top Hill and Mount Royal typically serenaded through their villages and eventually ended up in Windward; Windward singers sang their way from the northern end of Carriacou southward to "town"—the centrally located main village of Hillsborough. Gaby MacFarlane also remembers Windward singers beginning in Hillsborough and working their way back to Windward, arriving home as late as three or four in the morning, having walked the entire distance (interview, 1997). Often two Hosannah bands, each holding their banners, would meet en route. Filled with lighthearted humor, a friendly "competition" would typically erupt in which the two groups would attempt to outsing each other. As much a social event as a performance opportunity, Hosannahing is often described by participants as pure fun, offering the sheer pleasure of group singing and visiting friends and relatives through a celebration of the holiday season. Offering a break from life's routines, Hosannah bands strengthened inter- and intra-village bonds and, in doing so, reinforced social and community coherence in Carriacou.

THE DEMISE OF HOSANNAH BANDS

The fading of Hosannahing in Carriacou began in 1955 with the devastation wrought by Hurricane Janet. A storm of enormous destructive force, Hurricane Janet destroyed entire villages in Carriacou. Shortly after, emigration from Carriacou to England sharply increased. In contrast to earlier waves, these emigrants consisted largely of women and children, due to increasingly restrictive legislation in England concerning men (Hill 1977: 227). Because Hosannahing was primarily a women's activity, this particular pattern of emigration made a significant dent in the tradition. Younger Hosannah bands continued a simpler version of the tradition that they called "caroling," which left out the traditional banner and matching costumes (MacFarlane, interview, 1997; Lendore, interview, 1996). From the 1970s through the mid-1980s, the tradition waned; by the 1990s, Hosannahing had become only an occasional activity undertaken by a handful of individuals.

Much of this decline is attributed by Kayaks to the sharp rise in the acquisition of televisions and the availability of cable networks such as CNN in Carriacou, which tend to remove both adults and children from participation in more community-oriented activities such as Hosannahing (Fortune, interview, 1997; G. Bullen, interview, 1997).[5] Television—and telephones— have altered Carriacou's social and aural landscape: "When we had no television and things like that, you'd go visiting friends . . . you'd have moonlight picnics or moonlight walks. But now you don't have that. . . . And I think that television and everything is taking away those things. Like long ago, you wanted to get a message across, you'd take a walk and you'd go visit. But now you have telephones and everybody stay at home and they call on the phone. It's really putting people apart I think" (MacFarlane, interview, 1997).[6]

Another factor since the early 1990s that contributed to the decline of in-

terest in Hosannahing is the physical barrier of locked fences built around
the new, larger Carriacouan homes. Many of these homes represent a significant portion of the life savings of retired Kayaks who have returned to the
island after living abroad in England or the United States for upward of
twenty-five years. While some returning Kayaks construct fences to prevent
theft, others, particularly those who live in more modest homes, increasingly erect them to keep free-roaming livestock out of their gardens and
yards, a perennial problem in Carriacou. Needless to say, negotiating a
locked fence poses difficulties for Hosannah singers: " [It's] not as easy as it
used to be, because so many people have fence. They property's fenced out
and there might be big dogs in there. [Laughs] . . . And it's not easy to call at
somebody's gate, one in the morning, to have him or her come out to let you
in" (C. Bristol, interview, 1997).

For all of these reasons, then, Hosannahing seemed to be a thing of
the past already by 1989, until the Mount Royal Progressive Youth Movement took action, according to its president, Wallace Collins: "People used
to go from house to house serenading just around the time Christmas was
coming. . . . [But] this year, no serenading bands were pass by my doorstep,
you know. . . . So we say, that is a problem. Okay? And we cannot afford for
it to die. So let's start something, let's start to get in this Friday night thing
involved in the Parang by getting the Hosannah Bands involved. And so we
started and we get a good response. The first year we had Hosannah, we had
about seven, eight bands, you know?" (interview, 1997).

Between 1989 and 2000, the Hosannah band competition opened the
Parang Festival. Each year's Friday-night competition featured bands
competing in both the senior (adult) and junior (children) divisions. Unlike
traditional Hosannah bands, Parang Festival Hosannah bands in the senior division are limited to just eight singers, typically two individuals per
vocal part. (The junior Hosannah bands are allowed more than eight, to
encourage the younger generation to continue this tradition.) In addition
to a "test" piece selected by the Parang Committee, each Hosannah band
also performs a "choice" piece, typically taken from a variety of Christmas
carols learned from cassette recordings or from broadcasts by regional religious radio stations. As was once the tradition, members of each Hosannah band at Parang wear matching outfits on stage, but they carry no banner. Instead, they set up a few small stage props to dramatize the content of
the test piece.

CONTESTING THE CONTEST: AUTHENTICITY
AND CULTURAL REPRESENTATION

The Parang Committee, the members of the Hosannah bands, and the judges all continually raise the question as to what is authentically Carriacouan in the weeks surrounding the Parang Festival. Some feel that the Hosannah band competition is clearly rooted in Christianity, given its non-Afro-Caribbean imagery. Others, however, see Hosannah bands as a rich part of Carriacouan culture boasting long-established local performance aesthetics. This struggle between Western notions of a Christian-derived tradition versus a more localized Kayak aesthetic is played out repeatedly in the weeks leading up to the competition.

Preparation for the Hosannah band competition begins in late October, when the Parang Committee holds a series of public meetings. Members of both Hosannah and string bands who wish to participate in the Parang Festival are apprised of any changes in the rules. They are also able to question notions of authenticity and challenge the authority of the Parang Committee, such as in this exchange at the October 1996 meeting:

Hosannah band singer: Can we do modern calypsos, Christmas calypsos for the test piece?

Parang Committee member: No. We must make it as authentic as possible.

Although Caribbean-style carols are more germane to Carriacou culture and local identity, the Western Christmas repertoire and aesthetic retains supremacy. In a subsequent debate at the same meeting, the question of authenticity arises again, this time over whether the junior Hosannah bands ought to continue to be allowed to have instrumental accompaniment, as opposed to performing a cappella:

First Hosannah band singer: Where is your authenticity? The juniors copy the seniors. Juniors are the seniors of tomorrow, the seniors are in tomb. No instrument should accompany Hosannahs.

Second Hosannah band singer: They lose timing without backup.

First singer: Accept them at their level! They are children!

String band competitor: If you lead them to depend on it, they will.

Another participant: They sing well without the guitar. They should know how to sing in parts.

First singer: No instrument.

Third Hosannah Band singer: If you attempt to change [by not allowing instruments], it will be difficult.

While part of this debate is about encouraging the children who participate in the junior Hosannah band competition, there remains an underlying tension between those who would allow change and those who insist on the old ways. While the inclusion of accompaniment is common in some Protestant churches, the Anglican Church, and some Catholic churches in Carriacou, the tradition of Hosannah singing itself is specifically a cappella. Like many debates surrounding the Parang Festival, nothing was resolved; both junior Hosannah bands that year performed with guitar accompaniment.

In 1996, affirmation of what is authentically "Kayak" was played out during the opening performance of the Hosannah band competition by a folkloric Hosannah band. This four-member ensemble was not part of the competition; instead, they offered a presumably more authentic performance of local Hosannah singing. This presentation was jointly supported by the Parang Committee and folklorist Winston Fleary, who personally deplores the competitive aspect of the Hosannah band competition and is concerned about the preservation of Carriacou traditional culture (interview, 1997). The group—which included Mr. Fleary—appeared on stage with a banner that harkened back to the days of strolling carolers. They sang in a distinctively older style of highly melismatic two- and three-part harmonies sung with a thick vocal quality devoid of vibrato. In this case, authentic meant an older vocal style, one not commonly associated with contemporary church choirs. This style, however, was not necessarily the winning formula and would be tested by others throughout the competition that followed the folkloric band.

Representing a range of performance styles, five Hosannah bands, each consisting of four men and four women, competed in the 1996 Parang Festival. The New Tide Carolers from L'Esterre followed the folkloric band and in some ways resonated with them: their style was highly melismatic and featured a slightly unpolished "thick" vocal quality. They paid little attention to dynamics and tended to slip in and out of the local English Creole ("de" instead of "the," and so on). Most importantly, they sang a four-part vocal arrangement that reflected a distinctly local Carriacou style: the soprano melody was accompanied by a high harmony (above the soprano line) by the "altos," and the tenors sang below the sopranos, often doubling the altos' melody an octave down, while the basses sang a distinctive bass line. It was, in effect, a folk style derived from a religious genre: a beautiful singing aesthetic that lends itself to some lovely and at times unusual vocal blending.

The archrival of the New Tide Carolers is the Windward band called Splendiferous. The New Tide Carolers took first place over Splendiferous each year from 1989 through 1992; in 1993 and 1995, Splendiferous beat the New Tide Carolers (in 1994, another Hosannah band, the Harmonites, took first place). The members of Splendiferous have cultivated a smooth vocal delivery with some vibrato, and they make great use of vocal dynamics. In general, their sound has a more pronounced contemporary church choir style, featuring three- or four-part harmony singing: the sopranos sing the

FIGURE 4.1 The New Tide Carolers performing at the 1996 Parang Festival Hosannah band competition, Carriacou.

melody, the altos sing a harmony under them, and the tenors and bass sing a combined part suitable for their vocal range. In all, Splendiferous performs in a more polished, conventional, and less local style than the New Tide Carolers.

At the far end of this spectrum of authenticity is One Love, a Grenada-based ensemble that frequently travels to Carriacou for the Parang Festival. One Love is both a string band and a Hosannah band, and it routinely places last or second to last in both competitions. One Love's Hosannah singing has little to do with local Carriacou style, and although they perform well, they do so in a church choral style replete with seemingly trained voices, standard four-part harmony arrangements, vocal vibrato, a near total absence of melisma, and an overall smooth delivery. In the 1996 Hosannah band competition, One Love won third place out of four but received the prize for "best costume." The final competing group that year was the Carriacou pop band X-Trak, a band that normally plays soca, calypso, and reggae on electric instruments. The members of X-Trak clearly had done little by way of preparation, joining the competition at the last minute reportedly to show support for the event. Unlike the other bands, who wore matching costumes and sang from memory, the members of X-Trak performed in street clothes and sang from lyric sheets. Their presence provided good humor, however, and an important vote of confidence, given that so few Hosannah bands competed that year.

BEGGING THE QUESTION OF AUTHENTICITY: THE FIELDWORKER AS INSIDER/OUTSIDER

Because my husband and I lived in L'Esterre at the time, I hoped to observe the New Tide Carolers as they prepared for the competition. I made the necessary inquiries and was invited to attend rehearsals.[7] From the start, everybody in the group was very friendly, and it looked like a comfortable research situation. I went to several rehearsals at the L'Esterre RC Church and sat in a pew as the members of the group stood and sang. I took notes. Sometimes I tape-recorded their efforts. I smiled eagerly if I understood their jokes. Mostly, I was—and felt—disconnected. The experience was, to quote Nicole Beaudry on some types of fieldwork observation, "meaningless because . . . it (was) asocial" (Beaudry 1997: 74).

Until 1996 the New Tide Carolers had largely relied on L'Esterre musician and teacher Lionel Stiell to serve as musical director. Stiell arranged parts, taught the singers their lines, and rehearsed the group in preparation for the competition. In November 1996, however, Stiell was pursuing a certificate program for schoolteachers in Grenada, returning to Carriacou only on weekends, and the New Tide Carolers were stymied in their attempts to prepare for the Parang Festival. Several members had also joined New Horizons, another choral group that was not involved with the Hosannah band competition but wanted to put together a Christmas concert. (The group folded after a few rehearsals for lack of participant interest.) My husband and I were assisting New Horizons at the time, and in late November we were in turn asked by the New Tide Carolers to help them prepare for the Hosannah band competition. While I (and many other ethnomusicologists) have often performed and otherwise worked with the musicians who are also the subjects of the research, this particular situation seemed difficult, if not untenable: on the one hand, I wanted access to the group so that I could observe them. On the other hand, what would be the point of studying and documenting a musical performance process that I was, essentially, orchestrating?[8]

But I could not say no. Carriacouan culture is built on a complex system of giving and reciprocity, which comprise a daily social interaction that redistributes oftentimes scarce resources while reaffirming community cohesion. Volunteerism and assisting others are the norm in Carriacou, and it was clear to all that I had the skills and the time to help. To try to explain my perceived need to remain aloof would have been entirely inappropriate, even antisocial. I attempted a compromise: I urged Lionel Stiell to compose the individual harmony parts while limiting myself to consultation and helping to teach his arrangements. But with Stiell pretty much absent from Carriacou, the idea of just giving my opinion when asked did not work. Soon I was teaching harmony lines and vocal parts, rehearsing the group, and drilling the singers so that they kept their tempo steady, got their phrasing right, and so on. What I did not tamper with was the singers' local vocal style, and I stayed out of their repertoire selection, costuming, set design, and other components required for the competition. In the process, there was plenty of good humor and laughter. If I was manipulating cultural expression, so be it: we were having fun.

I also became better friends with many of the band members, despite my clear outsider status as a white American and my new position of authority as the music coach. Indeed, working on a project with a shared goal united us. I particularly grew closer to the women in the group. In prior field trips to Carriacou, I had little access to the women's culture, because I had been so focused on the exclusively male domain of string band musicians. What opened doors, too—particularly with the women singers—was my afore-mentioned pregnancy. After each rehearsal, when we "jes' relax," my out-sider status diminished as the women swapped pregnancy and childbirth stories, gave me advice, surmised what the gender of the baby would be, and generally reveled in the universal delight and fascination of bearing life.

After I began coaching the New Tide Carolers, I tried to broaden my perspective by approaching the Windward band, Splendiferous, to see if I could watch them prepare for the competition. I was immediately refused, although I did conduct a delightful interview with one member of the group, Gaby MacFarlane, and I was invited to observe the Windward jun-ior Hosannah band. Members of the New Tide Carolers suggested that I might have been seen as a spy. I had clearly underestimated the intensity surrounding the competition.

A few weeks later, however, I was surprised to receive a phone call from a singer in Splendiferous. The band members were having trouble with their parts. Could I come to Windward and help? I told the caller I would think about it.

Ultimately, I chose not to go to Windward, because at that point I had become part of the competition, like it or not. My allegiance was clearly with the New Tide Carolers: I had been made welcome, and in turn I put aside my previous concerns regarding so-called objective fieldwork practice in the interest of sharing my skills with the community; these were my friends and L'Esterre was where I belonged. I had, in essence, successfully negoti-ated Tim Rice's notion of the "hermeneutic arc," moving, in my case, from my own preconceptions of how things ought to be through a learning pro-cess of how things actually are to a new cognition of the relation of self with others (Rice 1997: 117).

What I did not know at the time was that in preparing for the competi-tion, virtually all of the Hosannah bands rely on a coach to assist them with the music. My role with the New Tide Carolers, in fact, cohered with these pre-existing expectations, and most of the competing bands had, at some point, received assistance from a trained musician outside Kayak culture.[9] For example, a retired music teacher from the United States had, for several years, assisted Splendiferous, and before that the New Tide Carolers (Mac-Farlane, interview, 1997). Splendiferous also routinely received help from various cultural officers at the Ministry of Culture in Grenada, including one who regularly served as a judge of the Hosannah band competition, an apparent conflict of interest that was, needless to say, appalling to the New Tide Carolers.[10]

That these singing groups looked outside of Carriacou culture for assistance is consistent with Donald Hill's (1977) analysis of Carriacou's overall social structure as divided into metropolitan and folk institutions. In postcolonial Carriacou, Kayaks have taken over from the colonial elite the administration of what were once metropolitan institutions such as local government and the educational system. There also continues to be a fairly constant presence of volunteer teachers from the Peace Corps and other service organizations, and while the school system is run by Carriacouans, there is an understood and accepted place for American and/or European volunteers within this system.[11] Similarly, the presence of the Catholic and Anglican churches in Carriacou dates back centuries. Catholic priests and Anglican ministers are typically white and hail, respectively from Ireland and Canada; most of the Catholic nuns are from outside of Carriacou, if not the Caribbean, as well. With this historic reality of white, non-Kayak teachers and clergy comes the long tradition of outsider authority and involvement in Carriacou's educational institutions, and their expressive cultural forms associated with Western religion. Assistance from the "other" in this context is thus considered neither foreign nor inappropriate. My role as a Hosannah band coach was more or less customary and, if anything, served on some small level to further reinscribe the authority of outsiders in the realm of education and non-African-derived cultural expression.

REFIGURING THE TRADITION: JUDGING CRITERIA AT THE HOSANNAH COMPETITION

Perhaps the Hosannah bands' reliance on outsider assistance has less to do with custom than with necessity, for when the Parang Committee established the Hosannah band competition in 1989, contestants were faced for the first time with a set of written aesthetics and judging criteria. Their rank in the competition is absolutely dependent on meeting these criteria, most of which have little to do with traditional Hosannah band performance practice. Apart from the criteria of "Parang Spirit," such considerations as lyrics (phrasing and breath control), melody, arrangement, interpretation, stage presence, and diction are more congruent with the aesthetics of formal choral singing than with what was once a spontaneous, community-based religious tradition.

To generate appropriate judging standards, the Parang Committee turned to Derick Clouden, Music Tutor and Cultural Officer of Grenada's Ministry of Culture. A classically trained Grenadian composer and singer, Mr. Clouden served as a judge at the Parang Festival for many years; in 1996, four others joined him to judge the Hosannah bands: Kayak businesswoman and singer Glenna Bullen; Elwyn McQuilken, an award-winning Grenadian calypso artist and Cultural Officer at Grenada's Ministry of Culture; Hillsborough Secondary School music teacher George Cox; and Theo Jerome, Manager of Operations in Carriacou of Grentel, the national telephone company. In 1997 interviews, I asked the judges to comment on the published criteria, beginning with "melody":

> Derick Clouden: Melody is the tune. . . . It must be accurate. And you as a judge are supposed to know the melodic structure of the test piece. . . . You must have an idea of what is a good melody because a good melody has its ways, has its ups and down. You see, you getting different waves. It keeps the listener [wanting] to hear more. That's a good melody.

> Glenna Bullen: Most of the people really have beautiful voices but you know some of them . . . are tone deaf. They would start off really well and then just went completely off.

> RSM: Should melody be the primary voice heard?

> GB: No. . . . It must blend and everything must harmonize.

> Theo Jerome: Melody is supposed to be a nice flow from one thing to the next.

While the judges had variable senses of what constitutes melody, they uniformly agreed on the specifics of vocal production, including breath control, tone, and dynamics:

Derick Clouden: What comes to mind is the words. And how the words are connected. Let's take "Joy To the World, The Lord Has Come." They might sing "Joy to the World [breath], the Lord is come." Like, bad phrasing. It had to be a sentence, everything in a block. So that what we look at is phrasing. . . . [The Hosannah Bands'] tone wasn't good. I have noticed that the people take shouting for singing. You know you supposed to be able to project your voice. . . . Some of the band[s] at times, they let go of themselves, as we say, locally, and they started to shout.

Elwyn McQuilken: My interpretation would be how you phrase the lyrics, so your rendition and your diction, intonation and all that, articulation, enunciation, those kinds of things I look for. And your breath control. Your breathing will affect all those other things.

Glenna Bullen: I would listen for a particular break . . . some singers would breathe really badly, like they would break right in the middle of a word . . . because it's like in speaking, just like how your sentences have to make sense, you don't chop it up. . . . Which here is quite easy based on how people speak. I hear it quite often in reading, even reading at church, like they would break a sentence right in the middle where there is no comma and then you go on and it makes it like a total different meaning.

Enunciation, tone, and, to a lesser extent, breath control are stylistic considerations largely associated with Western vocal training—aesthetics often imposed from the outside, from those who have some formal training or experience with church choirs. None of these things reflect the traditional local performance style. "Shouting" here refers to the characteristic vibrato-free tone as well as a tendency on the part of local singers to largely ignore dynamics in favor of "making a joyful noise unto the Lord." Thus the institutionalization of the Hosannah band competition brought with it an aesthetic shift away from the local and toward a more stylistically homogenized church choir style. Nowhere is this more evident than in the following judging criteria—the polemic surrounding the performance of Hosannah bands who sing using the "Queen's" (standard or Metropolitan English) versus the local English Creole:

Derick Clouden: You look for a Queen's English . . . all the words—your "Ts" and your "Ds" and your "-ings," all that should be expressed in your singing. . . . When you pick up a song, let's say a carol, you are looking at the Queen's English. You have to pronounce it properly.

RSM: So if you hear the band singing "da Lord is come" as opposed to "the Lord is come," would you take off points?

DC: Yeah.

Glenna Bullen: It's very hard for diction if you don't know how to sing. Because you're singing words with "d" that ends with "d," like "Lord" . . . you can't say "oh lor'" you know because you lose that "d" completely or "ing." Sing "ing" and just say the words like you're singing about the king, so that you actually have to pronounce your words slightly different. But people without training won't know that and they just go and sing just the way they would.

RSM: When I was listening to the groups get ready for the competition . . . instead of saying "the" they say "de." Should they force themselves to use a word they don't often use in everyday speech?

GB: I think they should because this is an English-speaking country. If you're not going to do it properly, then to me, there's no point. I don't think there should be any half way. . . . I'm not saying you should put on an English or American accent but you pronounce words the way they are to be pronounced.

This shift from the local Creole English to Metropolitan English underscores the increasingly "outsider" nature of the competition. Carriacouan Creole English is the *lingua franca* of the island, and virtually all folk songs, aphorisms, and other oral traditions are firmly grounded in it.[12] In terms of language, then, the Hosannah band competition is premised on a contradiction between preserving what was left of Hosannah band singing—a tradition that largely utilizes local English Creole—and encouraging a Western set of aesthetics and performance practices.

Another complicated judging criterion is "interpretation," one that judge Elwyn McQuilken admitted to be "somewhat vague" (interview,

1997). Derick Clouden, on the other hand, explains that "interpretation" includes correct facial expression ("It's supposed to tell us what you're singing about"), a sense of religious history ("Bethlehem was . . . a town that brought forth the Christ"), and overall tone:

RSM: More of a church sound?

DC: Yes, uh-huh.

RSM: Am I putting words in your mouth?

DC: No, no, no. It's a feeling. Interpretation is the feeling. You have to present the song so that the audience gonna get that feeling from you.

Such a formalization of Hosannah singing threatens to replace a once local sound with a more general, non-specific church choral style. Perhaps this is inevitable, given the growing influence of mass media, which brings—via radio and television broadcasts—a hegemonic Western church choir style to smaller cultures everywhere. Nowhere was this better illustrated than during the 1996 Hosannah band competition: Windward's Splendiferous performed a very polished version of the test piece "Oh Little Town of Bethlehem," with a well-executed, standard three-part arrangement—sopranos on melody, altos on harmony, tenors/bass on low harmony. Their choice piece was a lovely Christmas round, also nicely polished. Their notes were true and sung directly on pitch, with little if any melisma, and they articulated their consonants and sang with a light vibrato using Metropolitan English. In contrast, L'Esterre's New Tide Carolers sang four-part harmony on the test piece as well as on their choice piece, "Ding Dong Merrily the Bells." They drew upon a more traditional Carriacouan style, singing primarily a Metropolitan English but occasionally moving to a Creole English pronunciation. Their singing style made frequent use of melisma and there was little if any vibrato. Thus merging Christian hymnody with a unique, local vocal aesthetic, the New Tide Carolers stood out in stark distinction to Splendiferous. Both ensembles sang beautifully for entirely different reasons, and the resulting competition essentially pitted an extant local Kayak singing style against a local style that has been substantially reshaped, even replaced, by a standardized church choral sound.

The 1996 Hosannah band competition went to Splendiferous, with the New Tide Carolers in second, One Love in third, and X-Trak in fourth. Although One Love performed much like Splendiferous, with well-rehearsed and polished harmony singing, nobody was surprised to see them take third, given their outsider status both to Kayak culture and to the tradition itself. I was, of course, disappointed that the New Tide Carolers lost to Splendiferous, but not surprised, given the latter's polished vocal blending and nuanced arrangement, performance practices that successfully transcended the local in its emulation of a contemporary, more global church vocal style.

COMPETITION

Although Hosannahing has always involved some competition (for example, when bands met at a crossroads while serenading), the nature of it has radically changed with the institutionalization of the form.[13] Some bemoan this, noting that the caroling "competitions" were simply friendly and boisterous, not tense, as they are at the Parang Festival (C. Bristol, interview, 1997; W. Fleary, interview, 1997; G. Bullen, interview, 1997; L. Stiell, interview, 1997). This perspective on Hosannahing as less competitive and more cooperative is poignantly embedded in an anecdote recounted by Hosannah competition judge Glenna Bullen in 1997:

> I had one comment made to me after this last competition given the fact that the Windward group won in the last three years. . . . And someone said to me after, "I think there won't be a competition next year." . . . I said why and the person said because every year Windward wins and I think even though you know that they should win, forget about being fair and maybe you could just change the points so that you could give the other group encouragement. And I said, "I can't do that." The judges are sitting apart. No one is knowing what each other has on the paper and if all the points come up that way, then they must be doing something right. So you can't just say, "Right, because Windward has won for the past three years, we gonna let L'Esterre have it just so they would come into the competition again." But this is the way most people see it and it's really sad, you know.

In its attempt to revive what was correctly perceived to be a dying folk art form, the Parang Committee inadvertently created a dynamic that placed undue emphasis on competition rather than on the social component that once fueled Hosannah singing in Carriacou. In order to do well in the competition, Hosannah bands must amend the local style to be more congruent with a modern, church-based singing aesthetic. Because some bands make this shift better than others, and because of deeply rooted village rivalries, the competition ends in anger and resentment between the bands: "When you go out caroling to the different homes, it is not a competition. . . . It is like bringing joy, you know, like the whole spirit of Christmas and a Christian value is what's it about. But on stage it's a competition. . . . But I don't think this competition is working very well. From what I've noticed the people here are very poor losers. Very, very poor losers" (G. Bullen, interview, 1997).

RACE, CLASS, AND VILLAGE RIVALRIES

Indeed, there were bitter feelings on the part of the New Tide Carolers after they took second place to Splendiferous. Members of the group discussed the possibility of favoritism towards Splendiferous by the judges, and some questioned the relative difficulty of each group's choice piece (Splendiferous's round was possibly easier to sing than the New Tide Carolers' carol arranged for four-part harmony). Along with this unhappiness, then, the Parang Festival also inadvertently brings into stark relief the historic reality of inter-village rivalry. Dating back centuries to the era of Carriacouan enslavement and plantation culture, these rivalries evolved to the point that, during the 1970s, they often resulted in the cancellation of inter-village social events (Hill 1977: 251). Though motor transport on the island and an overall reduction in each village's relative isolation has mellowed things today, competition between Carriacou villages continues to inform island dynamics, particularly during cultural celebrations and events.

The flipside of inter-village rivalry is village loyalty, a historical reality apparent in all forms of Kayak discourse, informal and formal, including this comment in Briget Rao's unpublished history of Windward Village: "From all evidence, Windward still is the most picturesque of the villages in Carriacou." In a similar vein, Wallace Collins, the president of the Mount Royal Progressive Youth Movement, describes his village: "And history will tell you that Mount Royal is the village that has the most cooperation. That's it, the village in Carriacou that has the most cooperation. Anything that you want done within Mount Royal or anything you want done, and ask people from Mount Royal, you sure it be done. You know? That is generally known. It is not an opinion, it is statement, ok?" (interview, 1997). Indeed, Mount Royal does have an impressive history of community assistance dating back to at least the mid-1970s, and Windward is a handsome village. Such village loyalty translates into equally intense inter-village rivalry and, in the case of the Hosannah band competition, into acrimony that reached such a pitch that some Hosannah band singers declared they would not participate the following year.

Further complicating and informing the dynamics of inter-village rivalry is the issue of race.[14] In a discussion of this rivalry fomented by historical colonial association, Lorna McDaniel (1984: 185) notes that the population of L'Esterre was formerly referred to as the "French people," while those in Windward were the "*beké*" (white people). She argues that the lighter skin, Scottish-descended population in Windward can be considered a separate class due to a "self-imposed culture concept" that has resulted in endogamous marriage and physical isolation from the rest of the island. While Carriacouans are conscious of shades of coloring among the various village populations, McDaniel concludes that race does not form a particularly significant component of contemporary Carriacouan thought.

Others disagree. Parang judge and Grenadian calypsonian Elwyn McQuilken, for example, asserts that racial issues are very much at the heart of village rivalry, and of the anger often directed at the Windward ensembles during Parang: "In Carriacou, they have a racial problem . . . because you find Windward people are the light-skinned people. So there might be some jealousy or some sort of undertone. So you have to look at that too. . . . I feel that the majority of people wouldn't want Windward to win because of that" (interview, 1997). Equally significant here is the Kayak understanding of class difference, for the population of Windward is slightly better off economically than other Kayaks, thanks to their excellent boat building skills. L'Esterre residents, on the other hand, have a somewhat lower standard of living. As largely unspoken contributing factors to inter-village rivalry, the existence of class and racial differences explains in part the heightened emotions that surround the Hosannah band competition by virtually all of its participants.

EPILOGUE

In 1997 the New Tide Carolers took first place in the Hosannah band competition, an accomplishment they repeated each year until the Parang Committee, citing too few participants to warrant its continuation, eliminated
the competition altogether in 2001. Splendiferous declined to participate in
1997 but reformed with different members in 1998 as New Splendiferous,
taking second place to the New Tide Carolers for two years before disband-
ing. Since 2001, the Friday night of Parang offers a concert presentation that
showcases "local culture" and features carol singing by one or two Hosannah bands. Participants receive ginger beer, sorrel, wine, and cake at the
end of their performance—the traditional repast enjoyed by carolers in
years gone by. Then Santa Claus appears, distributing toys to children in the
audience.

As staged folklore, the Hosannah band competition distinctly altered
this tradition in terms of its performance practice, context, and meaning, a
cultural phenomenon found both regionally and globally. Burt Feintuch argues that staged folk music revivals are better conceived of as "musical
transformations," in which the recreated tradition achieves a new level of
momentum encompassing a standardized repertoire, a performance style,
and a "selective view of the past" (Feintuch 1993: 184). In the case of Carriacou Hosannah bands, the groups' repertoire indeed became increasingly
standardized, given that all of the bands performed the same test piece (always a well-known Christmas carol). The sheer variety of traditional repertoire was reduced, as the competition favored Christmas carols over the
more localized sankeys and hymns. Changes in performance style were also
palpable, as Hosannah bands moved from a local, folk-based aesthetic toward a more formal and generalized church choral style. Finally, the
Parang Committee's selective view of the past privileged certain performance criteria (for example, matching costumes and strictly a cappella
singing) that signified an older—and presumably more "authentic"—style.
Cast aside were local vocal aesthetics and language use, traditional rather
than standardized part arrangements, and the inclusion of a banner that
once emphasized village belonging.

That participation in the Hosannah band competition waned was, in
part, a result of the unrealistic expectations imposed on the bands by the various performance criteria—a set of aesthetics not at all in keeping with the

local style of singing. As a recontextualized tradition, then, the Hosannah band competition was moving toward a Western, more standardized church style, altering the traditional manner of learning, arranging, and performing this music.[15] Whereas Hosannah bands once functioned as independent entities organized by community members who sang familiar carols in a style they knew well, the new ensembles were forced to turn to outsiders for help with more formal (and difficult) vocal arrangements. And while the influence of outsiders in both local and national institutions is by no means anathema to Carriacou society, given the legacies of colonialism in educational and religious institutions, it nevertheless alters the tradition from one born entirely within the community to one that is largely fashioned from without.

5

⊚⊚

BREAK-AWAYS, **LAVWAYS**, CALYPSO, AND MORE
An Ethnography and Social History
of Carriacou String Band Music

EARLY IN OCTOBER 1996, *string band leader Harrison Fleary mentioned that he had been asked to organize some string band music for an upcoming fête—the anniversary party of Mr. and Mrs. Bartholemew of Belvedere. He invited my husband, Tom, and me to play with the band. We agreed to meet at the Bartholemews' small store/rum shop around 7:00. The fête was in full swing when we arrived. We were greeted by the domino-playing men who sat outside the rum shop and then by the Bartholemews themselves, a warm and outgoing older couple who took us inside to join Fleary and the other musicians. The band this evening would consist of three violinists, two guitarists, a banjo player, and a triangle player, all of whom were men except for me. From time to time, members of the audience added rhythmic layers by clapping along or by playing* chac-chacs *(maracas) made on the spot from empty small soda bottles filled with pebbles and sand. Or they might rhythmically scrape the ridges of an empty Fanta soda bottle with a thick Eastern Caribbean coin, producing a sound much like a Cuban or Puerto Rican* güiro.

Older people and young mothers with their babies sat on chairs that lined the walls of the Bartholemews' store. A long counter divided the store in half; we were told that the musicians were to play in front of and behind the counter—a bit awkward but not impossible. It was amazingly crowded. The hosts and party-goers were very cordial and excited about the music, always making sure that the musicians were comfortable. Watching us intently as we tuned our instruments and started playing, the audience members called out comments of approval and chatted and laughed with us between numbers.

String band music has long provided an aural backdrop in Carriacou for social and life-cycle events. Indeed, string band music is fairly ubiquitous across Carriacou; nearly every village has musicians who have entertained their neighbors and families for as long as they can remember. From informal but intensive serenading in the days prior to Christmas and New Year's to semiprofessional performances for visiting tourists, Kayak string band players contribute to the folk cultural fabric of Carriacou year around. Between occasional paid performances, most string band musicians play informally at music sessions or "practices" in rum shops, stores, or homes, attracting numerous enthusiastic onlookers. Indeed, only one or two eight- to twelve-piece Kayak string ensembles regularly play on a semiprofessional basis. Because string band music is secular, it is rarely heard at life-cycle events honoring the dead, such as gravestone-raising ceremonies; typically, a family organizes a Big Drum ceremony to honor the ancestors instead, unless the deceased was a string band musician or a particularly enthusiastic string band fan. More typically, string bands perform for events that celebrate the stages of life, such as anniversary parties like the Bartholemews', birthday parties, weddings, christenings, celebrations connected with homecomings, *maroons*,[1] other fêtes, boat launching ceremonies, the odd funeral, and, for some string bands, occasional paid performances for tourists. String band players are rarely paid, save perhaps for a small honorarium that covers transportation and other expenses.

Carriacou string band musicians learn repertoire and playing style by ear through listening and imitation. This vital and active tradition continues to attract players—almost exclusively young men, many of whom are aspiring calypso singers. In fact, there are very few women who participate in Carriacou string bands, with the notable exception of Cora Blair from Petit Martinique. Additionally, two members of the Central Serenaders string band, bass player Bernice Bristol and vocalist Shama Dixon, perform publicly during the Parang Festival but, in general, not at other events during the year (B. Bristol, interview, 1997). This gender imbalance arises from the traditional divisions within Carriacouan cultural life. Because instrumental performance is associated with manhood and virility as well as alcohol (L. Stiell, interview, 1997), women have traditionally been largely excluded from instrumental music of all types; if they participate at all, they do so as dancers or singers.

String band music is not specific to Carriacou; indeed, ensembles that combine string instruments with percussion are widespread throughout the Caribbean and South America. In part a relic of European colonialism like quadrille music and dance, Caribbean string bands epitomize syncretic cultural expression. Enslaved Africans throughout these island cul-

tures appropriated elements of European-derived music performed for
and by their owners and combined them with African and Latin American (primarily Venezuelan) styles and instrumentation. Over centuries,
this Afro-Caribbean hybridized genre was steadily infused with local creativity and innovation, resulting in idiosyncratic performance practices
that vary from island to island. In some cases, such as in eighteenth-century
Cuba, string band music entertained all social and racial strata (excluding
rural slaves; see Manuel 1994). Elsewhere, string band music remained the
province of upper-class Creole populations, as in early-twentieth-century
Haiti (see Averill 1997 and Yih 1995), or the Creole elite in post–World
War I Guadeloupe and Martinique (see Spottswood 1988). More often,
however, string band music retained a historical association with the aris-
tocracy but was appropriated by the lower classes.[2] This model holds true
for cultures throughout the Caribbean, in particular St. Lucia (see Guilbault 1984), St. Martin (see Sekou 1992), and the Puerto Rican *jibaro* population (see Singer 1988).

Carriacou string band music merges Euro-American and Anglo-
Caribbean melodies and songs with Latin American and African-derived
musical characteristics, such as rhythmic hocketing and interlock, and stratified rhythms. Once used largely to accompany social dancing, string bands
today generally play for a listening audience, although occasionally couples
dance along to waltzes and polkas. Playing a diverse repertoire that ranges
from old, traditional tunes to recently released calypsos, Kayak string band
musicians combine European-derived instruments such as the violin, mandolin, and guitar with regional instrumentation, such as the Venezuelan
cuatro and a larger type of mandolin called the *bandolin* (or *bandonéon*). Most
string bands also include some combination of tenor banjo (four-string)
and/or a locally made and finely crafted three-string banjo. An acoustic bass
guitar is often improvised by restringing a regular six-string guitar with the
four lowest strings on which bass lines are played, locally referred to as "the
background." A layer of African-derived polyrhythms is provided by a
wide range of "found" percussion instruments, including the triangle, the
chac chac, the brake drum (struck with a piece of iron), an overturned barrel
that becomes a bass drum, the Fanta bottle-turned-scraper, and others. Together with the rhythm provided by the string instruments, the percussion
serves as a driving accompaniment to the melodic lead of a violinist or mandolin player.

LOCAL TUNES AND PLAYING STYLES

Although the Bartholemews' anniversary party had been in full swing for several hours, we didn't begin playing until nearly 8:00 P.M. Following the lead of Harrison Fleary and the late violinist Norris George, we played through a range of tunes and songs, including waltzes, cacians, spritely polkas, and popular numbers from throughout the Americas ("La Bamba" and "Save the Last Dance for Me," among others), light jazz standards ("Besame Mucho"), country western songs ("Before the Next Teardrop Falls"), and old and new calypsos. But the main audience pleasers were clearly the many local tunes commonly performed by string band musicians, including the waltz "Whispering Hope," "Magica Polka," and the particularly prized "break-aways."

Improvisatory, up-tempo, and full of musical possibility for both melodic and rhythm players, break-aways form the centerpiece of string band sessions. According to Harrison Fleary, the term "break-away" is derived from street marches: "It . . . can (be) use(d) for a street march, a street 'jump up.' And this is why it's a called a 'break-away,' in that if you gonna put words to a break-away, you set the words in such a way that it can be chanted easily by the masses. And so if you were going to play it on the street you can have a lot of people just joining in and jumping and dancing, 'wining down' [partying], you know, enjoying that. To break away, actually, means to loosen up and dance in that kind of fashion" (interview, 1995).[3]

Led by the violinist, break-aways are typically in 4/4 time and consist of a simple melodic theme of eight or sixteen bars. The theme is then restated with variations, melodic improvisations, and rhythmic improvisations that might include syncopations within the measure and over the barline, as heard in Canute Caliste's playing (see transcription 3.) Using the rhythmic improvisation of three against two or six against four to create variation and musical excitement, Caliste improvises for eight bars, restates the theme, then improvises again.

A Kayak violinist's ability to improvise over chord changes and play inventively, but within the local style, is highly admired. A well-executed solo is typically met with shouts of "brave" (the local term for "smart"), "good man" (even if the player is female), and—at least in my experience—proposals of marriage. In addition to rhythmic and melodic variation, break-aways feature sliding into notes and occasional playing "in position" (that is, high on the neck of the violin). Transcription 3 also details the performance practice of Mr. Caliste's accompanists—the late Marxman Joseph on *cuatro*,[4] Ronald Jones on six-string guitar, and Enel James on twelve-string guitar. The three accompanying instruments are played in tightly interlocking, stratified rhythms in a style common to Carriacou string bands and locally called the "roll and chop." Harrison Fleary describes the roles of each player, using as an example the performance practice of his bandmate, banjo player Godwin

FIGURE 5.1 Transcription 3: "Break-Away," Canute Caliste (violin). ©1997 Canute Caliste.

FIGURE 5.1 *(Continued)*

Moses: "[The violin player] just does just about everything, just making sure that he fits back into the chords.... [The rhythm players play] roll and chop ... yeah, in fact, you would hear [banjo player] Moses like he's going wild during a break-away song.... But he just keeping the run of chords. As long as he maintains the run of chords, then he can experiment with all sorts of strums" (interview, 1995).

FIGURE 5.2 String band practice, Six Roads, Carriacou, November 1996. Left to right: Welcome Cummins (guitar), Norris George (violin), Ronald Jones (banjo).

The backup instruments in string bands privilege rhythmic variation and interlocking over harmonic complexity. Transcription 4 is a break-away as played by the late Norris George in May 1997.[5] One of Mr. George's signature tunes, this break-away relies on a simple chord progression—typically V–I or I–V, or occasionally I–IV–V–I. Here again, harmonic accompaniment is less important than the creation of a multi-instrument rhythmic bed over which Mr. George's melodic improvisations soar. Having performed semiprofessionally in England for nearly thirty years, Mr. George's playing style reflects years of involvement in European popular music and big band standards—music he brought back to Carriacou when he retired in 1995. His return, paralleling that of guitarist/banjo player Ronald Jones, reinvigorated Carriacou's string band music community; the two introduced new repertoire, an expanded musical aesthetic, and broadened local playing styles.

RELIGIOUS SONGS

Religious songs and church hymns also form a part of the string band repertoire in Carriacou, including such familiar melodies as "Amazing Grace" and "When the Saints Go Marching In." "Whispering Hope," transcribed here, is one of the most frequently heard songs in Carriacou and is played or sung in virtually every acoustic music context. A hymn written in 3/4 time by Alice Hawthorne (Crum 1960: 535), "Whispering Hope" is often sung in two- or three-part harmony in Carriacou church services, or by small groups of women carolers during the Christmas season, and it is performed during religious and life-cycle events such as wakes or funerals. Quite popular among string band musicians, "Whispering Hope" works well as a lovely, melodic waltz.[6] This slippage between the religious and the secular or social reflects a strategic response to an island-wide history of meager resources. While Kayak musicians do have more opportunities to learn new repertoire (from radio broadcasts or the increasing availability of cheap, pirated CDs and cassettes, for example), they continue to recycle and reconfigure repertoire from disparate sources to suit audience demand and their own musical aesthetics. Given the importance of Christianity in the lives of Kayaks, it is no surprise that string bands continue to rely on recontextualized hymns and other religious songs.

THE NORTH AMERICAN INFLUENCE:
COUNTRY WESTERN, FOLK, AND POP

Beginning in 1971, Peace Corps workers from the United States introduced schoolchildren at the Hillsborough Secondary School to Anglo–North American folk tunes such as "Red River Valley," "Get Along, Little Cindy," "My Bonnie Lies over the Ocean," and others. Most of these songs came from *Music around the World, Book Six* (Mursell 1960), and Carl Sandburg's *The American Songbag* (1927), two of the few music books available for students up until the mid-1990s (Moses, personal communication, 1995; H. Fleary, interview, 1995). Many of these North American folk tunes and songs made their way into the local string band repertory, particularly through those players who attended Hillsborough Secondary School in the 1970s.

The late violinist Norris George remembered as a child hearing American popular music broadcast over the wireless from stations on nearby islands beginning in the 1930s (George, interview, 1997). He and other Kayak instrumentalists, in turn, adapted what they heard on the radio into string band repertoire. Today, a large part of Carriacou string band music derives from North American popular musics, including popular dance numbers, R&B, and rock 'n' roll from the 1950s and 1960s. Wide ranging in style and aesthetic, string band musicians might follow Wilson Pickett's "Wait 'til the Midnight Hour," with the Tin Pan Alley classic, "Let Me Call You Sweetheart." John Denver's "Leaving on a Jet Plane" might segue into the theme from *Dr. Zhivago* ("Somewhere My Love" ["Lara's Theme"]). And many string band players enjoy jazz standards such as "Sentimental Journey." Although many of these tunes were learned from older recordings, younger

FIGURE 5.3 Transcription 4: "Break-Away," Norris George, violin. ©1997 Norris George.

FIGURE 5.3 *(Continued)*

players today most often learn this type of repertoire from older players. When asked where they learned these American pop standards, many string band musicians have no specific memory of where the tunes came from. They just "pick it up."

Like American pop music, country western music has long been heard on radio stations throughout the Lesser Antilles. Because Carriacou is well within receiving range of Trinidadian radio broadcasts, Kayaks have been listening to country western music from Radio Trinidad and Trinidad's Government Broadcasting Unit. Thanks to broadcasts of country and western music since the the 1930s by such entities as Caribbean Caricom, the Grenada Broadcast Corporation (GBC), Radio Antilles (Montserrat), Radio Barbados, Radio St. Vincent, and later Carriacou's own KYAK, many generations of Kayaks have grown up listening to older country songs such as "The Tennessee Waltz," the 1950s "New Nashville" sound of George Jones, and other styles. Harrison Fleary notes that much of the repertoire he has brought to his string band over the last three decades was learned from listening to country western music on the radio: "Since I was in my teens really, I had a kind of liking for country music. So I used to take them as I hear them and just learn the words particularly and take up my guitar because the guitar was my thing then. Some of [the music] I taped . . . just to learn the words and the tunes . . . And then I would take my guitar and per-

FIGURE 5.4 String band practice, Hillsborough, Carriacou, January 1995. Left to right: unknown player, Godwin "Mose" Moses (locally made banjo), Harrison Fleary (violin).

haps while I tending my animals, just sit on a stone or something and just sing. And I liked following those country programs, actually. I don't know, maybe I was a little sentimental in my youth" (interview, 1995).

SMOKE FOOD, HOT MUSIC, AND THE CALYPSO CONNECTION

At about 9:30 P.M., Mr. and Mrs. Bartholemew served supper to the many assembled guests, musicians, and others who happened by. Locally called "smoke food" (food prepared in large iron pots and cooked over open fires), the plates were typically Kayak: cou cou (boiled corn meal balls), rice balls, goat or pork served in gravy, and peas (beans). After supper, we played music—mostly calypsos— until past midnight. As we packed up, the hosts and those who remained thanked the musicians profusely, making sure to find out where the two Americans lived in Carriacou and, in true Kayak fashion, inviting us to return soon to visit.

Carriacou's string band tradition can be traced, in part, to Venezuela, a result of the extensive migration to and from that country by Kayaks in search of work beginning early in the twentieth century. Additionally, Kayaks historically have heard traditional and popular Venezuelan musics, as well as other South American genres, from coastal Venezuelan radio broadcasts. It is from these broadcasts that Carriacou string band musicians such as Country Boys' leader Anselm James found Latin American rhythms and Spanish-language songs to adapt to Carriacou string band instrumentation and performance practice (James, personal communication, 1996). Kayak string band music can also be traced to Trinidad, a culture with a rich history of string band music whose own roots also lie in the Venezuelan string band tradition, given remarkable similarities of instrumentation and repertoire (see Szwed and Marks 1988).[7] It was this tradition that provided the basis for early calypso music: in the late 1890s, Lionel Belasco, a well-known Trinidadian pianist, composer, and orchestra leader, popularized the use of Venezuelan instrumentation to accompany his early calypso songs. By the turn of the century, Trinidadian string bands were providing the basic accompaniment to these early calypsos. The prevalence of string bands in Trinidad during this era is clear from a 1912 article entitled "The Carnival" in the Trinidadian newspaper *Argos,* which describes the songs as "carisoes" accompanied by an ensemble of "guitars, quatros, *shac shacs, veeras,* and two short pieces of bamboo which they strike one against the other. Occasionally a stray violinist is seen among them" (cited in Rohlehr 1990: 49–50). At the same time, string bands began accompanying indoor Trinidadian musical traditions, such as contra dances, reels, and couple dances (known in Trinidad as Lancers, quadrilles, reels, jigs, and *paseos*). Early Trinidadian recordings of string bands feature an array of string, woodwind, and percussion instrumentation, including the piano, violin, guitar, *cuatro, chac chac,* bottle and spoon, flute, and clarinet (the latter reflecting a pervasive French Creole influence).

String bands served as the main accompaniment for calypso music until the 1940s, a time of stylistic transition when calypsonians in both Grenada and Trinidad increasingly began to favor larger ensembles with wind and horn sections and, eventually, amplified and electric instruments. Calypsonian Elwyn McQuilkin (aka "Black Wizard") recalls hearing his uncle, also a calypso singer, accompanied by string bands as late as the 1950s: "In those days you had what you call string bands . . . so my uncle, he used to be a lead singer in a band. So then I grew up in a house with a calypsonian, you could say. . . . In the band you have people who play instruments, then you have the lead singer, and the rest of the group who sort of respond" (interview, 1997).

Today, calypsos and the related but less political soca calypsos[8] are highly produced vocal numbers, complete with horn arrangements, electric guitar, bass, synthesizers, drum kit or drum machine, and other instruments. Contemporary calypsonians typically compose the lyrics and melody and then hire professional arrangers and part writers to orchestrate the song for big band ensembles. The calypsos are, in turn, produced in studios in Trinidad and Grenada and distributed via radio and CD throughout the English-speaking Caribbean. Despite this sophistication of instrumentation and arrangement, most Carriacou string band musicians draw on this historic calypso connection and aesthetic by continually appropriating and adapting the popular calypsos of the day into their repertoire, updating their sound.

It is these contemporary calypsos—those composed within the last ten or fifteen years, at any rate—that Kayak string bands perform for their local audiences. In their hands these calypsos are recontextualized to suit string band instrumentation and address the performance practices of the musicians as well as the limitations of the stringed instruments. For example, string band musicians rarely play chords more complicated than major and minor triads; chordal voicings specific to popular music are rarely heard in the context of string bands. Moreover, what might be complicated chord progressions are routinely simplified to suit the string band style. Finally, popular calypsos uniformly privilege lyrics, whereas string bands retool them largely as instrumental numbers and favor those with particularly memorable melodies or interesting rhythmic patterns. On occasion, however, string band audiences will sing along with a popular calypso. In 1996 and 1997, for example, the soca calypso heard almost constantly on the radio, sung by schoolchildren, performed by steel bands, and played by all the string bands was "Bouncing Low," named after a particular strain of flu that had been circulating throughout Carriacou and Grenada at the time. Like most soca calypsos, "Bouncing Low" is an up-tempo song with simple lyrics containing double entendres and sexual connotations. Almost everybody in Carriacou knew the song.

TOWARD A SOCIAL HISTORY OF KAYAK STRING BAND MUSIC

Virtually nothing is written about string band music in Carriacou prior to the 1960s, aside from the anecdotal news accounts in early newspapers documenting the presence of string instruments and supplies in Grenada (and, by extension, Carriacou).[9] For example, a notice dated May 16, 1894, in the *Grenadian Government Gazette* listed a guitar and "five demijeans rum, about five gallons in all" among the items seized for a customs sale due to "breaches of the Revenue and Excise Laws." Similarly, the *Grenada Free Press and Public Gazette* reported in its July 13, 1831, edition that one "Daniel Gibbs . . . imported, per brig *Dorothea,* from London . . . violin strings." Apart from the historic association of music with strong drink, there has clearly long been a demand for stringed instruments and accessories in the region.

Oral histories by Carriacou elders fill in some details about Kayak string bands since the early years of the twentieth century. Eslyn "Tateen" Stiell (b. 1917), for example, remembers that when she was growing up in L'Esterre, string band music was, along with quadrille and Big Drum, one of the only sources of musical entertainment available to the community (E. Stiell, interview, 1997). So common was this music that most Carriacou villages had at least one string band. L'Esterre's string band, for example, was by the 1940s one of the most active on the island. At the time, guitarist Sonnelle Allert was the youngest member of this group; he remembers performing calypsos, break-aways, and other types of tunes at community dances in Hillsborough:

> We have only one band in L'Esterre. We have older head with us. We had Marxman Joseph [on *cuatro*] . . . Canute Caliste [on violin], Gurine Joseph on violin as well. And we have Wilfred Thomas. He play the banjo very well. And Sidney Joseph . . . he was best of the young fellows playing guitar. . . . I play guitar as well. We start practicing with the elder head and then we come perfect for we-self. Yeah, well when . . . elder be gonna die out, well we get somebody to fit in the space and so we keep on going.
>
> In those days . . . they ask you to come and play in the hall in Hillsborough. Maybe fifty . . . peoples come in to dance, or maybe more than that. You know they paid to the door and come in and dance while we play. They collect money in the door for who come to dance and they has their bar on the side, sell drinks and so forth. (Allert, interview, 1997)

In the years following World War II, Sonnelle Allert's band regrouped in response to changing aesthetics and emigrating members. Like other groups on nearby islands, their string band was influenced by the new sounds emanating from Trinidad. Violinist Gurine Joseph soon began to double on saxophone, clarinet, and, according to his son, Dennis "Poco" Joseph, "just about everything else" (interview, 1997). With its more versatile repertoire that reflected modern musical influences (for example, big band jazz), this L'Esterre-based band was in steady demand as one of the "hot" string bands in Carriacou.

String bands continued to play an important role in Carriacou society in the years leading up to the 1960s, providing music for social, ritual, and celebratory occasions (Allert, interview, 1997; Fortune, interview, 1997; Caliste, interviews, 1995, 1997). M. G. Smith documented the performance of string band music in 1953 while doing fieldwork in Carriacou, noting that string bands played at christenings, *saracas,* at weddings, and for dances (Smith 1962: 95, 126–27). Smith's account includes tune types such as the "reel-engagé" and the "Scotch," both of which are rarely played in Carriacou today.

Stimulated by the popular musics of both North America and the greater Anglo-Caribbean region in the 1960s, some string band musicians followed their predecessors' lead and moved even further away from an acoustic string-based sound, this time toward a popular, combo instrumentation that included electric guitars, bass, and organ, among other instruments. Poco Joseph was a founding member of a prominent Carriacou combo, the Sunblisters, which went electric despite a profound lack of material resources: "You had to start as a string band because actually there was no electricity. Then, there was electricity but we had no electric instruments, we had no amplifiers. . . . We went in the woods to cut trees to make the drums that they used to use. We used to use radios. The type radios they had, you can use them like amplifiers, that's what we used to begin with. And then after we started, made a little money . . . we were able to buy [our] first amplifier" (interview, 1997).

The Sunblisters' repertoire included calypsos, country western songs, and other popular musics they heard on the radio. Because electricity first came to Hillsborough only in the late 1960s, villages such as L'Esterre would wait for it until just after the revolution nearly a decade later (C. Bristol, interview, 1997). The Sunblisters therefore used a portable generator or rehearsed in Hillsborough. Despite these limitations, they were in high demand and played often in Hillsborough at dances and concerts as well as on nearby islands such as Petit St. Vincent (PSV) and Union Island.[10]

ON PLAYING STYLES AND THE LOMAX TAPES

In 1962, the late American folklorist Alan Lomax arrived in Carriacou to document and record for future generations many hours of traditional music and song. Many of these recordings were of different styles of acoustic string band music and quadrille dance tunes. Lomax's tapes document only a portion of what Kayaks were then listening and dancing to, and, in doing so, preserve a truly distinctive and beautiful collection of string band styles. With few cars in Carriacou at the time (people traveled on foot or by donkey), Lomax found the northernmost village of Windward in a state of relative isolation from the rest of island.[11] He observed a stylistic difference between the string band music there and in the more southern villages of L'Esterre and Six Roads, noting in his logs that it was "poor stuff, interesting because of stiffness, lack of rhythmic interest and out of tune-ness. A Scotch settlement, now blending with Negro population" (Lomax, unpublished notes to the recordings, 1962). Lomax seemed to prefer the string band music he recorded in L'Esterre, noting that it was a more "Africanized" playing style, with a heightened polyrhythmic accompaniment and an emphasis on variation as played by violinists Canute Caliste and Gurine Joseph.

What Lomax found is still somewhat the case today, for Windward string band players tend to play slower and with greater deliberation (what Lomax heard as "stiffness") than musicians elsewhere on the island. And while Windward musicians play many of the same tunes, they also have a handful of unique pieces, including English and Scottish country dance tunes (such as "The Ashgrove," which dates to the eighteenth century), the odd Irish waltz (such as "Believe Me for All Those Endearing Young Charms," known locally as the "Windward Waltz"), and others. While no one knows exactly how these tunes found their way to Windward (or Carriacou generally), Scottish settlers of the late nineteenth century certainly could have had something to do with it.

Although "Windward Waltz" is limited more or less to the village of Windward, its instrumentation in transcription 5 (from 1995) is common to contemporary string bands throughout Carriacou (transcription 5 features both Windward and Hillsborough musicians). The lead melody is played by the violin or mandolin in a fairly straightforward manner, both melodically and rhythmically. The three-stringed banjo, *cuatro,* guitar, and percussion supply the rhythmic complexity. The percussion section features a musician playing an empty soda bottle struck with a heavy stick or metal tool in a hocketed pattern against the rhythm supplied by the bass (drum), which sounds on the first beat of every three-beat measure. The guitarist's fairly simple strumming pattern is offset by the banjo player's rhythmic variations, particularly when he substitutes very rapidly strummed sixteenth notes in places of eighth notes. This variation punctuates the ends of melodic phrases (see, for example, measures 7 and 8). The *cuatro* often plays a variation of the banjo rhythm but in a different timbre (the *cuatro* player uses his fingers to strum, whereas the banjo player uses a plectrum).

FIGURE 5.5 Transcription 5: "Windward Waltz."

FIGURE 5.5 *(Continued)*

"HEEL AND TOE POLKA"

Alan Lomax's 1962 field tapes also included one of Carriacou's most re-
quested polkas, variously called the "Heel and Toe Polka," "Go Tell Me
Mama," or "Magica Polka" (see transcription 6). This tune is derived from the
sixth figure of the English quadrille, and it appears to be the only tune that
has moved into popular usage outside of the quadrille. Apart from the *lavways,*
"Heel and Toe Polka" is also one of the few local Kayak string band pieces
that have lyrics.[12] Lucy de Rochet grew up in a French *patois*–speaking
community in Petit Martinique in the 1930s and recalls the following lyrics:

FIGURE 5.6 Transcription 6: "Heel and Toe Polka."

Me Mooma send me in the pon' for wahtah,
The Dominica man come feel me la la.

When I go, I go tell me mooma,
De Dominica [did/gone] feel me la la. (L. de Rochet, interview, 1995)

Lyrics with explicit sexual content are not uncommon in Carriacou expressive culture.[13] Similar sexual allusions exist in many Big Drum lyrics,
and there is suggestive choreography in some of the dances. Lorna Mc-
Daniel writes that there are thirty-three terms for genitalia in Carriacou but
attributes it not to some sort of Carriacouan hypersexuality but to a culture

of openness and humor: "Children and even the elderly are invited into light sexual banter between age groups. The greeting 'How is it?' may be accompanied with a genital gesturing. When asked about this extreme familiarity, culture bearers remarked thoughtfully to me that 'all things cannot be explained; it must be love'" (McDaniel 1986: 177–78).

Apart from the sexual imagery contained in "Heel and Toe Polka" (not to mention the implication of sexual violence and/or pedophilia), at least one version of the "Heel and Toe Polka" contains a sense of regional bias, for the man is from the island of Dominica. Other versions substitute "nigger man" or "damn nigger man" for "Dominica man" (Alexander, personal communication, 1997), including the version Lomax collected. A tape-recorded question/answer session followed the performance of this tune on these archival recordings:

Alan Lomax: What's the name of that tune?

Man #1: A polka, pond for water. My mother send me to pond for water.

Man #2: Dumb nigger man come to cut me la la. (Laughter.)

Man #2: My mother send me pond for water / Dumb nigger man come to cut me la la. / When I go, I go tell me woman, / Dumb nigger man cut me la la.

AL: That's really a calypso.

Man #2: That's the thing, but the name of it is a polka.

AL: Where was it composed?

Man #2: Right here.

AL: How old is it, Mr. Wilson?

Man #2: It's about, over eighty years old, or around there.

AL: Who composed it? Why?

Man #2: No, I don't know.

AL: You know the story of it?

Man #2: No I don't know. The mother send her daughter in the pond for water / And the nigger man meet him and they took up she la la.

AL: Uh-huh, I see. (General laughter.)[14]

Unlike many other string band tunes, "Heel and Toe Polka" almost always inspires couple dancing. To this day, "Heel and Toe Polka" is played at virtually every public performance or "practice" session by string bands, often more than once.

KAYAK WEDDINGS AND DANCING THE FLAG

Since the 1950s, scholars have noted the significance of string band music in Carriacou weddings. In 1953, for example, M. G. Smith observed that hiring a string band instead of hosting a Big Drum ceremony saved the groom money but necessitated the enactment of many Big Drum rituals (Smith 1962: 126–27). Some twenty years later, Donald Hill noted the combination of secular and sacred elements at weddings, observing that a Big Drum ceremony traditionally took place outdoors in the yard while a string band played inside the groom's family home on the night before the wedding (Hill 1980: 5–6; see also Hill 1977: 286–94). Carriacou Big Drum performer/teacher Christine David describes the participation of string band musicians during the ritualistic meeting of the flags and dancing of the cakes, two events that precede Kayak weddings (David 1985: 42–43). In turn, my field notes from weddings between 1995 and 1997 record the continuing significance of contemporary string band music on the morning of the wedding day at the home of the groom's parents:

August 1995: Around 8:30 A.M., I ride up to Mt. Pleasant with my musician friends, Harrison Fleary, Godwin "Mose" Moses, and others, in the back of Harrison's truck. The Central Serenaders was one of the groups asked to play for the pre-wedding celebration; the other group was led by Milton "Tailor" Coy of Hillsborough. We are quite late, so by the time we arrive, the "meeting of the flags" (also known as "fighting the flags") has already begun. The band members hurry from the vehicle and unpack their instruments.

The meeting of the flags divides the participants into two sides, those related to the bride and those related to the groom. Each side is led by a man holding a tall flagpole, and each has its own string band playing a tune of its

FIGURE 5.7, 5.8 Competing string bands at a pre-wedding ceremony, Mount Pleasant, Carriacou, August 1995. Violinist Milton "Tailor" Coy is at far right, lower photo.

choice. As the two ensembles approach each other, the contrasting tunes create an exuberant, if not cacophonous, atmosphere. Dancing up the street behind each flag is a crowd of onlookers. With much excitement and good humor, the audiences shout words of encouragement to their respective flag bearers. When the two groups meet, the flag bearers begin their "fight," swinging their poles toward each other and attempting to subjugate the other's flag. The intention is for the groom's flag to remain above the bride's, an act that symbolizes the dominance of the man over the woman in the marriage: "Then they tie the two flags together. . . . However, the flag of the groom will be slightly higher than that of the bride. Which has its obvious reason, of course. There could be only one head" (H. Fleary, interview, 1995).

Patriarchal domination is also the theme of the dancing of the cake, which takes place after the meeting of the flags. Symbolically demonstrating the domestic role of women in Carriacou life, two women dance facing each other, each holding an entire, perfectly iced wedding cake. Surrounded by onlookers, the women place the cakes on top of their heads and dance, gyrating their hips to the music provided by the musicians, who by now have joined together in one large ensemble. Midway through, the two women remove the cakes from their heads and hold them one underneath the other, with the groom's cake always held above the bride's. After the dancing of the cakes, a processional led by the musicians escorts the bride and groom back to the groom's home, where they prepare for the church service and marriage ceremony. Outside, in the yard, the musicians continue to play music for several hours.

Donald Hill's research from the early 1970s describes many ritual activities at a Kayak wedding but notes in contrast to M. G. Smith's research some twenty years earlier that the event "is less elaborate than it once was," as a result of changes in Carriacou's social structure (see Hill 1977 and Hill 1980: 6; see also Smith 1962: 129). By the mid-1990s, the wedding party undertook even fewer of the rituals described by Hill. Hill also recorded that in the early 1970s, steel bands had begun to replace string bands as the music of choice during the evening reception (Hill 1977: 292). Today, steel bands have been replaced by a deejay who spins discs of popular Anglo-Caribbean musics such as soca and calypso as well as Jamaican reggae, raggamuffin ("ragga"), slow ballads regionally called "lover's rock," and pop and funk musics from the United States.

The partial abandonment of the string band in the Carriacou wedding

FIGURE 5.9 "Dancing the Cakes" at a pre-wedding ceremony, Mount Pleasant, Carriacou,
August 1995.

ceremony reflects the creeping hegemony of the recorded music industry
both regionally and internationally and concomitant loss of traditional culture for Kayaks. However, folk culture is defined by the fact that tradition
evolves over time—that change is inevitable. Thus it is perhaps more con-
structive to contextualize this change with the question of cultural agency
and collective creativity. Increasingly, young Kayaks pick and choose among
elements of their traditional culture, replacing what they discard with a
contemporary, mediated pan-Caribbean musical aesthetic that is reflected
in the records spun by the deejay at the wedding reception. This generation,
like the generation just before them and like their counterparts elsewhere in
the Caribbean (see Bilby 1999), thus engages in the notion of tradition as a
progressive, empowering set of choices between the old (string band music,
for example) and the new.

SERENADING

The embrace of new technology and larger regional musical aesthetics affects other string band performance contexts as well. Carriacou string bands

were once most active in the weeks leading up to Christmas, but today only a handful continue this tradition. Like Hosannah bands, string bands from each village traditionally serenade or "parang" at the homes of friends and relatives in their village and beyond. In years past, serenading began as early as October; today, if it happens at all, it is during the week prior to Christmas, on Christmas Day, and on New Year's Day. Serenading bands range from six to twenty people, and the bands increase in size as they move from house to house. While most of the instrumentalists are men, women do much of the singing and play percussion instruments, as do the many children who join in.

While both serenaders and Hosannah bands stroll from home to home and perform for the occupants, serenaders consist of string band musicians and singers, while Hosannah bands technically are strolling groups of a cappella singers who sing strictly Christmas carols. Traditionally, serenading bands included parang instrumentation such as the guitar, banjo, *baha* (a mouthblown cardboard tube), *dub* (or *dups,* a cardboard barrel used as a bass drum), and *pan* (steel drum). By 1997 the *baha* had disappeared and serenading instruments had grown to embrace several guitars, mandolin, *cuatros,* occasionally a steel drum, violin, and myriad percussion instruments ranging from plastic soda bottles filled with stones to overturned boxes and plastic barrels fashioned into drums.

String band serenaders might sing a Christmas song or two but usually stick to a wide range of secular songs, including the infamous *lavways* or improvised songs containing local news and gossip, according to singer Brian Lendore:

BL: I guess you go to sing carols, so you say Hosannah. If you don't go to sing carol, [you] serenade.

RSM: What do you sing if you are serenading?

BL: (Laughs.) Social issues. Yeah. Anything that happen in the community. Now anything that anybody do in the community, they do compose a song around that. And that is what you sing if you go serenading. You don't sing Christmas carol. (interview, 1996)

Serenaders range in age from children to the elderly. A child's first instrument is typically "found" or homemade, perhaps fashioned by an older member of the community, as Sonnelle Allert recalls from his boyhood in the 1930s:

> We used to have this small, little *boule,* calabash, right. [Uncle Canute Caliste] used to make that for me and put a piece of board in it and put a screw. . . . Four [strings]. Like a ukelele. And I used to go serenading around Christmas time, say about three months before. We go to every village. And say when it come to four in the morning, we almost keep near to our village. Day could light us and everybody run out to see the serenading is coming back home, you know. . . . And we play 'til about seven. Yeah and then everybody go to their home. And then we start at seven in the night again and we go again. (interview, 1997)

Unlike community Hosannah singing, which is essentially moribund, some string band serenading does take place around Christmas and on New Year's Day. Because L'Esterre is one of the most musical villages in Carriacou today, my husband and I were not surprised (and quite pleased) to learn that there would, in fact, be serenaders on Christmas Day 1996, and we were invited to join in. What follows are excerpts from my fieldnotes from that day:

At home in the morning, Tom and I hear a wall of music as serenaders turn down our path. On guitars are Brian Lendore, Enel James, and Lionel Stiell, accompanied by Thora Stiell and other women on percussion. Dexter Lendore plays a "dups," that is, an open box hit with a stick. A pile of kids play various percussion instruments, such as empty drink bottles played with a rock or a stick, brake drums struck with a piece of metal, twisted pieces of metal which approximated a triangle or "steel," and soft drink bottles filled with stones and pebbles, used as chac chacs *or shakers.*

Cosmos Bristol had alerted us the day before that there'd be serenading, so I baked a currant roll and Tom bought a pile of drinks, including Jack Iron (rum), soft drinks, and beer. We were told that it is traditional to offer something sweet, something salt, and something pork. We have the sweet (currant roll) and the salt (peanuts) but skip the pork. The serenaders scarf down the currant roll and soft drinks. Henry Stiell wets the ground with the Jack Iron, followed by water as a blessing to the ancestors.

We join in, playing music as we walk. On the way, Enel finds some bass drums and gives them to teenage boys to play. Another Stiell brother, named "Fries,"

FIGURE 5.10   String band serenading on Christmas Day 1996, L'Esterre, Carriacou. Left to right: Brian Lendore (guitar), Bernice Lendore, Dexter Lendore (*dups*), unknown singer, Bradley Thompson (percussion [rock on bottle]).

plays a broken but loud snare drum. Lionel Stiell picks up a cuatro when we pass his house.

As we walk, we play popular calypsos like "Bouncing Low" with improvised lyrics about the season: "Bouncing low, working to the Parang." When we arrive at the homes, we play a variety of songs, including parang socas such as "The Cat Ate the Ham," "In da Parang Band," and "I Want Me Some Pork" by Scranta, one of Trinidad's leading soca artists:

> *I want me some pork, I want me some pork,*
> *I want me some pork for me Christmas.*
> *I don't want no manicou, you can keep the callaloo,* [15]
> *I jes' want me some pork for me Christmas.*

Produced and broadcast over radio for the Christmas season, parang socas are seasonal songs that, unlike regular socas, feature lyrical melodies in keeping with the folk parang style (Mathison, interview, 1997). "In da Parang Band," for example, by the Grenadian calypsonian and soca star Ajamu, filled the airwaves for months leading up to Christmas, celebrating the season and the tradition of string bands (often referred to as parang bands). Because of its propulsive beat and general accessibility, not to mention its seasonal relevance, the serenaders sang it at almost every house. In general, however, serenading repertoire is selected to suit those who are being visited. While the overall atmosphere is celebratory—often irreverent—there is also a sense of the dignity of Christmas, particularly when the serenaders visit older or more religious residents. Bass guitarist Bernice Bristol notes that she and other musicians adapt their music to the house: "If sometime we pass by someone house and they might be religious, we might just play a few hymns or Christmas carol, real nice and slow. Make a toast and just go" (B. Bristol, interview, 1997).

From my fieldnotes:

We play other songs, including one having to do with "sweet/salty": "Something sweet to pass through me teeth, something cold to pass through me throat, somet'ing salt to pass through me mouth." Another song we sing is "Going to a Christmas Party," to the tune of "Mary Had a Little Lamb" with improvised lyrics: "In the kitchen, baking, baking" and "Everybody's dancing, dancing." At this point, we form a loose circle, and everybody takes turns dancing solo in a big dance ring. Tom does an admirable solo; I am let off the hook because I am so hugely pregnant.

This type of social dance genre is called "pass plays." Traditionally, on holidays such as All Saints' and All Souls' Night (November 1 and 2), unmarried teenagers and sometimes children gather at crossroads (intersections) throughout Carriacou. There, the dancers form a ring, in some instances with boys on one side and girls on the other. As the group sings, a boy or a girl dances in the ring, singing and clapping, then dances over to the edge and touches a person of the opposite sex, who takes the dancer's place. Participants dance until everybody has had a turn in the ring. The songs feature call and response with a repeated chorus, often sung in two- or three-part harmony and sometimes accompanied by handclapping. Pass plays of this type are rarely performed today; this was an exception.

We sing lots of Christmas songs, such as "Silver Bells," "We Wish You a Merry Christmas," and "Jingle Bells," among others. In addition to various calypsos, we also sing another genre of song that I can't immediately recognize—one consisting of call and response lines.

This type of serenading song, it turned out, was called a "road march" (or, at times, a *lavway* or a parang)—that is, a song sung during a procession involving musicians, masqueraders, and merrymakers. Typically associated with Carnival and Christmastime events in Trinidad, Grenada, and Carriacou, these song types are probably descended from or at least related to the late-1890s *lavway* and the earliest form of calypso, which were played while musicians and masqueraders processed down the street during Carnival. Donald Hill defines this early type of *lavway* as "a litanous tune sung informally in outdoor festivals" and notes that most of them were "single tone," meaning that the song has only one melody, as opposed to separate verse and chorus melodies (Hill 1993: 3–4 and 1977: 384). Maureen Warner-Lewis notes that these early *lavways* could be descended from the Yoruba people of Africa, whose minor-key melodies are litanic in structure (Warner-Lewis 1986).

The modern *lavway* is no longer a simple call-and-response but instead a four-line, strophic verse. As the core of the serenading repertory in Carriacou, the *lavway* has traditionally been an improvisatory form; today, while some serenaders still improvise lyrics that reflect the moment, most *lavways* are composed prior to the Parang Festival's string band competition. Many Carriacouans have assured me that they know how to improvise *lavways,* and some singers still do so (B. Lendore, interview, 1996; W. Fleary, interview, 1997). Whether composed or improvised, the modern Christmastime *lavway* airs gossip, reports on inappropriate behavior, and discusses other local items of interest regarding the occupant of the home, thus holding him or her up to public scrutiny or ridicule. Folklorist Winston Fleary describes a "leggo"-style *lavway* from years past:[16]

Local composition[s], songs like "Raphael want to married, he no have money and they want to hold him to married." Thing is, he was having a kid with a girl and he had no job to marry, he had no money. . . . And the people made a song on that, you know. "Raphael want to married but he no have no money, so they must let Raphael shadow go." Let him go, you know? Don't bother the boy because he have [no] money to marry. Leggo Raphael shadow:

> *(singing) Raphael want to married, he no have no money.*
> *Why, why, why and a ohhh, leggo Raphael shadow.*
> *Leggo, leggo, leggo, let go Raphael shadow.*
> *Why, why, why and a ohhh, leggo Raphael shadow.* (interview, 1997)

From my fieldnotes:

As we approach each house, the occupants come out and welcome us. When we arrive, one of the serenading men—typically Henry Stiell, the principal of the Hillsborough Government School and the son of the late "Boy" Stiell—recites an improvised welcome to the owners of the home. The owners offer us drinks and food, ranging from snacks to full spreads of fried fish with ketchup, lambi (conch), mutton broth (made from sheep or goat), lobster, chicken, pork, cou cou, bread, cakes, sweet buns, fruit cakes made from brown sugar, white cakes made from white sugar, hard candies ("sweeties"), etc. Soft drinks, beer, rum, and liquors are always offered. The amount and variety differ from home to home; sometimes only liquor and soft drinks are offered; at other times, the spread is enormous.

As the kids drink their beverages, they retain the bottles to turn into percussion instruments. This is good, because the bottles break and need to be replaced.... After we eat and drink, we play two or three more songs; then Henry Stiell offers an improvised toast after which we leave the house with much laughter and thanks from the occupant. We move on to the next one, singing songs, drinking, eating and "making merry."

As we move toward the L'Esterre crossroads, we meet another band of serenaders, also from L'Esterre. We are singing one song; they another. We come up against each other, singing and playing louder and louder in an effort to drown out the other group. Everybody is laughing and carrying on and eventually we are all singing their song. We soon move off in different directions, our band up the hill toward the "pon'" and the other group toward Harveyvale.

Decades ago, when many string bands serenaded throughout Carriacou, informal friendly competitions were common when one strolling ensemble met another en route. After our string band encountered Poco Joseph's at the crossroads in L'Esterre, I was sure that his group had "won." Later, when he and I compared notes, he assured me otherwise:

PJ: We were competing then! You had more voices, so you won.

RSM: But we wound up singing your song!

PJ: I know, yeah. (Laughs.) So they like that, that's what makes the whole thing so interesting. They like that competing. Those girls, they wouldn't have come with us at all. Because they want to have the competition, they want to see who can out-do.

RSM: What girls?

PJ: Mrs. Stiell, all them. They deliberately stayed away from our band because they wanted to compete with us! Well you all beat us! (Laughs.)

RSM: Why? Because you left?

PJ: No, you all had the better voices . . . we gave up! (Laughs.) We had more instruments, but you need the voices. These girls, they can sing! (D. Joseph, interview, 1996)

From my fieldnotes:
After about six hours of serenading, Tom and I return home; the others carry on to other parts of L'Esterre. They later tell us that they serenaded for hours after that, going all the way to the neighboring village of Harveyvale. All in all, it is a great day.

ROAD MARCH TO MODERNITY

Oral histories gathered since the 1970s are the only extant records of how serenading came to Carriacou. However, many Kayaks believe that "visiting" on Christmas Day was typical of Carriacou society even before emancipation. String band serenading may have come from Trinidad via migrant Carriacouans beginning in 1838 and continuing after emancipation. Whatever its origins, serenading in Carriacou has historically been an integral part of the Christmas season, which it extends by weeks (or even months). For musicians, serenading offers an opportunity to play music with others within and outside of one's village. For those visited by the musicians, serenading becomes an affirmation of community belonging and responsibility, an act of social reciprocity between the serenaders and the serenaded.

Albert Fortune (b. 1953) remembers Christmas time serenading as one of the main activities that everybody in his village of Belleview looked forward to:

Like in my parents' days they don't have no TV or anything, so the musical instruments, the string bands, that was the thing. . . . We used to go all around the place, serenading, playing the guitar and so

on. I was a very tender age and a lot of people used to admire us playing. Whole band of us. We used to be up to around eight, ten [in the
morning]. And there's something call a "road march," start up as
little children, just start up the serenading, and we start around October in those times.

Well, in those times Christmas had meaning. Now this year, [chil-
dren] don't know anything about Christmas. When you start serenading from October right up to Christmas and probably night after
night, going village to village and people used to appreciate very
much. It was very nice. (Interview, 1997)

Beginning in the 1960s and continuing into the early 1980s, extensive migration away from the island, coupled with the increasing popularity of
modern and transnational musics such as reggae and steel band, led to a
large decline in serenading, but it did not spell the end of the tradition. Donald Hill's (1977: 289) fieldwork reveals an active string band community in
Carriacou in 1970–71, with musicians serenading at Christmastime, in
Easter processionals in the main village of Hillsborough, and during various parts of the extended Carriacou wedding celebration. Kayaks generally
agree that this amount of interest in serenading has become more the exception than the rule in contemporary Carriacou. Certainly musicians continue
to serenade in their villages, but both the number of the individuals and the
overall time spent serenading has declined drastically from several decades
ago. Some musicians note that pressure to rehearse for the Parang Festival
results in less time to serenade. Others point to a general decline of interest
in traditional music making, or to the increasing dominance of recorded
musics in Carriacou's sonic landscape.

As one style of expressive culture fades from practice, a contemporary
version fills the vacuum. The tradition of serenading on foot from house to
house, bringing music, song, and cheer to families and friends, and enjoying friendly face-to-face sing-offs with competing serenaders, is increasingly being supplemented—or supplanted—by large mobile sound systems
that serenade via a "motorcade" on Christmas and New Year's Days. Since
the mid-1990s, Kimberlin Mills, a well-known Carriacouan businessman,
award-winning calypso artist (professionally known as Kim Da King or DJ
Kim), and founder of Carriacou's most popular radio station, KYAK,[17]
loads up a flatbed truck with sound equipment. He and his assistants then

slowly drive through each village in Carriacou. Broadcasting soca, parang socas, calypso, and other popular musics, they sell beer and soft drinks from a bar at the end of the truck. With music played at ear-piercing volume, the motorcade attracts a steadily expanding following of young people who "jump up" alongside the slowly moving truck, dance, drink, and celebrate the Christmas season. The impetus for the motorcade arose in the early 1990s, when Mills saw that the island was too quiet on Christmas Day: "Everybody was home and I think that we needed to go out and be merry. And show people that we merry. And the only way to do that and attract the attention was the DJ's system on top the trucks. And you would hear this noise coming and then you would see it . . . [and] a whole bunch of people would like [be] very merry" (interview, 2001).

While younger Kayaks enjoy the motorcade as both observers and participants, the flatbed approach to Christmas cheer is clearly generational, as Theo Jerome explains: "Every Christmas Eve, 4:00 A.M., they parade around the island on the vehicles, blasting music. To me, it kills the Christmas spirit. This is why we don't have many string bands and many young people involved in string bands. That thing, they go until they drunk themselves and they get so tired. They sleep wherever they fall off the truck. . . . This is not Christmas" (interview, 1997).

It is, however, the road march of modernity, when public musical performances no longer mandate local knowledge, creative energy, or cooperation. Increasingly, music making and consumption on Christmas and New Year's Day in Carriacou is dominated by technology and the capital investment in sound equipment—a variation of Krister Malm and Roger Wallis's notion of "mediazation," when "a music is changed through [its] interaction with the mass media system" (Malm 1993: 344). In this case, recorded music is replacing an entire tradition of community music making, much the way deejays replaced string bands during Kayak wedding receptions. While opinion differs as to the aesthetic value of this type of road march, most Kayaks acknowledge that the role of string bands, participatory music making and consumption, and Christmas traditions in general have all changed in Carriacou.

The growing presence of the media and musical technology in the lives of Carriacouans creates what Mark Slobin terms an "industrial intercul- ture" (Slobin 1992: 42), whereby the Carriacouan aural landscape is now increasingly dominated by recorded music produced elsewhere in the Caribbean and North America. Although musicians continue to play string band music in the rum shops, they must first turn off the ubiquitous record-ings of highly produced non-local musics playing over the sound systems. Contrasting with the popular indulgence of the remaining few strolling groups of serenading musicians is the rising popularity of the Christmas-time motorcades. With less physical and social space for string band musi-cians to create live music, Carriacouans increasingly share the worldwide trend of passively experiencing and consuming mediated, non-local musics.

TOURIST AUDIENCES

While Kayaks find themselves with fewer and fewer opportunities to hear and perform their musics, the few tourists who visit Carriacou come with precisely this expectation. Their desire to sample "native culture" provides opportunities for Kayak string band musicians to perform on a limited but regular basis. These tourist settings have impacted aspects of string band style and performance practice and will continue to do so as the tourist in-dustry grows, as many in Carriacou hope it will.

No firm figures exist as to the exact numbers of tourists visiting Carri-acou, but it is clear from the relatively few accommodations that the num-ber is quite small compared to many other Caribbean islands (J. Bullen, interview, 1995). In an effort to attract foreign capital, more and more Kayak business owners and political leaders have become active in devel-oping the tourism industry (M. Bullen, interview, 1997; Nimrod, interview, 1997). The tourists who do venture to Carriacou come largely via tour packages or on board the *Mandalay* or the *Yankee Clipper*—smaller cruise ships that have dropped anchor on a monthly basis in Hillsborough Bay since 1987. These predominantly North American and/or European audi-ences are often entertained by local Kayak string band performances, work that is arranged by the cruise ships' bursars. In addition, Grenadians on holiday, visitors from other Caribbean islands, and returning Kayaks who live abroad often visit Carriacou during Carnival (in February) and Regatta (in August), events that often feature performances of string band music. String band musicians will also occasionally perform on neighboring Petit St. Vincent, an exclusive resort island a stone's throw from Carriacou and Petit Martinique.[18]

Carriacou string band musicians distinguish between performing at a community event for free (or almost free)—"playing"—and performing for tourists audiences for a fee—"working" (H. Fleary, interview, 1995). Inherent in the latter is a power dynamic skewed towards the financial exploitation of the musicians. In 1996–97, a six-to-eight-member string band on board the *Mandalay* was paid $100 (U.S. dollars) for a three-hour set (plus a bag of ham sandwiches and cans of Budweiser beer to bring back to shore), whereas guests on the cruise ship paid upward of $1,500 apiece for a thirteen-day cruise.[19] String bands of the same size at the Kayak-owned Silver Beach Resort were paid $94 for their three-hour set, while guests there paid around $85 per couple per night.[20] String bands playing a three-hour set on Petit St. Vincent were paid $112–150 (U.S. dollars), whereas a night on the island cost paying guests $740 per couple.[21]

It is obvious that the pay per musician is exceedingly low, even at the Carriacou resort, and the string bands were in fact the lowest-paid groups hired by the *Mandalay* and on Petit St. Vincent. The *Mandalay,* for example, hired a six-piece band in Antigua for $250 for a three-hour set;[22] Petit St. Vincent regularly paid approximately $206 for a weekly performance by a European jazz duo and about $299 for a ten-piece steel band from neighboring Union Island.[23] From this fee schedule alone, string bands were clearly not considered as valuable a commodity as other musical genres.

Specific repertory changes are immediately discernable when Carriacou string bands perform for tourists. While string bands certainly perform some portion of their standard repertoire, they also respond to requests for songs long associated with the greater Caribbean, such as the Cuban *guajira* "Guantanamera" or old calypsos popularized by Harry Belafonte. Recognizable to European and American audiences as relics of the calypso craze that swept the United States in the 1950s, songs like "Yellow Bird," "Jamaica Farewell," or "Island in the Sun" are largely lighthearted and apolitical, unlike contemporary calypsos that often carry messages of contemporary political or social significance. While most string band players enjoy playing for tourist audiences (Chase, personal communication, 1996; Coy, personal communication, 1996; McGillivary, interview, 1997), many, like Harrison Fleary, do not relish playing these older songs over and over again: "When I go to [play on cruise ships], I play songs that I don't even enjoy. You have some little things, folk songs, that we play just for the tourists . . . "Miss Mary Anne" . . . "Island In The Sun" and this kind of thing. I don't play that locally, I mean, for my own local folks. All those things, I doing for tourists, very often. Very often" (interview, 1995).

In privileging these older calypsos, string bands are forced to neglect local Carriacou tunes and current calypsos, displacing contemporary expression and local aesthetics in favor of the image of a homogenized Caribbean. Carriacou then could be any other Caribbean island with, as Stephen Stuempfle eloquently writes of Trinidad, "the soundtrack of an exotic experience of tropical, palm-fringed beaches and carefree living" (Stuempfle 1995: xiv).

The interaction between Carriacou string bands and tourist audiences can best be described as the "primitive gaze," whereby first-world audiences judge the "natives" based on culturally biased, ethnocentric, or simply erroneous assumptions. In addition to recognizable older calypsos, string bands also play American folk and popular pieces for their tourist audiences. These tunes are rendered with an entirely different set of aesthetics from that of North American ensembles. Their intonation, for example, although similar to a Euro-American aesthetic, is closer to that found in various West African musical systems, which, according to Koetting are "free of the confines of a standardized pitch, tempered-scale tuning system" (Koetting 1992: 73). Someone unfamiliar with this tonal orientation will hear music that sounds "out of tune" and conclude that the musicians are not proficient because the music sounds "wrong." Additionally, Carriacou string bands reconstruct North American popular tunes to suit their instrumentation, which is a far cry from a big band with horn sections and amplified guitars. The addition of percussion instruments such as the keg drum, conga, triangle, or soda bottle scraped with a dollar coin presents a very different aesthetic than does the more visually familiar trap set or the synthesized percussion of a drum machine.

Unaccustomed to this type of intonation, and to stratified polyrhythmic string accompaniment played on found percussion instruments, European and American audiences tend to interpret the musicianship as unskilled and "rough" and the music as somehow "natural" or "funky." That most Kayak musicians cannot afford expensive instruments and thus play on old, beat-up guitars and violins as well as on "found" instruments adds to the sense that the musicians are "earthy" but unskilled. According to the Bursar on board the *Mandalay,* Carriacou string bands are "one of the high points of the cruise" because "they're so rough, so folkie" (Sarah, personal communication, 1995). Despite this, local music on cruises creates a "better atmosphere" for the guests, notes Captain Mike Taylor of the *Mandalay:* "[The string band has] a fairly unpolished sound, don't they? Yeah, they're unique really. A bit like Zydeco, I suppose. But certainly different to the run-of-the-mill bands you get. They're less polished. They look as if they're enjoying it. I mean they all seem to be having a good time. You look at 'Soldier' playing the guitar there. He's got his guitar strung normally, but he plays it left-handed. Sometimes he's got six strings, sometimes he's only got four. They got atmosphere" (M. Taylor, interview, 1995).

Poking fun at the musicians' artistry and damning them with faint praise are fairly typical of the comments I've heard from tourist audiences. In a similar assessment of string band music as being somehow "natural," Hazen Richardson, the owner of Petit St. Vincent, explains why he hired Cora Blair's string band from Petit Martinique for several years:

HR: [String band music] was pretty much, kind of funky but kind of fun.

RM: Funky?

HR: That's not quite the word. A very natural group 'cause this is what they played at home. . . . Well, it wasn't so fabricated the way I feel electric guitar music is or say a synthesizer or something like that, which I think is so artificial. . . . I think the guests enjoyed the naturalness of it. You don't very often see guys walking around playing violins. Kind of unusual. (Interview, 1996)

The trope of "natural" is constantly reiterated by outsiders to Carriacouan (and indeed, Caribbean) culture and reinforced by media depictions of the region. A 1979 article in *National Geographic,* for example, describes Carriacouans as living a "freewheeling rhythm of life," apparently free of responsibilities and thus representing something "natural" (Starbird 1979: 417). This notion of Afro-Caribbean culture is also inherent in the hiring policies that affect Kayak musicians: they are associated with the primitive and as such must necessarily be culturally regressive. Whereas European jazz musicians are expected to master and integrate electronic technology into their music, Kayak musicians pay a price if they introduce any progressive change to theirs. For example, Harrison Fleary's string band played at

Petit St. Vincent for a year and then was joined by multi-instrumentalist Peter Quashie of Petit Martinique:

> When Peter got involved, it was his idea that we use some electronic instruments as well. We had electronic drum, we used the bass guitar, we had rhythm guitar. . . . And we had an amplifier and so on. Very much to the distaste of [the manager of Petit St. Vincent]. He almost asked us not to come back. Like he did say, if he wanted electronic music, he could find that. What he wanted was to see a man behind a drum, beating and get this acoustic kind of sound. He said that's what he wanted! That's what he was paying for. And not this electrical thing. (H. Fleary, interview, 1995)

Eventually, these musicians were fired because their interest in integrating technology with traditional music was rejected as "artificial" and contrary to an outsider's sense of what Caribbean culture ought to be (Quashie, personal communication, 1996). While the notion of change and innovation may serve as an inherent component of the academic definition of "folk," in practice the representation of Kayak folk culture by outsiders (the owners of Petit St. Vincent) for outsiders (European and American tourists) is limited to that which is old and "rough."

The only individual in a position to hire Carriacou string bands to play for tourist audiences who does not subscribe to this aesthetic of apparent primitiveness is native Carriacouan Judy Bullen, the former assistant manager of Silver Beach, one of Carriacou's largest resorts. During Ms. Bullen's tenure at Silver Beach, she regularly hired the string band led by violinist Milton "Tailor" Coy of Hillsborough: "I like it personally, I like the music . . . and this is what Carriacou has to offer. And I think the guests are quite receptive to it. It is part of our culture and seeing these old guys still going on, continuing this thing, I think that's quite appealing to them. They play good music, you know?" (J. Bullen, interview, 1995).

String band music in the context of a tourist performance, then, takes on a meaning wholly unintended by the performers. For outsiders "gazing" at the musicians, the music locates the local inasmuch as the musicians are Carriacouans; however, the demand for them to play familiar, pan-Caribbean songs and calypsos contradicts that distinguishing sense of locality in favor of a more homogenized regional orientation. Their region thus becomes "the Caribbean," a single cultural zone where the people live lives free from the responsibilities, constraints, sophistication, and cares experienced in the "first world." In short, the population of this Caribbean is on vacation, just like the tourists they entertain.

TOWARD AN EVOLVING TRADITION

It is a challenge to interpret the effect of modernity on traditional culture. On one hand, change as a result of technology, globalization, and other contemporary forces is often seen as somehow damaging, altering folk traditions to the point of their extinction or, at best, some loss of their "authenticity." Yet traditional music is by definition adaptable and subject to transformation, a process which, when read in a more positive light, can comprise an empowering set of choices made in response to social and economic circumstances, not to mention community aesthetics. Still a vital part of Carriacouan culture, string band music, to be sure, has undergone a major transformation in terms of its performance context and practice. It is nevertheless appreciated by audience and performers alike as a source of entertainment and artistic creativity, and as a continuing beacon of Kayak identity. A creolized form that historically has combined found instrumentation and disparate musical traditions and repertoire, Carriacou string band music is eminently adaptable to local circumstances and changing aesthetics. This adaptability bodes well for its continued practice in Kayak society into the twenty-first century.

Most folk traditions worldwide undergo long periods of widespread popularity as well as periods of disinterest. Some of these traditions die out; others rebound on their own; still others are reenergized through the efforts of individuals or groups committed to the maintenance of heritage. Cultural revival occurs when a so-called "dying" tradition is actively and self-consciously reinvigorated, usually for political, social, or ideological reasons that might include the maintenance of an ethnic identity, the perceived repercussions of cultural encroachment, and the changing sociopolitical landscape. Such is the case with Carriacou string band music, a genre that precipitously declined for several decades until the late 1970s, when the Mount Royal Progressive Youth Movement's Parang Festival captured the imaginations of both string band players and audiences alike. Since then, the Parang Festival has imposed certain aesthetics and conditions on the participating string bands, subtly transforming, in the process, the tradition and its players. Given, however, the enormous popularity of the Sunday evening string band competition, these transformations have alienated neither Carriacouan audiences nor the musicians. On the contrary: string bands continue to serve as an expressive tool of Kayaks for presenting values and societal norms in increasingly recontextualized settings, simultaneously evoking tradition, modernity, and regional belonging.

6

MELÉE!

The Sunday Evening String Band Competition

They vex with we, they vex with we,
they vex with we, but we happy.
Me en' lie [I don't lie about] on nobody,
but dem people drivin' we crazy.

They vex with we, they vex with we,
they vex with we, 'cause we happy.
Me en' lie on nobody,
so we have no damn apology!

—Parang band BBH, 1996

STANDING IN A ROW ON THE BRIGHTLY LIT stage in Hillsborough's Tennis Courts, the musicians in the parang band BBH dig into their *lavway* chorus with an energy that brings the audience to its feet. The band's eight members are dressed in matching, amazingly colorful costumes—bright yellow flowing blouses and pants edged with sparkles that catch the stage lights. All of the band members have vibrant head scarves that flow down their backs. The effect is one of color, light, and motion in contrast to the aggressive energy of the tight, polyrhythmic playing and the strong lead and harmony vocals. This powerful moment is not lost on the audience, as the band members' dazzling appearance is offset by their stance and edgey messages embedded in their lyrics.

As part of the Sunday evening string band competition, the performances of BBH and the other ten or so parang bands map how Carriacouans locate themselves in relation to each other and to the greater Caribbean region. Vying for substantial cash prizes, bands from Carriacou's villages are pitted against each other while presenting gossip and the social issues of the

FIGURE 6.1 BBH performing at the 1996 Parang Festival string band
competition, Hillsborough, Carriacou (partial view of band; video
capture).

day. These bands reiterate themes concerning village/locality/community
throughout the event, reinforcing collective understandings of identity and
belonging, inter-reliance, and social control. Regionalism is similarly signaled, most obviously in the very name of the event: Parang. Despite the traditional local use of the term to describe a Christmas-song style and a seasonal activity, its transference to the context of a staged competition also
recalls the Parang tradition and competition of Hispanic Trinidad. The
local and the regional meet most profoundly in the work of the competing
bands, many of whom consciously integrate various Latin American musical emblems into their performances while highlighting traditional Carriacou string band style. Much debated among musicians, judges, and audience members, this integration of local with regional styles, on one hand,
underscores and reinforces community bonds, mores, and aesthetics. On the
other hand, this climactic event of Parang weekend also highlights an ongoing connection to Grenada's revolutionary past as well as a contemporary
thrust toward regional affinity and cooperation.

The buzz surrounding the Parang Festival begins to grow among musicians, organizers, and the general public about two months before the actual
weekend. During this time, representatives from participating bands partner with the Parang Committee in a sometimes uneasy dance of collabora-

tion and contestation. While the musicians frequently criticize the process and chafe at the administrative control, most ultimately work together with the Parang Committee toward the mutual goal of a successful competition.

OCTOBER: MEETING WITH THE PARANG COMMITTEE

String bands who wish to compete in Parang must conform to a set of regulations and expectations—rules that are clearly delineated by the Parang Committee and handed out as judging criteria to both string band and Hosannah band members at the early October meeting. Many of these rules are at odds with the typical performance practice of non-competition string bands, such as the limit of eight players per string band (ad hoc ensembles range from three to ten or more). Such standards construct musical, vocal, and aesthetic expectations that participants in turn routinely challenge at the October meeting:

> Hosannah band singer: What is this "Parang Spirit"?
>
> Parang Committee official: [It means that] performances should be lively, make it look like a festival.
>
> String band musician: The test piece [a Christmas carol] is very slow—what kind of "Parang Spirit" can you see there?
>
> Parang Committee official: You need to project [your voices].
>
> Hosannah band singer: This is where people feel bad after judging. You have to have people who *know* Parang Spirit in order to judge it. . . . You want to say, "They must portray happiness, brightness, joy, felicity, and upbeat." Is that what you want to say?

In fact, the vague notion of "Parang Spirit" often does prove to be a problem, because many of the musicians project seriousness of purpose on stage rather than the upbeat spontaneity enjoyed by all during informal village serenading. As Parang bands move from the community to the stage, the musicians instead focus on the competition and, in some instances, their stage fright. With an eye toward marketing the festival to Carriacou's fledgling tourist industry, the Parang Committee attempts to spruce up the performances and professionalize the stage presence of the participating musicians. This extends also to visual imagery that the Parang Committee hopes to

integrate into the Parang Festival, such as Nativity scenes, shepherd costumes, and other icons that highlight imported notions of Christmas:

> String band musician: Best dressed? What is the "Most Cultural"
> outfit? Some people last year dress as shepherds. Is that really [our]
> culture?
>
> Parang Committee official: It mean Christmas colors.
>
> String band musician: But shepherd outfit is not a cultural thing to
> Carriacou.
>
> Hosannah band singer: Shepherds equal Christmas culture. But I've
> never seen a parang band where each member dress alike. They are
> well dressed, because each person has a personality . . . but [wearing
> the same clothes] is departing from fundamental authenticity. [One
> year] Mount Pleasant was the best band in all ways, the most
> authentic, but L'Esterre got it because they had flowers, et cetera.
> People come from England, New York, they say "What is that?" We
> must be aware of [the] economy and the tourist dollar. They must see
> who we are. (A lot of "shtoops"[1] from the assembled musicians.)

There are two conflicts here. The first arises from traditional images of
Christmas that have little or no bearing on Afro-Caribbean reality or on images of the Caribbean/Kayak self.[2] Despite Christmastime being a time-
honored tradition and an important holiday in Carriacou, the Parang Festival attempts to present local Kayak culture with all its attendant tropical
imagery—representations that clash with traditional Christmas images
(Middle Eastern deserts and shepherds). And, as the Hosannah band member points out, if tourists come to Parang, they would *expect* to see "traditional" island garb rather than costumes that locate a more conventional interpretation of the Nativity.

The second conflict is between actual local practice and the invented
image of parang bands proposed by the Parang Committee. String band serenaders traditionally wear street clothes, not matching costumes. The problem here is how best to represent Kayak culture during the Parang Festival
to tourists, either as a Euro-American conception of a Christmas "show,"
complete with matching outfits, or as a less staged and more accurate representation of Carriacouan traditional culture.

Despite some grumbling, each band ultimately winds up appearing in matching original costumes; some bands even make two sets of costumes, one for the test piece and one for the choice piece. The costumes range from matching jeans and shirts to more elaborate matching shorts and shirts to bright, colorful costumes that evoke a celebratory atmosphere akin to Carnival. There is an incentive: the band with the best costume wins a special cash prize at the end of the festival.

NOVEMBER: VILLAGE ORGANIZATION

Like the Hosannah band competition, the string band competition also underscores the historic and oftentimes intense rivalries between villages. Village loyalty is manifested in the names of each string band: for example, BBH, the winner of Parang 1995, is an acronym for Belmont, Belleview, and Harveyvale, three neighboring villages on the southern end of the island. Members of the Central Serenaders live primarily in Carriacou's main town of Hillsborough or next door in Beausejour, both located in the central part of the island. Other string bands locate themselves geographically while promoting a competitive image of their musical skills. Eastern Bees leader "Babu" Callender explains the derivation of this name in the location of their village, Mount Pleasant, at the eastern end of the island, coupled with the potency of the group's *lavways:* "Bees, they sting. When we come out, we sting the audience" (Callender, interview, 1997).

Historically, Carriacou society has been organized at the village level, and, as demonstrated earlier, as strategic units for political organizing during Prime Minister Bishop's administration. The Parang Committee puts this preexisting structure to use, appealing to musicians to represent their villages in a string band, and when necessary, approaching musicians and helping to organize a band for the upcoming Parang Festival (W. Collins, interview, 1997; G. Collins, interview, 1997). Thanks to these efforts, the Parang Festival typically features a fairly good representation of villages. Indeed, representation by a string band brings a sense of pride to village residents, as can be heard in the constant (and raucous) audience response as villagers cheer their band on.

The Parang Committee also utilizes Carriacou's village structure to generate interest in the festival itself. In addition to financial support from local businesses, national sources (government grants and Grenadian-based

businesses), and international donations from Kayaks overseas, the Parang
Committee/MRPYM fundraises by producing dances and string band concerts in villages throughout the island. A pre-Parang night at the Community Center in Hillsborough presents string bands that perform *lavways* and
related songs from prior years, which "puts people in the mood" for Parang
(H. Fleary, interview, 1995). The pre-festival night also highlights business
sponsors; in 1996, for example, the main sponsor was Grenada Breweries,
and they paid the three participating bands for their performance, in contrast to most fundraisers, where bands play for free, and Parang night itself,
when bands must place in order to win one of the cash prizes.

NOVEMBER/DECEMBER: THE BANDS REHEARSE

One of the criticisms levied by musicians against the Parang Festival is that
competing bands have no time to participate in community serenading in
the weeks leading up to Christmas, because of the time needed for rehearsal
(Fortune, interview, 1997; C. Bristol, interview, 1997; MacFarlane, interview, 1997). Bands must learn, arrange, and then memorize the test piece—
usually a Christmas carol of four or more verses—and they must compose
a lengthy, two-part *lavway*. (The first part is either a jingle that advertises
each band's business sponsor or a seasonal introduction to the *lavway* itself,
usually in the style of Trinidadian or "Spanish" parang music. The second
part of the *lavway* consists of approximately ten original verses, each followed by a repeated chorus.) Some of the participating musicians are also
civic leaders whose responsibilities at other Christmastime events preclude
them from attending parang band rehearsals; others work during the week
in Grenada and are in Carriacou only on weekends. For some, there is little
time to rehearse for the competition, let alone to go out serenading. In this
sense, the staged version of parang has supplanted the community grass-
roots activity of serenading.

The concept of "rehearsal" (also called "practice") is itself a changing tradition. It was once as social as it was musical: until 1995, most string bands
rehearsed for Parang in rum shops, in stores, or at homes with the doors
open, so that people came by to listen—a sort of reverse serenading. Harrison Fleary described the Central Serenaders' rehearsals around this time,
particularly in regard to the *lavway:* "People would come around, just
gather around. Actually days before the Parang are perhaps the more excit-

ing time, you know. People will just come by, vehicles will just come by to hear some of it before it actually goes on stage. And we happy to have them hear it because they going to be chanting it while we are singing it, and so you have the backup" (interview, 1995).

By allowing the *lavway* to be heard in advance of the festival, bands created a buzz about the "stories" (gossip) contained in each verse—who might be "named," and why. Moreover, it offered the audience the opportunity to learn and sing along with the chorus during the competition. In this way, public rehearsals were very much in keeping with the calypso tradition in Grenada and Trinidad, where the music is broadcast on the radio for months before the competition to create excitement and share the material.[3] While Carriacou parang bands did not go to the expense or effort of their calypso counterparts, their open rehearsals encouraged the essential social component of Parang between musicians and audience. Still, this arrangement eventually proved impractical: by 1996 bands started to rehearse behind closed doors, if only to stay focused, says Central Serenaders bassist Bernice Bristol: "You can't get anything done! . . . Like sometime we go to [Harrison's] shop and then we can't do anything because somebody comes in and they start go, 'I want to hear this song, I want to hear that song.' You have to stop and play that for that person. We decide that it's better to practice somewhere far away, where you can concentrate and just keep your mind on what you want to do and what you planning for" (interview, 1997).

The Ghetto Boys are equally concerned about the interruption factor, but as the band's leader, Kenly "Rhyno" Joseph, notes, there is a more pressing reason for private rehearsals: "The lyrics we have to sing, I mean we don't want everybody to hear it because at least then everybody would know what you singing about, so that's why you keep it secret. . . . So normally the night of Parang, that would be the first time everybody would hear the lyrics" (interview, 1997). This is a fundamental change from when bands wanted to share the choruses and stories contained in the *lavway*. Some worry that melodies and "stories" must remain fresh for the actual competition; others worry that their material might be "tief" (stolen) by another band, according to Albert Fortune of BBH:

> If people hear you practice before, they will try and go and sing the song out. So then now we try to move away so they don't get the words of the whole song. You see, when you will hide the things,

when they got out, they know the issues, but when they start hearing what you saying, is sweeter. . . . And again, for other people passing, they might get [the] tune, go to another band and expose it and probably might even take somebody, the words from our tune or probably part of the tune and make theirs better. So I think other bands do the same thing. They try to be in secluded places so the people won't really know. (interview, 1997)

Maintaining secrecy, according to Harrison Fleary, is critical in preventing other bands from imitating or "improving on" the chorus. The melody and lyrics, notes Fleary, "might be your only edge on them" (H. Fleary, interview, 1997). Others, such as Andy "Leftist" Mathison of the Ghetto Boys (frequent first-place winners), demonstrate a calypsonian-like bravado concerning the possibility of other bands tiefing their music and/or lyrics: "If you gonna steal our chorus, when we get on stage, you're gonna be devastating, because . . . Ghetto Boys rehearsing Ghetto Boys' music. When the other Parang [bands] come [on stage], if you want to stand up in front of us and compete with us, you gotta be good" (interview, 1997).

Bands eventually still go public in the days leading up to the Parang Festival weekend. The Ghetto Boys make a point of serenading in their village to boost "Parang spirit" prior to leaving for the string band competition: "We do a last rehearsal before we come into town. If we inside, we come out, so that the village will hear us . . . to get the boys out, going down to Parang. 'Cause they always come down [to] support us. Somebody passing, I hear guys say 'I hope you are win tonight!'" (Mathison, interview, 1997). Likewise, the Central Serenaders pile into Harrison Fleary's pickup truck and play music as Fleary drives through the villages on their way to the string band competition. The crowd behind their vehicle grows steadily larger as they arrive at the Tennis Courts.

SUNDAY EVENING: AT THE TENNIS COURTS

Outside the Tennis Courts, the atmosphere is charged with excitement; concertgoers pack the streets hours before the string band competition begins. Food vendors sell barbequed meat on skewers, snacks, and a variety of soft drinks and beer. Recorded music blares from the many rum shops nearby—soca, calypso, and reggae dominate portions of the street, blending together at a distance. Packs of thin and unhealthy-looking terrier-type dogs break into fights over discarded food scraps. The line to buy $25 tickets for the string band competition is long, but the event is on Carriacou time: advertised to begin at 9:00 P.M., it doesn't actually get underway until well after 10:00.

A large, brightly lit stage dominates one end of the Tennis Courts. The back of the stage is decorated with paintings of musical instruments overlaid with colorful posters advertising a brand of Grenadian dark rum. Soca music blasts from the enormous speakers on either side of the stage. Flapping in the breeze are rows of small, colorful, triangular flags that hang from the top of the stage. Occasionally the breeze and the beat of the music somehow synchronize, giving the appearance of hundreds of dancing flags. About ten feet back from the stage sit the four judges' tables, each with a chair, pads of paper, and pens for scoring. Behind them are two rows of chairs reserved for political leaders and other VIPs, and behind those are the rows of chairs for the audience. While some prefer to sit, most of the audience stands behind the last row of chairs offering commentary and loud good humor throughout course of the evening.

After introductory and welcome speeches by the president of the Parang Committee as well as some words by the local VIPs, the hosts of the evening are introduced. In 1996 comedians Errol Fabian and Nicky Crosby from Trinidad delighted audiences with their charisma and subversive bantering. The MCs eventually get around to introducing the string band test piece and, amid cheers, applause, and whistles, the first band takes the stage. Band members stand in a single row, each musician behind a microphone that may or may not be turned on or loud enough to be heard in the mix. Their individual stances often hint at something akin to stage fright, until they get down to the business of performing.

"AND HEAR THE ANGELS SING!": THE TEST PIECE

The notion of authenticity is often debated among string band musicians in the weeks before and after Parang. Some bands perform in a style true to the perceived Latin American and Trinidadian origins of Parang, while other bands insist that Carriacou's own style of parang music is authentic in itself. This issue crystallized around the performance of the 1996 test piece, "It Came upon a Midnight Clear." Most of the bands performed it in a fairly

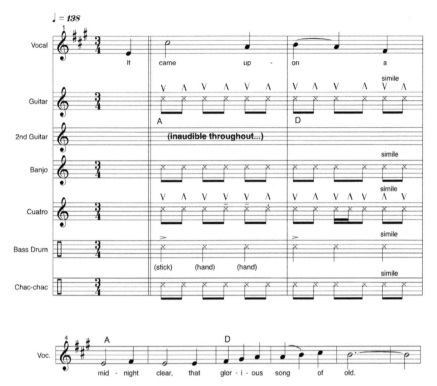

FIGURE 6.2 Transcription 7: "It Came upon a Midnight Clear," as played by the Royal Determinators.

conventional, local string band style: standard triple meter, moderate tempo, and straightforward vocals, with one or two lead singers and one or two others adding occasional harmony (see transcription 7, as played by the Royal Determinators). There is little by way of polyrhythmic interplay among the instruments: the guitar, banjo, *chac chac,* and *cuatro* all play three sets of eighth notes, with the *cuatro* adding an occasional flourish to the second beat.

Emerging on stage dressed as shepherds, the Central Serenaders began their rendition of the test piece. With melody, harmony, and lyrics well in place, the carol sounded new and different, for the musicians had completely reconfigured it from a traditional triple meter into duple meter. Underscoring this metrical oddity, their version was propelled by the addition of the syncopated half of a clave rhythm. Originating in Afro-Cuban music,

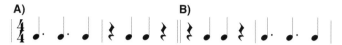

FIGURE 6.3 Clave rhythms.

FIGURE 6.4 Modified clave (*tresillo*).

clave is heard worldwide today in traditional and popular Caribbean, Latin American, and African American musical forms (notably salsa). The three-two clave is indicated in figure 6.3, example A; the two-three clave (a reversal of the two measures) is indicated in example B. A modified clave, as played by the Central Serenaders and other string bands in Carriacou, eliminates the quarter notes measure, resulting in a *tresillo* (roughly, "three-let") beat that pervades much of Afro-Caribbean and Afro-American music (see fig. 6.4).

Because even a modified clave beat cannot translate into 3/4 time, the only way to incorporate it into the Christmas carol "It Came upon a Midnight Clear" is to convert the time signature to duple meter, which is precisely what the Central Serenaders did (see transcription 8). Played by the bass guitarist and in variant form by the bass drummer, this modified clave is *the* Trinidadian parang beat, according to members of the band. While playing an "authentic" Trinidadian parang rhythm is not limited to the Central Serenaders—indeed, many string bands incorporate similar musical elements from the Hispanic Caribbean into their performances—the Central Serenaders were the only band that year who reconfigured the Christmas carol to duple time in order to introduce a Latin feel into the music. With an eye toward framing their performance "authentically" (that is, from Hispanic Trinidad), bass player Bernice Bristol observed, "I feel that if it's Parang, and you're dealing with Parang, I think it's only fair that you should do it in a Parang beat" (B. Bristol, interview, 1997).

While the incorporation of a modified clave links the music to the greater Caribbean region, the Central Serenaders' rendition of the test piece also neatly demonstrates a specific local aesthetic. Their music features an extensive (and virtuosic) rhythmic interlocking between the instruments—particularly between banjo and *cuatro* players—locally referred to as "roll and chop." These interlocking rhythms are produced on the first and third beats in the *cuatro* and banjo parts (see transcription 8): the *cuatro* "chops" (offbeat, accented strum) while the banjo "rolls" (an extremely fast strumming of the chord that is almost impossible to notate accurately). Highly prized among Kayak string band players, the roll and chop typically reflects the exceptional musical skills of two musicians who have played together for years, such as Central Serenaders' banjoist Godwin Moses and *cuatro* player Harrison Fleary.

Polyrhythmic interlocking between instruments is hardly specific to Carriacou; indeed, this rhythmic orientation is at the heart of many West and Central African musics and, as such, can be understood as one of this continent's many extant legacies in Kayak culture.[4] However, string band musicians prefer to link the roll and chop to contemporary string band performance instead, thereby underscoring the importance of a local, Kayak aesthetic (H. Fleary, interview, 1995; J. McGillvary, interview, 1997; G. Moses,

FIGURE 6.5 Transcription 8: "It Came upon a Midnight Clear," as played by the Central Serenaders.

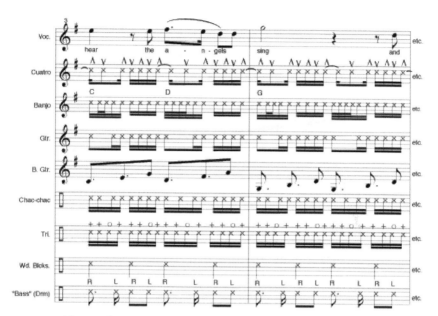

FIGURE 6.5 *(Continued)*

personal communication, 1995). Given the presence of the modified clave and the roll and chop, the Central Serenaders' test piece reflects three components of contemporary Kayak identity: a local musical aesthetic (probably rooted in a West African aesthetic); the ongoing significance of Christianity via the carol itself; and the integration of Kayak culture with the larger Caribbean, in this instance, the Hispanic Caribbean through the immediacy of an aural link.

ROUND TWO: THE CHOICE PIECE

The atmosphere inside the Tennis Courts grows even more charged as the last of the competing bands finishes their test piece. As the MCs return to stage to banter with the audience, lightly insult the judges, and generally entertain in their off-color way, the competing bands are changing into new costumes for the second half of the string band competition, or gathering in a corner together to practice quietly before their moment back on stage. Members of the audience mill about, buying beer and soft drinks from vendors inside the Tennis Courts, comparing notes on each band, and perhaps predicting the final outcome of the competition. After reintroduction by the

FIGURE 6.6 The Central Serenaders at the 1996 Parang Festival string band competition, Hillsborough (partial view of band; video capture). Left to right: unknown triangle player, Godwin "Mose" Moses (banjo), Jerry McGillivary (guitar), Harrison Fleary (vocals/*cuatro*), Sharma Dixon (vocals), Bernice Bristol (bass/vocals).

MCs, the first band again takes the stage to the cheers and applause of their friends and family. Despite this show of support, it is clear that most of the string band musicians are unaccustomed to formal staged performances: they stand rather stiffly in front of their microphones, and few make eye contact with the audience. The exceptions are the stage-savvy calypso singers, for calypso performance prizes a charismatic stage persona that spills over into the Parang competition. With no spoken introduction, the first band launches into their choice piece, the long awaited *lavway* that marks the climax of the Parang Festival weekend.

Unlike traditional *lavways,* which are typically improvised on the spot as string bands serenade through the villages, the competition-style *lavway* is composed prior to Parang by two or more members of each string band. Most *lavways* stick to fairly formulaic melodies and harmonic progressions. Some bands pen new lyrics to the same (or a quite similar) melody from the year before, or one band's melody might be reconstituted by another band the following year. The latter practice troubles Albert Fortune of BBH: "If you listen to Parang songs, they basically the same thing.... And that is something I'm against too. I think some people say that's the reason they re-

ally don't want to take part in Parang, because there's no change. Everything's the same thing. Just change the words. And then you have a slight
change in the chorus. But all the rest is (*shtoop*) basically the same thing. Is
Parang" (interview, 1997).

What *lavways* may lack in melodic and harmonic imagination is made
up for by their lyrics, however, which form the centerpiece of the competition. To highlight these lyrics, bands must strategically limit themselves to
instruments that provide rhythmic accompaniment, such as bass guitar fashioned out of an acoustic six-string guitar, Venezuelan *cuatro,* guitar, mandolin, three- or four-string banjo, one or more *chac chacs* (maracas), brake
drum struck with a piece of metal, bongo drum, triangle, sandpaper blocks,
and bass drum. One or two lead singers are joined by a chorus of three or
more. Lead players, such as a mandolinist, play rhythm and incidental
melody lines at transition points. Harrison Fleary, for example, notes that he
replaces his violin—normally the centerpiece of a string band—with a *cuatro* to avoid competing with the singers: "The gist of the thing is to get the
message out. The people want to hear the story. They want to listen to what
you say and jump to what you're saying and they become interested in the
words more than anything else" (interview, 1995).

"WHEN YOU'RE SHOPPING, THINK WISE"

Prefacing the *lavway* is one of two types of introductory songs: an upbeat
piece relating to the Christmas season or a jingle written and sung on behalf
of the band's sponsor. The seasonal song typically celebrates the holiday or,
on occasion, criticizes how people observe Christmas. The business jingle,
on the surface, simply advertises a specific business in Carriacou; in fact, it
becomes part of a complex cycle of giving and reciprocity that underscores
the significance of the Parang Festival and reflects fundamental values of
Kayak cooperativism and community.[5]

The Mount Royal Progressive Youth Movement organized the Parang
Festival so that all participating bands receive some financial support. To
this end, Kayak businesses either volunteer or are asked to sponsor their
local band. The business underwrites the band's expenses, including costumes, instrument repairs, and the purchase of strings, as Central Serenader
Jerry McGillivary observes: "You get $700 so you could get yourself a nice
uniform. And then buy youself some strings and you know, nice up your

guitar, your mandolin, or your *cuatro,* your banjo. And then you kick from there" (McGillivary, interview, 1997).

In 1996, BBH had two Harveyvale sponsors: Alexis Franchise and Baba's Auto Rentals. Using a lot of call-and-response between the lead singer and other band members, their jingle gives equal time to both businesses (which incidentally are owned by the same family):

> *If you have something in mind,*
> *if is now or anytime,*
> *check out the Alexis franchise.*
> *(Chorus) Alexis fran-chise!*
> *If you want to do some shopping,*
> *or you want to go a'sailing,*
> *check out the franchise, satisfaction guaranteed.*
> *Alexis franchise!*
> *(Chorus) Alexis fran-chise!*

> *Baba's Auto Rentals,*
> *you can always give us a call,*
> *When you in the country,*
> *and you feel [want] to spree.*
> *You can get a four-wheel Tracker,*
> *or a nice nice luxury car,*
> *Baba Auto Rentals, you won't regret at all,*
> *Baba Auto Rental,*
> *(Chorus) Baba Auto Rentals!*

> *For these are our sponsors,*
> *(Chorus) For these are our sponsors.*
> *For these are our sponsors!*

In 1996, the Central Serenaders performed a jingle on behalf of their sponsor:

> *When you're shopping, think wise,*
> *shop at Mallick's Enterprise.*
> *Whether for grocery or for clothes,*
> *remember Mallick is a goes.*

You can have a look around,
try the other stores in town,
there's one thing you see for sure,
here your dollar gives you more.
(Spoken) Mallick's Enterprise, our sponsor, phone 443–7203.

Advertising jingles neatly illustrate a cycle of reciprocity and community responsibility that defines the Parang Festival. By voluntarily underwriting the preparation costs of their village Parang band, local businesses ensure that their village is represented in this island-wide event as impressively as possible. With this support, the bands make preparations that enhance both the quality of the music and the visual component of their performance. The Parang Festival thus becomes increasingly professional in appearance, and ticket sales increase every year, in turn raising more money for the Mount Royal Progressive Youth Movement (MRPYM) that is then given to those in need. The return for the sponsoring local businesses is that they are publicly acclaimed and promoted on stage and via radio broadcasts of the event for weeks to come.

This inter-relationship between businesses, cultural institutions (the MRPYM), Kayak musicians, and members of the larger community is yet another example of a historic and ongoing cycle of sharing and giving that has sustained Carriacou society on many levels for centuries. Lorna Mc-Daniel (1986: 110–11) notes this cyclical "economy of giving" in Carriacou society, particularly when shopkeepers and fishermen give gifts of food despite the fact that their livelihoods depend on selling it. The business jingle is also very much reflective of the revolutionary era in which the Parang Festival was born, for the Bishop administration sought to create the means and consciousness for community self-help. As expressive and artistic embodiments of Carriacou's long-standing community tradition of mutual aid, business jingles reinforce the unspoken understanding and expectation that just as one gives to others, so shall one receive.

This "economy of giving" is further underscored by the fact that all Parang Festival bands have a business sponsor whether they perform a jingle on their behalf or not. Indeed, some bands skip the business jingle and instead bow to an older Trinidadian parang tradition of composing and playing a song that reflects the Christmas season. While Trinidadian parang bands traditionally perform more formal, religious songs concerning the

Nativity, Carriacou parang bands generally favor lighter, cheerful songs that convey wishes for a happy holiday.[6] In 1994, for example, the Central Serenaders performed the following:

> *Merry Christmas to all, and I know,*
> *We can have lots of fun.*
> *There is room for everyone,*
> *So join and sing a happy song.*
>
> *(Chorus) Oh Merry Christmas, wish you a Merry Christmas,*
> *and a happy New Year!*
> *So come and join the band and sing a sweet Parang.*
> *And spread the merry Christmas cheer.*
>
> *Buy some little toys for the children,*
> *be nice and treat them kind.*
> *So their sorrow keep and whine,*
> *keep them smiling all the time,*
> *and let them sing a little rhyme.*
>
> *(Chorus)*
>
> *Don't forget your Granny and Nanny,*
> *they will love the Christmas too!*
> *Send them greetings in a card,*
> *that will make their spirit glad,*
> *and they will know it's Christmas time.*
> *(Chorus, two times)*

In contrast to this lighthearted message of Christmas tidings, the Ghetto Boys in 1996 used this opportunity to chide Kayaks for neglecting the spiritual and communal aspects of Christmas. They asked listeners to look inward and examine their values while enjoying their traditional Christmas-time rum cake and ginger beer (see transcription 9):

> *Christmas is a season, celebrate without a reason,*
> *with a real strong rum cake and ginger beer.*
> *And so while we celebrating, we forgetting the true meaning,*
> *and is these things what we do year after year.*

FIGURE 6.7 Kenly ("Rhyno") Joseph of the Ghetto Boys performing at
the 1996 Parang Festival string band competition, Hillsborough (video
capture).

I can't hear no carol singing, no bands, no serenading,
and this is what a Christmas used to be.
Long ago it wasn't so, the way Christmas now go,
I want my friends to know.

(Chorus) You see on Christmas day,
we used to kneel and pray,
that one day and one night,
the Lord will shine his light,
and the whole world will be bright.
You see on Christmas day,
we got to kneel and pray,
'Cause Jesus is our Savior,
is our Lord and our Jehovah,
Born to save this world.
(Mandolin solo)

Pandemonium in the air,
Christmastime's already here,
let us all just say a prayer and sing a song.
Let us do it for a cause,

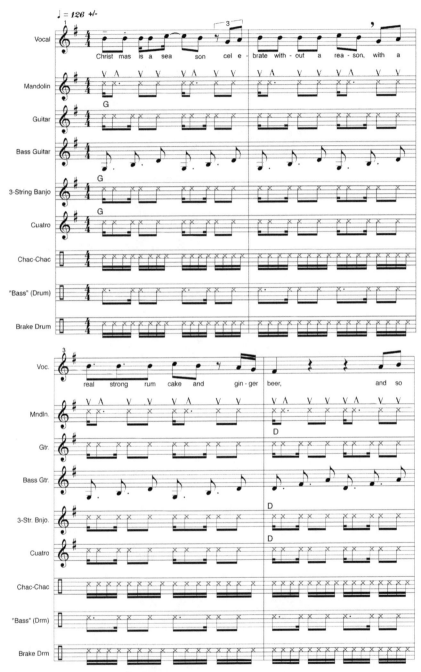

FIGURE 6.8 Transcription 9: "On Christmas Day," Ghetto Boys. ©1996 The Ghetto Boys.

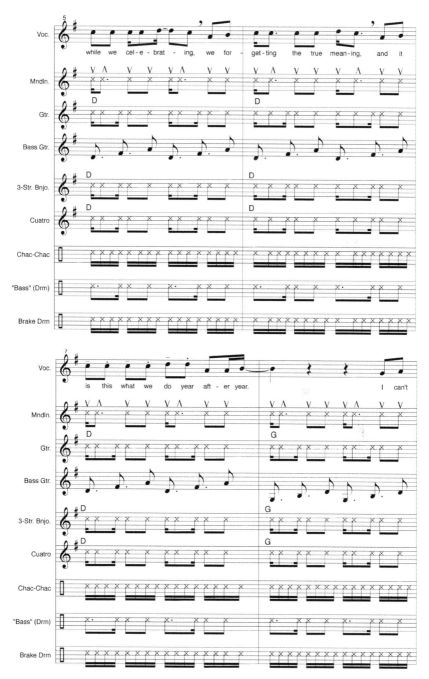

FIGURE 6.8 *(Continued)*

forget the old Santa Claus,
with his Rudolph bringing carols in the sleigh.
I can't hear no carol singing,
no bands, no serenading,
and this is what a Christmas used to be.
Guided by a star and three wise men from afar,
I want you remember.
(Chorus)

The Ghetto Boys's lament reflects a general gestalt that was sweeping the Anglo-Caribbean at the time; for example, the parang soca "Put Back de Christ in Christmas" by Grenada's top calypso artist, Ajamu, was played often on local and regional radio stations in the months leading up to the holiday.

REGIONAL TEMPO, LOCAL RHYTHM

The Ghetto Boys wrap up the first part of their competition choice piece with an extensive and complicated transition. Rhyno, on mandolin, plays an extended solo, punctuated by exclamations by band members such as "Gimme a rise"—that is, modulate to a new (higher) key (transcription 10, measures 9–13)—and "Oh God! It me [the Ghetto Boys] again!" (measures 18–24). Finally, a climactic musical sequence moves the tonal center from G major to D major (measures 17–18). Upon arriving at the next section of the choice piece, the Ghetto Boys reduce their overall tempo as well (measures 24–25). Excitement mounts as the music slows, signaling the beginning of the band's *lavway* or *melée*. In contrast to the first part of the choice piece, the *melée* section is most often much slower, signifying the band's switch from a Trinidadian parang style derived from Venezuelan string band music to a local Carriacou style that accompanies the *lavway* lyrics.[7] Also in contrast to the first part, the *melée* de-emphasizes the clave, if only because the tempo has significantly slowed. Rhyno notes the importance of the musical shift to Carriacou parang style: "The real Parang would be the Venezuelan. . . . Parang would be international and that would be the beat. So if you had to go out like let's say Trinidad to play Parang, you'd have to play that Venezuelan beat. Play it, say look, this is the original and then this our Parang" (interview, 1997).

FIGURE 6.9 Transcription 10: Transition into *"Lavway,"* Ghetto Boys. ©1996 The Ghetto Boys

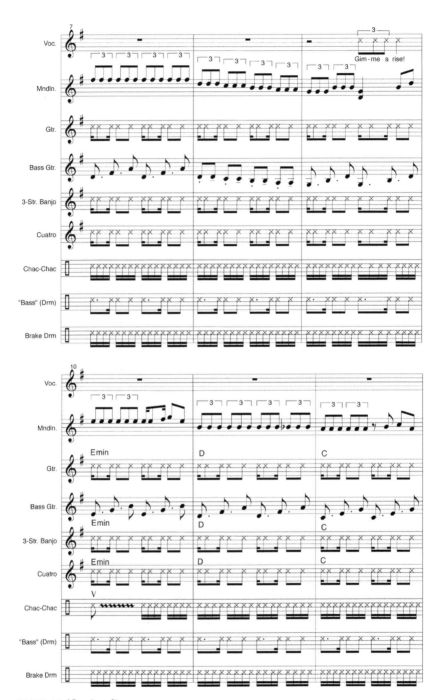

FIGURE 6.9 *(Continued)*

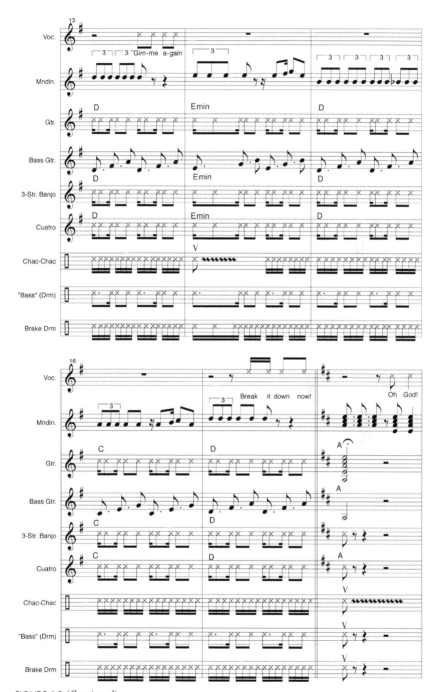

FIGURE 6.9 *(Continued)*

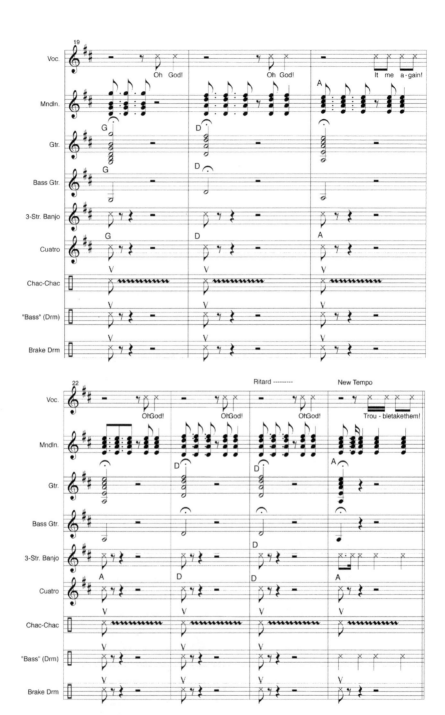

FIGURE 6.9 *(Continued)*

Despite the initial emphasis on the Trinidadian/Hispanic roots of parang music, the local Kayak musical style remains central to the festival's string band competition. Like Rhyno, Central Serenaders guitarist Jerry McGillivary observes that while it is important for Kayak bands performing at Parang to recognize and incorporate the Hispanic-Caribbean beat into their competition music, it is only one style of parang music, and not necessarily the most significant:

> The Parang Beat is the inspiration beat, come from way back from our foreparents, you could say. And like Christmas time, when the Christmas breeze coming in the air, that special beat coming to you. So then you just be in it, like . . . Is a feelings. We have a tradition, and just as Trinidad have a tradition. Right? Trinidad Parang and Carriacou Parang is two different thing. And look at what we calling *melée* in Carriacou, they call it parang in Trinidad. You go five minutes, start in the *melée* . . . like you did a little Spanish commenting and get a little break and then you come with a local. Well, that's a hint of [Trinidadian] Parang. But then we come back to we local culture. (interview, 1997)

LAVWAY CHORUSES

The essence of local Carriacou culture is encapsulated in *lavway* lyrics, which are the heart of the string band competition and, indeed, of the entire Parang Festival. *Lavways* reveal much about the mores, social expectations, community bonds, and changing realities of life in this small society. While the *lavway* portion carries with it the unspoken agenda of social control, the atmosphere surrounding the performance is anything but somber. On the contrary, audience and bands join forces to celebrate (loudly) the vagaries of human behavior and the bonds that unite Carriacouans. During the performance of their *lavways,* the members of the bands are often oddly stiff, rarely smiling, and extremely focused, communicating a sense of purpose rather than fun. Yet the *lavways* are intentionally hysterical—so funny, in fact, that loud roars from the audience after each verse often obscure the upcoming chorus.

Lavways are fairly simple single or double quatrains collectively composed by band members. One or two lead singers sing the verses, while the rest of the band harmonizes on the chorus, which is usually simple in structure and memorable. By the end of the *lavway,* audience members are often singing along:

> *Them people like tori [gossip, news], (oui!)*
> *the people like melée,*
> *if you come over here to stay,*
> *make sure that you learn to live the right way.*
> *Kayaks and Grenadians,*
> *they love their confusion,*
> *if you know what you did was wrong,*
> *listen for your name right here in Parang! (The Ghetto Boys, 1996)*

Other bands reiterate these lighthearted warnings to residents to watch their behavior or suffer the consequences at Parang.

> *When the Parang time come,*
> *and you do somethin' wrong,*
> *you can't make them get away,*
> *you have to be on Parang melée.*
> *I say, when the Parang time come,*
> *and you do something wrong,*
> *You can't make you get away,*
> *you have to be on Parang melée. (The Central Serenaders, 1994)*

BBH's *lavway* chorus in 1996 took on a different tone altogether while recalling the outcome of the previous year's competition. Despite being a first-time competitor in 1995, BBH took first place, an unprecedented feat. Many longtime Parang musicians were irritated with BBH's beginner's luck and with the judges for their decision, feeling that they should do their time as a participant in the festival before being awarded first place. The resultant grumbling was the subject of BBH's chorus in their 1996 *lavway:*

> *They vex with we, they vex with we,*
> *they vex with we, but we happy.*

Me en' lie on [I don't lie about] nobody,
but dem people drivin' we crazy.

They vex with we, they vex with we,
they vex with we, 'cause we happy.
Me en' lie on nobody,
so we have no damn apology! (BBH, 1996)

That other bands resented BBH's 1995 victory underscores the almost universal understanding that first place ought to go to a band with years of commitment to the festival and, by extension, the Mount Royal Progressive Youth Movement. A January 1996 article entitled "Ghetto Boys and Determinators Quit Parang" places into perspective the bitterness of members of veteran string bands with regard to supporting the festival and preserving Kayak traditional culture:

> Two of the most popular Parang Bands have decided to quit from participating in further Parang string band competitions. Ghetto Boys of Six Roads led by Calypsonian Rhyno, together with Leftist, another Calypsonian, and Determinators of Bogles with Sugar Patch and Skylark, also known entertainers, jointly said that the inconceivable judgment handed down by the judges at last month's Parang competition has virtually forced them out of any future Parang competition.
>
> Joseph (Ghetto Boys) said that it is very discouraging, *having put your all into building the stand of the culture,* only to have the judges totally disregard the efforts. "I'm still shocked that the first band BBH Serenaders came ahead of the Ghetto Boys and, to make it worse, by 35 points," said a puzzled Joseph (*Grenada Voice,* January 13, 1996, emphasis added).

Contesting the judges' decision is a constant from one year to the next, as is a show of bravado among the bands. BBH repeats "They vex with we" several times in each of the two quatrains that made up the chorus, which is itself repeated after each verse of their very long *lavway.* If last year's losing bands weren't vexed before, they surely were by the end of BBH's *lavway.*

"THEM PEOPLE LIKE *TORI*": *LAVWAY* VERSES

Tori, meaning news or gossip, brings people to the Parang Festival. It ranges from gossip to social criticism and occasional commentary on local political issues from the past year. In contrast to traditional *lavways,* which are improvised on the spot, competition *lavways* are composed and rehearsed, to some extent in response to the Parang Committee's rule that no *lavway* can exceed ten minutes in length. Underscoring the Parang Fesitval's connections with calypso, the verses are often ribald and scandalous and contain an element of *picong* (from the French word *piquant,* to bite, to sting, as in an insult).[8] Parang judge and calypso singer Elwin McQuilkin sees little difference between the stings underlying both *lavways* and calypso and locates them in the age-old tradition of West African derisive singing via another name for calypso, *kaiso,* which is derived from the West African word *kaito:* "[Kaito] means it serves them right . . . that's the reason why it's supposed to prick you. Because if you behave in a certain manner, then it's like a punishment, so it serve you right for someone to sing on you. . . . In Grenada, you might hear a child say 'A *picong* juke me' . . . how do you call it, um, 'pricker.' So the song's supposed to do that. If sing something on you, supposed to prick you [laughs]. For instance, well it's semantical business. If somebody interferes with an animal, for instance, when they hear the song, that song is supposed to prick their person" (interview, 1997).

Critical or derisive singing arrived in the Caribbean along with enslaved Africans three centuries ago. Africanist scholars have long noted the cultural importance of satire and the role of the derisive song as mechanisms for social control. William Piersen, for example, argues that "derisive songs . . . discouraged unpleasant and dangerous face-to-face confrontation . . . [and] allowed a safer, more effective, and certainly more entertaining manner of criticism" (Piersen 1977: 2). Among various African cultures, songs of a critical nature are sung for entertainment or because their performance is mandated by the ancestors. The Nzema of southwest Ghana, for example, believe that their young male singers are entrusted by their ancestors with messages that critique those in power (Agovi 1995: 49). Urhobo men of southwest Nigeria sing abusive songs featuring exaggeration or near fabrication of fact as a form of entertainment in competitions among villages (Okpewho 1992). In Yoruba society, satirical singing, theater, and other expressive genres serve to exercise social control; public ridicule serves as an "important character-molding device" and becomes an art when given imaginative treatment in a formal performance setting (Adedeji 1967: 62).

Related traditions are found throughout the black Atlantic: "trading dozens" or "playing the dozens" (exchanging insults) is an integral component of African American expressive culture, particularly in North America (see Gates 1988), and some rap music serves as a form of social critique and challenges those in power. In the Caribbean, Haitian *rara* and other local genres are based on a style of verbal signification known as *pwen* ("the point") or *chan pwen* ("the sung point"). Intended to ridicule prominent Haitians and authority figures, *pwen,* according to Elizabeth McAlister, is concerned with "both the distillation of knowledge and the deployment of power" (McAlister 2002: 167; see also Averill 1997). Similarly, singers in St. Martin have performed the fast-paced, rhyming *quimbés* since at least the end of slavery in 1848. Now a dying tradition, the *quimbé* was often performed in informal competitive formats or "contests" where singers sang of current affairs, local news and gossip, and tragedies (Sekou 1992: 31).

While the connections between *lavway* singing and calypso are clear, *lavway* singing also coheres in intent to Big Drum *piké* songs, a genre that "called names and exposed the anti-social, the haughty, the conceited, and those in high positions" (McDaniel 1986: 188). Another Big Drum song genre, the *chirrup,* according to anthropologist J. D. Elder, "gives 'picong' to . . . the people in the community" (quoted in Hill 1977: 366) and, like the aforementioned Nzema of Ghana, placates the ancestors. Historically, these genres of Big Drum songs served, in part, as resolutions to social conflicts through public shaming, much like the effect of the contemporary *lavway.* Lorna McDaniel (1986, 1998) argues that parang songs (and early calypsos) filled the niche for songs aimed at people's reputations and overarching social control after Big Drum composition of the *chirrup* became moribund in the 1920s. One genre replaced the other.

Contemporary *lavways* are not used to gain social status or simply hurl insults, nor do they necessarily relate to communicating with or placating ancestors. Mostly, they level the hierarchies within Carriacou society: anybody's behavior can be subject to scrutiny in a *lavway.* This collective culpability became all the more evident in 1991, when the Parang Committee, in response to several heated responses by individuals who had been "named" in a *lavway,* banned the outright use of names in the competition. Because the targets of *lavways* are now (mostly) identified in a roundabout way, *lavway* singing at Parang carries a sense of universalism in the sense that everybody is capable of acting outside of the norm.

"NAMING NAMES"

Carriacouans are awash in names. Not only are there baptismal and confirmation names on legal documents, there are also nicknames: children receive a "home name," perhaps a *jida* or a humorous name, at birth and some acquire another nickname as they grow up. Because of this (or in spite of it), "naming names" in a *lavway* is a source of great irritation for some and a highly conflicted issue for all. Although it has not actually happened, some Parang competitors fear that if they "call names" in a *lavway,* they could be sued by the person in question (McGillivary, interview, 1997). Thus new strategies have arisen to identify the *lavway* targets while adhering (more or less) to the rules set out by the Parang Committee.

Lyrics might identify a personal attribute, notes Jerry McGillivary: "If I know something about Becky and I just sing on Becky, I wouldn't sing like, 'Becky steal Jerry's purse.' I would say 'the white woman steal the black man's purse.' . . . I don't call no name. So then the audience know is the one who prove who do that [so then the audience knows who did that]" (interview, 1997).

Other strategies include using an individual's nickname:

Pumpledums sleeping in the red van,
to let your children sleep in the next one.
Because we en' have no place to live,
you have them running just like fugitive.
When you think the thing would over,
you have to take back your trunk to Canada.
The woman didn't like your behavior,
You 'shamed to pick up your furniture. (The Ghetto Boys, 1996)

Pumpledums is digging a pressure,
they throw all they clothes in the gutter.
Man, these things what make me sad,
it is that the mattress in the yard.
I take a walk up the Seaview,

when I see this thing was really true.
I see the dog playing with video,
and I see the pig with the radio. (BBH, 1996)

The unfortunate Pumpledums, a minibus taxi driver, was mentioned in almost every lavway during the 1996 string band competition. Apparently, he and his two sons were living in the village of Beausejour with his common-law wife, who, after an argument, kicked him out of her house, putting him and his boys on the street along with all of their possessions. Another version of the story from the same year, as sung by the Central Serenaders, names the local social worker, a school teacher named Lybon Phillip, who took up the case on behalf of the two boys.

Them two little boys on the run,
we have to send for Teacher Lybon.
On a bench, they nodding,
their father in the bus dere sleeping.

Look, we really sorry for Pumpledums,
he get thrown out.
The man going through a curse,
oh Lord, right now he sleeping inside the bus.

In traditional Carriacou society, a man in Pumpledums's position is rare. While Kayak men often have extramarital affairs and are responsible for the financial support of any children resulting from such a union ("born outside"), they rarely, if ever, reside with a mistress ("friend"), particularly if she is not the children's mother. It is also unusual for a man to have his children living with him rather than with their mother. Because of these inconsistencies, Pumpledums is not fulfilling an accepted and respectable Carriacouan male role, which explains why so many *lavway* lyrics were directed at him that year.

Another way to avoid direct naming is to describe the individuals in question in terms of their relationship to each other, their occupations, or simply their villages:

Two brothers arguing in L'Esterre,
who say no stranger should interfere.

He didn't like what he brother said,
so he took the guitar and he split the head. (The Central Serenaders, 1996)

This story refers to an intense argument that erupted between then seventy-year-old Sonnelle Allert and his younger brother, Gavis, over a family affair. Gavis smacked a guitar belonging to Canute Caliste over Sonnelle's head, resulting in injuries requiring medical attention at Princess Royal Clinic in Carriacou. Gavis also suffered a fractured arm and was dispatched to General Hospital in Grenada to have it set. This conflict was well known throughout Carriacou by the time the string band competition took place, and its mention evoked a massive audience response.[9]

String band competitors can also avoid naming names, to some extent, by using only the first name, though this works best if the name is a common one, notes Kenly "Rhyno" Joseph:

KJ: I can call, I can say "Tom."

RSM: You can?

KJ: Yeah, I could say "Tom."

RSM: But I thought the committee said no calling names.

KJ: Yeah, but if I say "Tom," right, who that be?

RSM: Because there's more than one Tom?

KJ: More than one Tom. (K. Joseph, interview, 1997)

In the end, some bands simply ignore the rule and explicitly cite an individual by name; this occurs several times in the course of every Parang Festival. BBH's Albert Fortune disdains this strategy: "If the person wants his or her name to call, fine. What if they don't want, we leave it out or we just talk as it could be anybody. Or we could just put a nickname to the thing. So . . . embarrassment, we not in that. I personally encourage the rest of the band not to be in that. And if they decide to call names without the person's approval, I'm offed from the band" (interview, 1997).

Aside from the fact that Carriacou is small enough so that virtually everybody recognizes the protagonist(s) in each of the stories and despite such censure by the Parang Committee, the Ghetto Boys, the winning band in the 1996 competition, sang the following during their award-winning *lavway:*

> *Mr. Warner*[10] *couldn't take the pressure,*
> *so he take a walk up by Nola.*
> *Before the man could enter the door,*
> *see how Nola hidin' Tobago.*
> *Tobago fold up in a spread [rolled up in a bedsheet],*
> *and she push him quite below the bed,*
> *If you see how far in she push him,*
> *not even Carmichael coulda find him!*

Identifying the subjects by name happens mostly with major figures in Carriacou, including politicians and others in positions of authority. Mr. Warner happened to be one of the judges that year for the string band competition and was seated directly in front of the stage when the Ghetto Boys "sang on him." Understandably irritated, Mr. Warner later told me that the entire story of his dalliance with the two-timing "Nola" was a fabrication; even Leftist, guitarist and back-up vocalist in the band, admitted that the final four lines were contrived for humorous effect (A. Mathison, interview, 1997). Civic leaders remain at the mercy of the string band musicians, however, notes Rhyno of the Ghetto Boys: "The people would inspire [you with] what they want to hear. Because let's say something happen in your village or somewhere, the people will pull on you and they will blow it out of proportion, so everybody would know that this happen. . . . And they will want to hear why you singing. You as a writer do spice it up! Spice it up for sure" (interview, 1997). Other musicians, like Bernice Bristol, take a dimmer view of this exaggeration: "I no like it. Because sometimes they may sing something or something might happen and what, sometime it not true and they just sing. And they don't care who get hurt in the process. I don't like that" (interview, 1997).

Despite this tendency toward exaggeration, *lavway* lyrics nevertheless must be based on public knowledge, an unspoken rule that both regulates the composition process and lends at least some integrity to the entire event. With reference to being sung on by the Ghetto Boys, Mr. Warner remarked, "Everything else in their [The Ghetto Boys'] lyrics, their choice piece lyrics, was based on public knowledge. And this is what really upset me about it . . . because what they talked about never happened. And it's not public knowledge, so why sing about it?" (interview, 1997).

What is considered public knowledge varies with the individual. Although a *lavway* story may not necessarily be immediately known to all, part of the audience's fun revolves around figuring out the gossip, according to Harrison Fleary: "Actually people are looking for a story—what's the story? And then they get the story and they want to know, who is that person they singing about. Who did that?" (interview, 1995).

There is one consideration agreed on by all: lyrics must be limited to local issues. Reflective of the *lavway*'s roots in Christmastime serenading, the lyrics refrain from more political and potentially serious issues of national and regional scope, such as those often found in calypso lyrics. In explaining how BBH composes their *lavway,* Albert Fortune notes that the band eschews lyrics about the Grenadian government, in part for practical reasons: "That is not relevant for the Parang thing. Because it's a Carriacou thing we talking about. . . . Because if you not in line with the issues you sing, nobody understands. So you must do something that people understand" (interview, 1997). Thus, one of the verses written by BBH for the 1996 Parang (it was rejected) aimed its *picong* at the Grenadian government:

> *The Government say they have a plan,*
> *so they going round seeking opinion.*
> *But you no hear what happening,*
> *they only seeking opinion from women.*
> *The custom man say he is not in that,*
> *'cause they importing too much private parts.*
> *So when I ask him what's the plan?*
> *They planning to castrate every man.*

With their emphasis on the local, *lavway* topics deal with issues of general social interest such as *tabanca* (heartbreak), adultery, domestic fighting, the arrest of local Rastas for growing marijuana, disagreements between local businesses, and, from time to time, bestiality. Derick Clouden, a cultural officer at Grenada's Ministry of Culture, serves as a judge for Parang's Hosannah band and string band competitions. He notes that such "wicked deeds" as bestiality are often gossiped about in Grenada and Carriacou: "Yeah, it happens in Grenada. At one time people said that they will never buy beef again! [Laughs.]" (interview, 1997). In 1996, the Central Serenaders sang the following *lavway* about one man's alleged proclivities:

> *That Belmont boy look he mind so big [he's so bigheaded],*
> *they catch him sleeping in the pen with a pig.*
> *We don't mind, he take a pig to bed,*
> *but he should pay for the three little ones that are dead.*

This lyric publicly shames both the act and the more potentially damaging social crime of arrogance. While bestiality is not condoned, what is more important to the fabric of Carriacou society is the breakdown of behavioral norms. This man's attitude of entitlement opposes notions of cooperative endeavor and unity, thereby threatening Carriacouan social structure.

Another recurrent topic in Parang *lavways* is the issue of "tiefing" (stealing). Theft in Carriacou is most often taken up locally, though police will intervene when substantial sums of money are involved. Because of this community self-mediation of tiefing disputes, the string band competition at Parang offers an ideal platform to air grievances, reiterate recent incidents, and report on the outcome:

> *Me partner that living in Six Roads,*
> *well this fella get out of control.*
> *He tief he uncle cow and he sell it,*
> *and had the man help them look for it.*
> *They looking all over the area,*
> *they can't find the cow in the pasture.*
> *And when they sister check out the matter,*
> *he sell it for nine hundred dollar! (BBH, 1996)*

Here one *lavway* verse conflates complex Kayak relationships of family, community, and property. On one hand, the man in question stole the cow; on the other hand, he helped his uncle search for it, knowing all along that he had sold it to his sister. This is an interesting example of how antisocial behavior can combine with the normal Carriacouan sense of reciprocity. The thief's audacious actions clearly warranted mention in the *lavway,* and the humiliation is his punishment.

Other lyrics serve as commentary or a form of reportage on changing

Carriacouan ways of life.[11] Since the early 1990s, increasing numbers of non-Kayaks have begun to buy land and settle in Carriacou, a reality reflected in the occasional *lavway* verse. In 1994, for example, Mama's Determinators "sang on" an American ship captain, his Canadian-born daughter and son, and his former wife, all of whom lived in Carriacou until 1998. The lyrics refer to his personal dealings with his European girlfriend (and boss), who owned a major shipyard in Harveyvale, and her assistant, an Italian reggae musician also of Harveyvale who later became her lover while the ship captain was sailing.

> *You captain, the white man cruiser,*
> *You little daughter come from Canada,*
> *we ask she, have you busy?*
> *Harveyvale man rubbin' the belly.*

On one level, this *lavway* is nothing more than gossip about infidelity. However, it also speaks to the growing number of North Americans and Europeans who are investing in Carriacou's relatively cheap, tropical land to live, establish businesses, or simply to retire and live tax-free. This *lavway* recognizes the beginning of what has recently become a complex economic and social dynamic in Carriacou. While there is growing resentment among Carriacouans toward white landowners, there is also the realization that there is quick and considerable cash to be made by selling off an acre of land.[12] *Lavway* lyrics about white people are rare, but their increasing inclusion indicates that everybody is watched in Carriacou, and nobody is immune to being sung on.

Other lavway lyrics report on much more serious events, such as crime, domestic violence (particularly when children are involved), and drug use. One of the most conspicuous topics in 1996 was an attempted murder using the herbicide Grammazome:

> *You try to kill a man with Grammazome,*
> *Never know you have a store room at your home,*
> *'Til Bullen and them boys discover,*
> *I hear they take down your antenna.*
> *People say it's courts come to take part,*

Bullen, Scotland Yard launch an attack,
They come and they take 'way everything,
They even take the bed where you sleeping. (The Ghetto Boys)

You tell us don't sing about the Grammazome,
because that thing happen too long.
We'll just advertise the electronics store,
Fathead selling video and stereo.

For this Christmas, you in the red,
if you know you shop by Fathead.
When you see he go make a jail,
send for Junior to stand the bail. (The Central Serenaders)

I hearing a thing about Fathead,
well this thing could really kill me dead,
because the fellow working with Mr. Bullen,
and it tiefing out every damn thing.
He tief three fridge and two stereo,
with some TV and four video,
and when you want to buy you soft drink,
check out Fathead by Mr. Bullen. (BBH, 1996)

These *lavways* chronicle the misadventures of one "Fathead," who first worked as a driver at Bullen's, one of the three major grocery stores in Carriacou. Fathead allegedly stole shipments of groceries ordered from Grenada and dropped them off at his house before returning to the store. His cohort, "Junior," apparently went to the police to clear his name and, in doing so, fingered Fathead, who was then arrested. For some reason, Junior stood bail for Fathead. Fathead was fired from Bullens but landed a job at the local hardware/appliance store, where his reputation did not improve. He got into a fight with another man over a woman and, in an effort to knock out the competition, tried to poison him by adding Grammazome to Guinness beer (H. Fleary, interview, 1997). Fortunately for him, the man did not drink the poison-laced beer, though Fathead was rearrested when another person tasted the beverage, realized what was in it, and went to the police. Ultimately, nobody was injured, but Fathead's evil ways were recorded in virtually every Parang *lavway* that year.

Since the 1990s, Carriacou has seen an increase in local drug use and in the drug trade:

When you takin' coke, you lost control,
what control your whole body have so,
takin' coke is not a joke,
I beg Sexy to stop take the whole. (Mama's Determinators, 1994)

While small by the standards of other Caribbean islands, Carriacou's drug trade is becoming increasingly apparent, particularly in the production and sale of marijuana by the local Rasta community, as well as the importation and use of cocaine. "Sexy" is the nickname of an alleged drug user and prostitute in Carriacou. Her lifestyle is often cited in *lavways,* primarily as a warning to others regarding licentiousness and drug abuse.

Every year, at least one band "sings on" the Parang Committee. In 1994 Mama's Determinators gently criticized their choice of judges:

Well this here something reminds me,
about the Parang Committee,
They want judges in Parang,
they bring judge like Boyouk and Beardman,
Wee ha!![13]

Bands more commonly take a sympathetic attitude toward the Parang Committee. In 1996 the Ghetto Boys' winning *lavway* contained a verse concerning the committee's efforts to renovate the Tennis Courts in time for Parang, as well as their struggles that year with the local radio station, KYAK. Newscaster Rawlie P. apparently approached members of the Parang Committee to appear on KYAK, but they declined, saying they were too busy working on the Tennis Courts. Rawlie P. evidently told his radio audience that the committee members simply failed to show up at the radio station, and then he spoke about the festival himself, angering them (W. Collins, interview, 1997). The Ghetto Boys capitalized on the incident, directly naming the subject not once but three times (see transcription 11):

The Committee working, all they know,
to get Parang and build de Tennis Court.

FIGURE 6.10 Transcription 11: *"Lavway,"* Ghetto Boys. ©1996 The Ghetto Boys.

While the Committee out there working,
the man Rawlie P. undermining.
Last Sunday, the radio program,
Rawlie P. representing Parang.
The Committee find out wha' happened,
members plan to slap Rawlie Pattison.

Some bands critique local government officials, although most tend to stay away from politics in general. Two of the members of the Ghetto Boys— Rhyno and Leftist—are award-winning calypsonians who honor this tradition with at least one or two verses of such criticism in their Parang choice piece every year:

Carriacouans laughing, they happy,
they glad we getting we own Ministry.
Now the whole Treasury get in the red,
see how Nimrod handle the affairs.
To fix the road in Brunswick where he from,
is only now he know where he belong.
Harveyvale, he give priority,
but one day he must come back to we.

Here the Ghetto Boys celebrate Carriacou's recently upgraded representation in the national government to a ministry post while simultaneously criticizing the new minister, Senator Elvin G. Nimrod, for allegedly choosing to repave only the roads (always a contentious issue) in those Carriacou villages that supported him in the recent election. The Ghetto Boys chastise Nimrod for his political favoritism, and for ignoring the needs of his own village (Brunswick), which also happens to be their home turf. Thus couching social expectation in a critique of local politics, the Ghetto Boys sang their *lavway* directly to Senator Nimrod, who, incidentally, was seated in the front row reserved for dignitaries. By the end of the verse, Nimrod was smiling; the rest of the audience was roaring.

Lavways end in a variety of ways. Some bands simply sing through their verses and choruses, play a short instrumental tag, and then end. Others add a final surprise verse that is known only to the lead singer, a technique borrowed from calypso. The final verse of the Ghetto Boys' 1996 *lavway*, for ex-

FIGURE 6.11 Andy ("Leftist") Mathison and Kenly ("Rhyno") Joseph performing at the 1996 Parang Festival string band competition, Hillsborough (video capture).

ample, was written by Rhyno, who surprised fellow band members by singing "on himself":

> *Leftist beg me not to sing on him,*
> *it's me alone that no way he hiding.*
> *Every year you sing for someone else,*
> *Rhyno, they say, sing about yourself.*
> *I hope you hear the talk that going around,*
> *I hear the town man have you [Rhyno] on the run,*
> *From leader you become opposition,*
> *I cannot handle it, kinky man.*

PROFILE IN PROGRESSIVE VOICES: STRUGGLERS

Other *lavways* end with a final section evoking an older local style. Coming to a full stop, the band begins anew with a slightly different rhythmic feel, and the lyrics move from rhyming quatrains to a call-and-response between the leader and the other band members. Here, the Strugglers from the village of Brunswick describe a 1996 case of domestic violence using this older, local style:

(Chorus) Bust him up, donkey, bust him up.
(Lead) Take your paws and rip he belly,
(Bust him up donkey, bust him up)
Lion that give you already.
(Bust him up donkey, bust him up)
The woman they give you already,
(Bust him up donkey, bust him up),
Take your claw and rip out belly.
(Bust him up donkey, bust him up),
Poor monkey fighting for donkey
(Bust him up donkey, bust him up),
Palante [Strugglers's lead singer] fighting for donkey . . .

This ending is essentially identical to the aforementioned single-tone (tune) "road march" (see chapter 5), an older style of *lavway*. Both resonate with Christopher Waterman's (1952) description of various West African musics that feature call-and-response vocals with a litanous response (meaning it remains the same). This type of *lavway* features an offbeat phrasing of melodic lines as voiced by the lead singer as well as an ostinato rhythmic orientation (e.g. timeline), in this case played by the bass drum, the triangle, and the *chac chac* (see transcription 12, measures 2 and 4, and transcription 13, the offbeat accentuation of the lyrics in measures 3 to 5). Performing in this older, local style, the Strugglers use the well-known signifiers of the lion and donkey to report on an abusive relationship. A man apparently beat a woman ("Lion that give you" means that the man had beaten her before), and she retaliated by fighting back ("Take your claw and rip out belly") (Charles, interview, 1997; C. Joseph, interview, 1997). While the use of signifiers such as "lion" and "donkey" is quite common to calypso,[14] the difference between the Strugglers' *lavway* and calypso is in the intent. Whereas calypso usually denigrates the woman (Warner 1982: 99–100), the *lavway* sides with the woman. The Strugglers have competed in Parang since the 1970s and have maintained a progressive political orientation such as this, since their inception.

Unlike other bands, the Strugglers use their entire choice piece less for gossip or remarks about the Christmas season and more as a call to social and political action. From the outset, the Strugglers skipped the business jingle/seasonal ditty altogether, instead voicing a progressive ideology that calls for Carriacouans to cooperatively work to support the Parang Festival:

> *This is Parang in 1996,*
> *to we the people must come together,*
> *to build our Parang.*
> *We building the Parang, we building the Parang.*
> *And we building the Parang, because it's cooperation.*
> *This is Parang in 1996, we, dis people, must come together,*
> *to build our Parang, we build the Parang,*

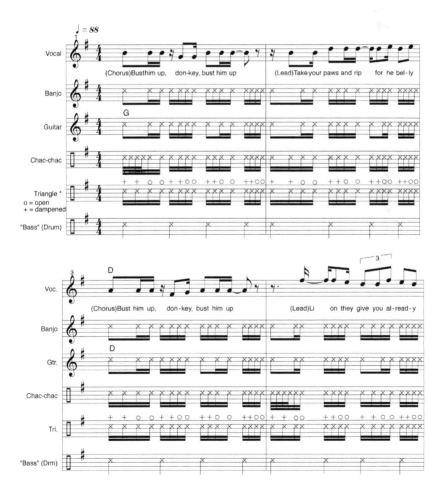

FIGURE 6.12 Transcription 12: "Bust Him Up . . . ," The Strugglers. ©1996 The Strugglers.

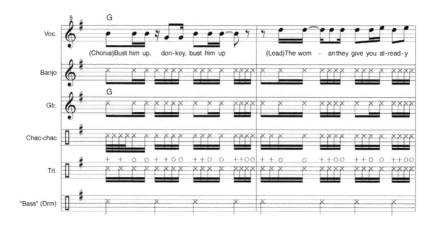

FIGURE 6.12 *(Continued)*

> *we build the Parang, we build the Parang,*
> *because it's cooperation.*

The Strugglers then condemned the forces that create the social ills that plague Carriacouans:

> *(Chorus) Man catching the hell in Carriacou,*
> *man catching the hell in Carriacou.*
> *Man catching the hell,*
> *man catching the hell in Carriacou.*

Money what we working for,
it can['t] even buy a pair of shoes,
Neither the children's schoolbooks,
neither the children's uniforms.
(Chorus)

Tanks [Thanks] to Carriacou Yankee,
that come back to Carriacou,
They come and build they house,
that is how the builders getting a job.
(Chorus)

[I/we] don['t] have the money,
to pay the whole population.
Man catching the hell,
man catching the hell in Carriacou.

Augustin Charles, a friend of the Strugglers who coauthored some of the *lavway* lyrics, explains that "Man catching the hell in Carriacou" means "We suffering to survive: no work, no money" (interview, 1997). With little by way of governmental help to supplement people's incomes, it is a struggle for many Carriacouans to educate their children: schoolbooks are very costly (all are imported from the United States or England) and children must wear uniforms to school, which is an enormous expense. The Strugglers point out that some strapped families and under-employed Kayak men have, in recent years, found relief via the "Carriacou Yankee"—that is, the emigrant Kayak who retires to Carriacou and builds a new house with re-tirement savings. These returnees have generated an explosion of construc-tion work, bringing much-needed revenue to the island. But the Strugglers correctly point out that this only partially solves the problem of poverty, be-cause overall Carriacou continues to lack the resources to help everybody. The Strugglers also insist that Carriacouans shoulder some of the responsi-bility for positive social change:

The nation has gone astray,
the nation has gone astray,
the nation gone astray,
They don't even care 'bout the Almighty.

Only cursing and fighting, raping and killing, raping and abusing,
and drugs that they selling . . .
No respect for nobody, they don't have no understanding,
They don't have no reason, only creating trouble. . . .

Look what is going on in this blessed country,
They taking over the country, yes, I'll tell you people.
Look what is going on in this blessed country,
They taking over the country, yes, I'll tell you people.
Take care of you body, I'll tell you people,
Take care of you body, I'll tell you people.

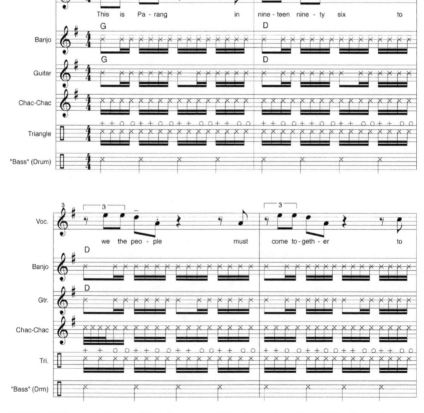

FIGURE 6.13 Transcription 13: "This Is Parang," The Strugglers. ©1996 The Strugglers.

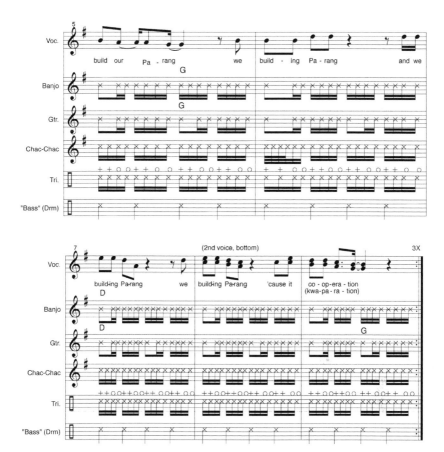

FIGURE 6.13 *(Continued)*

Using the body as a metaphor for the island nation, the Strugglers warn Carriacouans to look inward, toward their communities, and take care of their problems, or they will suffer the consequences of social and economic imperialism. This message very much recalls the revolutionary era and the birth of the PRG, specifically the time when Grenadians and Carriacouans were routinely asked to critique themselves and each other to solve problems from within, thereby advancing their self-reliance, cooperative engagement, and cultural autonomy. When asked about the meaning of "Take care of you body," Augustin Charles emphasized that "if you don't take care of what you have, somebody else is going to tramp on it" (interview, 1997).

Dressed in street clothes rather than costumes and with only six (as opposed to eight) members in the band, the Strugglers are clearly the least organized and least rehearsed band in Parang. With no smooth harmonies or rehearsed arrangements and little outstanding musicianship, the band appears disorganized and somewhat ragged onstage. Indeed, their reception is decidedly mixed: part of the audience greets the Strugglers with *shtoops* and laughter during their performance, while others cheer them on. The day after the 1996 string band competition, many people with whom I spoke laughed at the Strugglers' (last-place) performance. One woman, criticizing the overall quality of the string band competition, opined that "All the bands were Strugglers!"

But the band is held in high regard among many Carriacou musicians, who recognize them as the most authentic Parang band in terms of performing music with a strictly Carriacou Parang rhythm and playing style. Central Serenader Jerry McGillivary remarks: "You know the band Strugglers? They play the *real* Parang music. They do play the real, local Parang music. They don't have theyself organize together, so then they go out there and find drugging here, drugging there, on the stage. Stopping, singing, stopping. When I say drugging, you know, turning and twisting there. Like they don't organize, alright? So then that's why you know they all time come in the back [last place]. . . . You see this slow beat they have there. That's it, you know. That's it . . . because they have the ideal beat for Parang" (interview, 1997).

Unlike most of the other Parang bands, the Strugglers do not incorporate the syncopated half of a clave into either their test or their choice piece. Their bass drummer instead plays a simple, strictly on-the-beat pattern (see transcriptions 12 and 13). In addition, they play their entire *lavway* at the same slow tempo (quarter note = 88 versus the more typical tempi ranging from 94 to 110). Because they do not demarcate one section of their choice piece as rooted in a traditional Trinadadian parang rhythm, the Strugglers eschew any musical connection to Trinidad and the larger Hispanic Caribbean, reinforcing instead the primacy and significance of Carriacou's local style of string band music.

That the Strugglers reject regional stylings in favor of a local sound underscores a somewhat conservative gesture of preservation and cultural autonomy. Along with the band's lyrical emphasis on progressive social and political agendas, the Strugglers solidly reflect the ideologies of the revolutionary era, during which they (and the Parang Festival) were born. As one of the first festival participants, the Strugglers promote the political and social activism of an era when critical self-examination and cooperative endeavor held forth the promise of spiritual and cultural (as well as economic) growth.

"SO, TOM WANT TO KNOW / HARRY WANT TO KNOW / DICK WANT TO KNOW, / THAT IS WHY THEY COME TO THE PARANG SHOW"

After the last band's final performance, the MCs return to the stage and, over the shouts and cheers from the audience, announce that the judges are tallying their ballots. Filling time, the comedians banter with the audience about the competition, the bands, and the audience itself. When the judges finish, the MCs tease the audience for a few more minutes, then finally announce the winners: third place, BBH; second, the Determinators; first, the Ghetto Boys.[15] These rankings are greeted with more cheers and general rowdiness, but fairly soon afterward the audience files out of the Tennis Courts and another Parang Festival comes to a close.

Through its competition format and formalized staged context, the Parang Festival has essentially institutionalized what was once a community tradition of improvised *lavway* singing. Either composed or improvised, however, *lavways* serve as a quintessential example of Henry Louis Gates's notion of "signifyin(g)"—the African American verbal art of assessment or critique by indirection or by the language of trickery (modeled after the divine trickster figure of Yoruba mythology, Esu-Elegbara; see Gates 1988). This rhetorical device extends throughout the black Atlantic, dividing the insiders from the outsiders via its metaphoric speech, which is comprehensible only to members of the speech community (see, for example, Walters 1999). Given that the overriding point of the string band competition is to underscore community values and appropriate social boundaries for its audiences and perhaps reprimand people for their behaviors, it is fundamentally an event by and for Kayaks. Few tourists attend the string band competition—or the rest of the Parang Festival, for that matter—despite the organizers' hope that Parang might serve as a tourist attraction. If non-Caribbean tourists did attend the string band competitions, they would understand neither the local creolized English nor the gossip and "stories" presented in the *lavway*.

What strikes the listener at first is the undeniable social control that *lavways* offer. That anybody from a simple fisherman to a Kayak politician or wealthy person can be "named" in a *lavway* is in keeping with the stated

Kayak view that Carriacou is a classless society: "We is one family." Yet, while this reiteration of local mores and ethics ultimately benefits this small and somewhat ingrown society, the point of the *lavway* does not end at the *picong*. Indeed, *lavways* serve multiple purposes for Kayak audiences: their criticism of fellow Carriacouans is couched in humor, and even a public shaming is mixed with an (unspoken) empathy. *Lavways* promote an understanding of the human condition, focusing more on behavior than individual character and leaving the final verdict to the audience.

The *lavway's* immediacy imbues the Parang string band competition with a sense of fresh expansiveness and contemporary relevance. The lyrics are local, while the "authentic" Trinidadian/Venezuelan or Hispanic Caribbean rhythms and tempi point toward a larger regional belonging. Such regional affiliation is open to a wide range of interpretation by members of the audience and performers alike: some cite a "Spanish" influence in the competition, while others assert that the string band competition is just another form of calypso and is thereby linked to the Anglo-Caribbean rather than Latin America. Others, particularly those participants and visitors from Grenada, see the string band competition as "country style," exposing their ongoing and historical bias toward Carriacou as a backwater dependency. Still others assert that the event is at heart Carriacouan, a view shared by the Mount Royal Progressive Youth Movement, who doggedly reiterate the need to preserve this and other Kayak musical traditions.

This dual sense of belonging, local and regional, offers a contemporary postcolonial parallel to W. E. B. Du Bois's notion of double-consciousness, whereby black Americans see themselves through the "revelation of the other world" and "ever [feel their] twoness" (Du Bois 1969: 45). But whereas Du Bois wrote of a world where black Americans were subjected to the worst kind of racism, the double consciousness that I am postulating in Carriacou describes instead an emergent response to the growing global integration of world cultures. In short, the string band competition serves Kayaks as an expression of an evolving identity, one component of which insists on a cultural autonomy specific to Carriacou. The other is a decidedly postcolonial statement of Carriacouan culture that exists outside of its small island space, belonging also to the greater Caribbean region, contributing positively to the notion of unity there.

7

⊚⊚

"WESELF AS ONE PEOPLE"
Local Identity/Regional Belonging

"The culture is bigger than a man."

—Wallace Collins, Mount Royal Progressive Youth Movement, 1997

THERE IS A GREAT DEAL OF COMMENTARY, critique, and evaluation in the days following the Parang Festival. In the villages, on the minibuses, and in the shops, people discuss the merits of the various bands, their *lavways,* and other aspects of the event. Kayaks compare notes as to who was "sung on," argue about the veracity of the *lavway* lyrics, and debate the fairness of the judging for both the Hosannah band and the string band competitions. People also critique the overall musical skills and preparedness of the groups, often harshly. Those who have been "named" in a string band *lavway* defend their reputation by denying the action or, more commonly, by simply "shtooping" and then changing the subject. Others laugh it off or bask a bit in the glow of the attention—unless there was a major humiliation, being "sung on" briefly elevates an individual's status in the community.

The string band competition does not fade quickly from memory: radio station owner/calypso singer Kim "De King" Mills records each of the string band performances with an eye toward selling cassette and CD copies. Minibus drivers and rum shop owners snap them up and play them loudly from their vehicles and stores for months to come. The "stories" of the "named" thus become part of the aural landscape of Carriacou, eventually turning gossip into island folklore and further working to reinforce social codes.

FOLKLORIZING CULTURE AND THE BUILDING OF COMMUNITY

The Parang Festival strengthens overall social cohesion and community health in Carriacou by providing a platform from which community values and norms of behavior are reinforced and generated. The articulation of these values is framed in a performance context, one that depends on the process of folkloricization—the act of canonizing and, typically, standardizing what were once essentially community-based artistic expressions. The impromptu nature of serenading thus hardens into the formal composition of *lavways*. Rules and judging standards result in stylistic homogenization of the music, as bands conform to specific criteria in order to win. (The notable exception here is the Strugglers, whose insistence on performing in an older style coheres with their long-lived progressive political and social ideologies. They almost invariably place last in the competition.) Similarly, the Parang Festival's Hosannah band competition, in its last years, became less of a showcase for the local style of a cappella choral singing and more of a contest imbued with contemporary, non-Kayak, church choral aesthetics. Quadrille performances at Parang were limited to a set of specific, rehearsed dancers who perform two or three figures rather than the full set of six in order to fit a prescribed amount of time. Similarly abbreviated is the Parang Festival performance of Big Drum, which becomes less a semi-sacred ceremony for the ancestors than a gesture toward the Kayak cultural past.

This process of folkloricization is by no means unique to Carriacou's Parang Festival. In Cuba, for example, the folkloricization of Afro-Cuban religious music and dance by the state-sponsored troupe El Conjunto Folklórico Nacional de Cuba has resulted in the commodification of forms once considered sacred, which, according to Katherine Hagedorn, serves as the "elusive yet much-touted panacea for the Cuban economy known as tourism" (Hagedorn 1995: 313, see also Hagedorn 2001). In Haiti and among Haitians in the United States, the presentation of staged folkloric music and dance throughout the twentieth century has transformed these genres according to specific social and historical circumstances, particularly with reference to nationalist movements as well as changing discourses of race and class (Wilcken 1998). Similarly, Trinidad's Parang Competition has so changed the style and performance practice of parang music that the genre, according to Krister Malm (1978), has become "objectified" from a community event to a marketable entity sponsored by corporations and imbued with national symbolism.

The difference between these models and Carriacou's Parang Festival is one of methodology and intent. Parang is produced by a community institution composed entirely of volunteers; it is neither state-sponsored nor reflective of corporate interests. From its inception and for some years after, the Parang Festival was supported primarily by Kayaks.[1] And, like other examples of folklorized cultural expression, while the promotion and preservation of local culture certainly provides a large part of the impetus for the event, the Carriacou Parang Festival, in contrast to other Caribbean models, serves a greater need: to raise funds for charitable purposes in Carriacou during the upcoming year.

"WESELF AS ONE PEOPLE:" THE PARANG FESTIVAL AS A COMMUNITY BUILDER

As a major fundraiser for the Mount Royal Progressive Youth Movement, festival profits from donations and ticket sales go to the Carriacou population throughout the year in the form of charity to educational institutions, the elderly and the needy, houses for the homeless, improvements made to community centers, grants toward books and school uniforms for children, and other projects (J. Collins, interview, 1997; W. Collins, interview, 1997). Thus even musicians who bemoan the lack of Christmastime serenading today would nevertheless agree with Jerry McGillivary that the Parang Festival's benefits are far-reaching and important: "Parang is interest for the people itself. . . . People must support Mount Royal Progressive Youth Movement, the Parang Committee. Because poor people house fall down or what, they help them! Because they [the MRPYM] do it in the school, they do . . . community development. They help! . . . We all play a great role in Parang, whether win or lose [the competition]. We go. Because you know it not for our benefit alone—is for the other people out there" (interview, 1997).

At the hub of an intricate web of Kayak individuals, institutions, and businesses, the Parang Festival is thus a study in self-reliance: Kayaks support Parang, which in turn supports Kayaks through charity and financial aid. Parallel if less institutionalized systems of mutual aid have been part of Carriacouan society for at least two hundred years. As an expression of this historic system of assistance and support, the Parang Festival—and by extension, the MRPYM itself—continues a tradition of community-based responses to the long history of poverty and economic neglect wrought by Carriacou's status as a double-dependency society.

Thanks, in part, to the ongoing success of the Parang Festival, the

MRPYM has become more visible and effective in Carriacou, as well as more powerful.[2] While Kayaks often grumble about the group, the MRPYM nevertheless continues to garner widespread support, and their containment became something of an objective for the local Carriacou government in the mid-1990s. Beginning in 1997, Senator Elvin G. Nimrod, Minister of Carriacou and Petit Martinique Affairs, sought to consolidate Carriacou cultural activities by creating the Carriacou Cultural Association. This umbrella organization would include the Parang Committee, the Regatta Committee, and the Carriacou Carnival Development Committee, and it would be overseen by a cultural officer appointed by Senator Nimrod. Senator Nimrod saw this as an opportunity to organize cultural events and performances at a high professional level, under the auspices of local government: "We want to officialize, so to speak, a position of culture. In the past, it was just, well, you know, everybody do their thing in culture. But we want to really have a government person who would provide that kind of a guidance and guidelines and to execute policies that we believe would be enhancing culture in a sense" (interview, 2001).

As a potential attempt to co-opt power from folk institutions by the "metropolitan" power structure—that is, local government—this initiative met with resistance from all three cultural organizations and particularly the MRPYM (Nimrod, interview, 2001). Such a usurpation of control by Carriacou's metropolitan institutions was played out on some level in the fact that it took six years for the position to be filled. In 2003, however, Linton Lendore (a former singer in the New Tide Carolers Hosannah Band) accepted the post of cultural officer. He reports that collaboration between the Ministry and the Parang, Carnival, and Regatta committees works well, due perhaps to his own longtime involvement with all three events (Lendore, personal communication, 2007).

VILLAGE LOYALTY, ISLAND CONSCIOUSNESS/ISLAND LOYALTY, REGIONAL CONSCIOUSNESS

As with other youth groups and social clubs, the Parang Festival and the MRPYM initially were strategic responses to the myriad financial and civic needs of Carriacouans. But unlike most Kayak folk institutions, they have remained popular throughout the island for over thirty years. Parang is now a central component of expressive Kayak culture and its organizing group has arguably grown into one of the most powerful community-based institutions on the island today. Its island-wide popularity may indeed arise from its island-wide focus: one of the three objectives in the MRPYM's constitution is this relative expansion of orientation and perspective from the village alone—to "work towards the development of the community, the development of sports and culture on the island, and to make life comfortable for the less fortunate in the community," and to "allow young people to express themselves in local, regional, and international forums." The Parang Festival essentially moved Christmastime performances of traditional music and song away from individual villages to the main village of Hillsborough and, building on historic rivalries between villages, recontextualized them as competitions. In doing so, the members of the MRPYM, while based in Mount Royal and certainly loyal to that village, succeeded in building the broader and farther-reaching objectives of intra-island solidarity and self-help.

Such a rethinking of the notion of community in larger terms neatly parallels a central ideology embraced and furthered by Grenada's early radical political party, the New Jewel Movement, and then, after the 1979 socialist revolution, by Prime Minister Bishop and the People's Revolutionary Government. One of Bishop's accomplishments was the 1981 signing of the Treaty of Basseterre, as mentioned earlier in this study, which established the Organization of Eastern Caribbean States (OECS) as a regional institution designed to promote unity, solidarity, and economic cooperation among Eastern Caribbean island nations (Antigua, Dominica, Grenada, Montserrat, St. Kitts/Nevis, Saint Lucia, and Saint Vincent and the Grenadines). This shift in focus from the relative isolation of a small former colony toward a nation with a regional role figured into the ongoing formation of a new postcolonial identity among Grenadians and Carriacouans.

In the quarter century since, the pervasive discourse regarding unity among Afro-Caribbeans throughout the Eastern Caribbean continues to arise in local, national, and regional contexts to consolidate the political and economic power of these island nations in an increasingly globalized world. In Carriacou, this consciousness of pan-Caribbean unity is readily apparent during contemporary Parang Festivals when competitors and performers amend their performance practice to include non-Kayak musical inflections and styles. Significantly, these aesthetics are appreciated by Parang Festival audiences who have come to expect such an orientation.

FURTHER AFIELD: GLOBALIZATION

This postcolonial appreciation of an extended, transnational cultural identity is clearly limited to the Caribbean, however; popular culture from the United States and to a lesser extent Western Europe is viewed by members of the MRPYM and others as spelling the end for Kayak culture: "I think aspects of the old traditional culture is going away, trying to be more Americanized. . . . We trying to go into a world thing too much. Everything that we used to do before (shtoops) 'en make sense again. You know? And that's the whole . . . old attitude of our people, that we never like to maintain something that is indigenous to us" (Wallace Collins, interview, 1997). This fear of Carriacou becoming increasingly "Americanized" particularly affects those involved in education and cultural presentations, such as school teacher/guitarist Albert Fortune:

> [Carriacouans] have no time for [Parang] music. . . . I think the TV is the main reason, 'cause everybody has a TV or if they don't have, they go by their neighbors, sit down and look at the programs. And they get so Americanized because they don't do anything. The television don't really push out any local programming. Is more satelliting facts from America, even . . . advertisements and all these things.
>
> I will tell you that the children, sometimes they talk about [soap operas] *The Young and the Restless*—everything that went on. And when I am talking to them, they can't remember what I'm telling them. But they could remember everything they saw on the TV on the night before. (Fortune, interview, 1997)

The initial inspiration behind the Parang Festival—the preservation of traditional Kayak culture—was a response to the need of Kayaks to cultivate a new, postcolonial understanding of their heritage and identity. Today, interest in preserving what is seen by Parang organizers, performers, and audience members as traditional Kayak musical expressions is similarly high, but now more as an antidote to the homogenizing effects of globalization. For it is precisely the maintenance of Kayak cultural autonomy that forms the core meaning and impetus behind the Parang Festival of Carriacou. And because Carriacou is emerging from centuries of political, economic, and cultural domination, this assertion of cultural autonomy through traditional music, song, and dance is crucial.

There are both historic and contemporary implications for the success of Carriacou's Parang Festival. Born during an era of political and social revolution, the Parang Festival adapted—perhaps unintentionally—some of the prevailing revolutionary ideology that had benefited this small society. The pressing concern of cultural autonomy—once critical in forming a postcolonial identity from the wreckage of double-dependency status—is now, in the face of globalism and its homogenizing effects, equally urgent. Each year's iteration of Parang underscores the need to maintain this autonomy; it also reinforces the age-old expectation among Kayaks of the significance of cooperation and mutual support to preserve local culture and help those in need. As such, Carriacou's Parang Festival offers a lesson of cultural renewal and preservation as a response to political and social upheaval. It is also indicative of how folk culture can be manipulated to address political ideologies, changing aesthetics, and the ambivalence generated by varying levels of understanding and acceptance (or rejection) of a collective past. The event, its performers, and its audience together tell the story—the *lavway*—of Carriacou's past and present. Given the durability of the Parang Festival and its component parts, this augurs well for its continued role into the future.

Notes

1. INTRODUCING CARRIACOU AND THE PARANG FESTIVAL (PAGES 1 – 29)

1. I use "Carriacouan" and "Kayak" interchangeably throughout this study.

2. An earlier spelling of the island's name, "Kayrioüacou," was recorded in 1656 by Dominican missionary John Baptist Du Tertre, who visited the island and commented on its natural beauty in his *Histoire des Antilles*. Subsequent spellings from the late seventeenth and eighteenth centuries included "Kayryouacou" (Kay 1987: 8) or, as written on maps from 1784, "Cariuocou" (Devas 1974: 171; see also 1974: 166).

3. The earliest documentation of slaves in Grenada dates back to the occasion of the First Census in 1700; presumably, the first slaves arrived in Grenada some years prior to that (Brizan 1984: xiii). Indeed, very little is known about Carriacou during the first half of the eighteenth century, when the island was under French control. Donald Hill (1977) notes that by the time Britain solidified its control over Carriacou in the late 1700s, about half of the landholders and slave owners were British and half were French. The rest of Carriacou's population included a few mixed or free black estate and slave owners, free white indentured servants, landless free black tradespeople, isolated runaways, and the extensive slave population, which easily formed the largest subgroup on the island.

4. For more on Big Drum, see Pearse 1956b; McDaniel 1986, 1992, 1998; Hill 1977, 1980.

5. The derivation of *lavway* is possibly the French patois *la voix,* meaning "the voice" (Warner 1982: 19; also Gerstin, personal communication, 1998), or possibly *la vrai* or *la verité* ("the truth"). Hill glosses *lavway* as a "litanous tune sung informally in outdoor festivals" (1993: 4) and notes that it developed into an early genre of calypso. By 1905 Trinidadian *lavways* had become a form of street calypso and contained African-style call-and-response melodies (Hill 1993: 56). Some Carriacouan *lavways* are sung as a two-line call and response after a section of four-line verses.

6. Parang may have been introduced in Trinidad as well by Capuchin Franciscans, who settled primarily in the north of Trinidad between 1686 and 1689 (V. Martin 1982). Other scholars speculate that Christmastime serenading and the performance of religious songs pertaining to the birth of Christ are Americas-wide traditions with origins in the Spanish rural peasant music introduced by Spain's occupation of Trinidad from 1498 to 1797 and elsewhere as well (see Taylor 1977: 8, Hill, personal communication, 1999).

7. In Trinidad, the term "parang" also refers to the highly syncopated and up-tempo musical genre associated with seasonal serenading. Akin to Venezuelan *joropo* music (Girard 1980), Trinidadian parang music is played variously on the *bandol* or *bandola, bandolin* (or *bandonéon*), violin, cello, *cuatro,* guitar, mandolin, and *tiple* and is accompanied by *chac chac* (maracas). Carriacou's parang tradition is

mirrored elsewhere in the Caribbean. For example, Puerto Ricans traditionally serenade from house to house during the holiday season, singing *aguinaldos* (upbeat lyric compositions with strong rhythmic accompaniments) and other songs in a celebration known as *parranda* (McCoy 1968).

8. Religious songs also include narrations of the Annunciation and Nativity, the trials of the Holy family, the Crucifixion, and the Resurrection. Social and couple dances include the *castillian,* the *galerón,* the *estrebío,* the *vals* (waltz), and the *paseo.*

9. This separation formally took place in 1980. William J. Brisk (1969) notes that St. Kittians felt at times that Anguillans were poor "country cousins" in comparison to their more sophisticated "city dwellers"—a common attitude toward the population of dependency islands by the residents of the main island.

10. The Mount Royal Progressive Youth Movement now receives funding from the Grenadian National Government toward projects involving infrastructural repairs in Carriacou. The basis for this organization, though, remains rooted in the model of a folk institution generated by and for the community.

11. Melville Herskovits (1941) stressed the possible African origin of New World cultural and expressive forms and applied the notion of cultural syncretism to the black Atlantic. Noting that it is rare to find African traits in their "pure form," M. G. Smith (1965: 6) cited the process of creolization, as African contributions are overlaid upon or associated with European-derived elements. Others, such as E. Franklin Frazier (1957), asserted that any vestige of an African heritage was destroyed by slavery and, more specifically, by the American experience.

12. Our cistern ran dry about a week after we returned from Grenada with our newborn son, Sam. Fortunately, we were able to make arrangements to have the water pumped from an unused cistern into ours, a common practice in Carriacou during the dry season.

13. Because calypso has been studied extensively elsewhere, and because the Parang Festival Saturday-night calypso show reveals relatively little about the transformation of Kayak culture overall in comparison with other festival events, I limit my discussion of it here.

2. "FORWARD EVER, BACKWARD NEVER!": THE PEOPLE'S REVOLUTIONARY GOVERNMENT AND THE MAKINGS OF THE PARANG FESTIVAL (PAGES 30–59)

1. The NJM was formed on March 11, 1973, and combined members of the JEWEL organization (Joint Endeavours for Welfare, Education, and Liberation) with members of the Movement for Assemblies of People. The NJM mobilized the masses around the issue of independence. In response to this growing political activism, thugs from Prime Minister Gairy's notorious "Mongoose Gang" terrorized NJM members and were responsible for the assassination of Maurice Bishop's father in 1974 (Brizan 1984: 332–33).

2. Much has been written on the structure, development, and political and economic strategies of the People's Revolutionary Government of Grenada, Carriacou, and Petit Martinique. See Aberdeen 1986; Bishop 1983; Brizan 1984; Heine 1990a; Henry 1990; Lewis 1987; Payne, Sutton, and Thorndike 1984; Searle 1982 (ed.), 1983, 1984a, 1984b; Sunshine 1982, 1985; Thorndike 1985. For opposing perspectives, see Adkin 1989; Dujmovic 1988; Ledeen and Romerstein 1984.

3. Neither outgoing emigration nor incoming immigration statistics in the United States and Britain differentiate between Grenadians, Carriacouans, and Petit Martiniquans. Exact numbers of migrant Carriacouans are thus unobtainable, but it is reasonable to assume that patterns of emigration from Carriacou paralleled those of mainland Grenada.

4. Tony Thorndike notes that none of these institutions was completed by the time of the U.S. invasion. A fourth initiative, the creation of a new "People's Constitution," had also been introduced, but by the invasion, work on it had barely begun (Thorndike 1985: 84).

5. Donald Hill notes that this self-reliance dates back to plantation culture in the 1700s, when France ruled the islands. Cotton was then the major export—a labor-intensive crop that nevertheless required labor for only two or three months of the year. Enslaved Carriacouans were often released from the plantations at other times to work at other activities, thus fostering a sense of communal effort and self-reliance (Hill 1977: 208).

6. This project had its precedent elsewhere in the Caribbean, and particularly in Haiti. Between 1962 and 1968, left-leaning students in Port-au-Prince launched a struggle aimed at developing a peasant-style music and poetry in Haitian Creole (not French) in an attempt to build solidarity with Haitian peasants (Averill 1997: 94–95).

7. "She Alexis" means that the woman in question, Miss Raymond, is a member of the Alexis family, one of the two largest and most influential families on Carriacou.

8. While the NACDA assisted the development of local cooperatives, the PRG's national and transnational business initiatives occasionally undercut them, as in this account regarding a confrontation between Cosmos Bristol and a governmental official in charge of the Carriacou militia regarding Carriacou's fishing industry:

> Then, most of our fish was shipped to Martinique. Martinique was the new market. And, well, a lot of fishermen was able to have money that time, 'cause they could ship readily to Martinique. And so [the official] came on to say that we shouldn't ship the fish to Martinique, we should make the fish available to the people in Grenada. But many times, when the boats go to Grenada, they find a crowded market or . . . they would have problems at sea. By the time they get to the land, the fish is rotten already. . . . So having a Martinique market at your doorsteps was a credit.
>
> Moreover, I indicated to him then that in my concept, [a] thriving

economy . . . is when the country has something to sell. And if we have fish
to export, I think we would have some foreign exchange to back up on. And
he mad over that and he crack up [pull a gun] on me again. (Bristol, interview, 1997)

9. The NYO was modeled in part on Nkrumah's strategy to mobilize Ghana-
ian youth through the Young African Pioneers. Youth was not so much an age category as a distinct class—for example, "youth equals proletarian" (Collins and
Richards 1989: 41n39). This politicization of youth culture had worldwide precedents (the former USSR, China, and regionally in Cuba). In Grenada and Carriacou, the PRG organized other youth groups in addition to the National Youth
Organization, including the National Students Council, which sought to have its
membership become involved with "emulation" programs, work-study courses,
and community projects. Similarly, the NJM Young Pioneers attempted to organize the children of the nation, instilling in them "discipline, self-confidence, creativity, commitment, leadership, patriotism, and so forth" (Bishop 1981: 184).

10. Such modernization was not limited to Carriacou: years before in Trinidad
a wave of nationalism leading up to independence in 1962 brought new attitudes toward local culture that centralized the production of what had once been largely
community-based expressions such as calypso or the steelband movement. During
the 1960s and 1970s the latter in particular enjoyed a considerable increase of support from state and corporate sources for performances and competitions, support
that, Stephen Stuempfle notes, was "interrelated with an elaborate system of patronage and material rewards used to maintain political power" (Stuempfle 1995:
142). The institutionalization of culture in the name of modernization also took a
step forward in 1963 when Trinidadian Prime Minister Dr. Eric Williams instituted "The Prime Minister's Best Village Competition" as part of a rural development program. It was this particular competition that would alter the performance context and style of Trinidadian parang music, again through corporate
patronage and the centralization of the National Parang Championships by the
state (Malm 1978).

11. Another youth group in Carriacou is the L'Esterre South Striders Social
Sports Club. Formed in 1986, the South Striders focus on sports, cultural events,
and community development. Like other youth groups in Carriacou, the South
Striders aim to organize young people. As founder and group leader Brian Lendore
notes, "If you don't get the young people involved in something, then they're going
to get involved in something else" (interview, 1996).

12. This type of public criticism is common at Carriacou events. In 1995, for example, the chairman of the Regatta Committee, Henry Stiell, condemned at length
those in and outside of the committee who did not contribute to the mounting of
Regatta as they had promised.

3. CULTURAL AMBIVALENCE: THE CASE
OF CARRIACOU QUADRILLE (PAGES 60–98)

1. According to the 1750 census in Carriacou, the Kongo group comprised the largest segment of the Carriacou population (McDaniel 1998: 51).

2. Herskovits concludes that "socialized ambivalence" informed his informants' explanation of their participation in Vodou, a syncretic religious practice that blends West and Central African spiritual traditions with Roman Catholicism. He argued that Haitian peasants were socialized by other, non-Vodou-practicing Haitians to distance themselves from what was then thought to be a holdover from African ancestral traditions. Finding that people were reluctant to talk about their participation in Vodou, Herskovits decided that they were ambivalent about Vodou itself. Ethnomusicologist Michael Largey notes that

> Herskovits committed a common mistake of anthropological research by failing to account for the historical moment in which he collected his data. In 1934, the United States ended a nineteen-year occupation of Haiti in which U.S.-backed Haitian administrations sponsored what were termed 'anti-superstition campaigns' against Vodou practitioners. Houses of worship were burned, ritual objects were confiscated, and, most importantly, religious leaders were imprisoned. Herskovits began his research almost immediately after the occupation with the blessing of the Haitian government. When Herskovits asked peasants about their participation in Vodou, they were not, in fact, 'ambivalent'; they were frightened to talk to someone who was sanctioned by the Haitian government, the same government that sent soldiers into Vodou temples in order to destroy them. (Largey, personal communication, 2007)

3. The *cacian* (possibly from "Castillian") may be a product of the historical cultural exchange between Carriacou and Trinidad. From the 1830s to the 1960s, Carriacouans migrated to Trinidad and vice versa in search of work. It is quite likely that the Kayak *cacian* is Trinidadian, and thus Spanish, in origin.

4. Libations are common in everyday life in Carriacou. Prior to drinking a beverage, one typically spills a little on the floor "for the ancestors." Libations are particularly important during Big Drum ceremonies and other rituals relating to the ancestors.

5. Lancers quadrille (or simply "Lancers") is a variant of the English quadrille that was popular in the nineteenth and early twentieth centuries. Lancers derived even more of their music from popular songs and stage works. The name "Lancers" is derived from "Quadrille des Lanciers," which was introduced in Dublin in 1817 by the dancing master John Duval. This social dance virtually died out after 1870, except in England, where it found new life with a different musical repertoire and became known as "the Lancers."

6. The Albert quadrille, named after its inventor, French dancemaster Charles d'Albert, combined various choreographies into one set or figure, including the first figure of the quadrille, the second of the Caledonian (yet another variation of the quadrille that emerged in England around 1830), the fourth figure of the Waltz Cotillion, and the fifth figure of the quadrille (Richardson 1960: 72–73).

7. The *paisadé* step is also found in Big Drum Nation Dance choreography; Mc-Daniel describes it as the "single example of a musical cross-over from the Big Drum ceremony to the quadrille" (1986: 192). It is also commonly found in North American square-, contra-, and quadrille dance forms, however. For this reason, the *paisadé* is probably of European origin and was appropriated by Carriacouans into both the Big Drum and the quadrille forms more or less simultaneously. Carriacou quadrille, incidentally, shares another choreography with Big Drum: the "wheel," whereby each of the couples swings clockwise in a dance embrace or with an arm around each other's waist. In the Big Drum ceremony, the wheel is essential to introduce and exit dancers, and according to McDaniel it "is strangely incongruous with the movement and style of the Nation dances" (McDaniel 1998: 25).

8. Big Drum dancers also signal the end of a dance by touching the head drummer's lap. Since the three drummers provide strictly rhythmic rather than melodic accompaniment, the result is a less ragged ending than in quadrille.

9. Lorna McDaniel notes that Big Drum music is essentially immutable as well, because practitioners place a great importance on the maintenance of old repertoires and performance practices. She links this concept of cultural memory and static tradition to the music's function as entertainment for a spirit audience that is responsive only to "signals from the past" (McDaniel 1998: 169).

10. In contrast to western classical violin technique, this grip (and the highly tightened horsehair) is common among traditional violinists in Carriacou and fiddlers elsewhere. Violin bows are inherently ill balanced; "choking up" on the bow equalizes the weight between the heavier frog and the lighter tip, allowing for greater volume and ease of playing over longer periods of time.

11. The phenomenon of remembering and learning music in dreams is not limited to Carriacouans. The late Irish button accordionist, Tom Doherty, noted that upon awakening, he would feel an overwhelming urge to refamiliarize himself with the tunes he heard in his dreams (Doherty, interview, 1986). Dreams similarly inform the composition process of former Grateful Dead drummer Mickey Hart: "I get this stuff in dreams; that's where it comes from . . . I try to lay down whatever remnant I have on tape . . . [And when I can't remember] I use self-hypnosis and tell myself to remember my dream. It's a very powerful way of getting into the unconscious. And there are other techniques I use to mine the dream state" (as quoted in Catlin 2000).

12. Polkas and waltzes are more popular than the quadrille among dancers in Carriacou, probably because they require no specialized training. Its lack of accessibility has no doubt contributed to the fact that quadrille has become largely a performance genre.

13. The term "quadrille" is derived from the Italian *squadriglia* or *squadra* (a company of soldiers formed in a square), or from the Spanish *cuadrilla,* and it originally referred to a small company of cavalry. It later came to refer to a group of pageant dancers, and in French ballet the term *quadrille de contredanses* arose from the inclusion of a set of contradances in a ballet. Once it was imported to the ballroom, its name was shortened to "quadrille" (also to distinguish it from other *contredanses*) (Richardson 1960: 59).

14. The presence of quadrille throughout the Caribbean by the early 1800s is well documented, testifying to its appeal. It would undergo widespread and extensive local adaptations over the following century. John Szwed and Morton Marks (1988) provide an excellent overview of quadrille and related dances throughout the African diaspora. Jocelyne Guilbault (1984) examines the practice of *kwadril* in St. Lucia among various social clubs, while Gordon Rohlehr (1990) documents it as a popular ballroom dance in Trinidad. Paul Austerlitz (1997) draws a connection between *contredanse* and early *merengue* music and dance in the 1800s in the Dominican Republic. Gage Averill traces a similar connection: by the 1804 Haitian Revolution, European figure dances (*contredanse,* quadrille, and Lancers quadrille, among others), as well as "kongo-influenced African recreational dances," came to form a creolized genre known as *karabinè* (Averill 1997: 32–33; see also Yih 1995). This genre evolved eventually into Haitian *mereng* and later into the popular Dominican music and dance form called merengue. After the 1804 Haitian Revolution, planters and colonialists fled St. Dominque to Cuba and New Orleans, bringing with them the Haitian creolized *kontradans.* Peter Manuel (1994) notes that in Cuba, the Haitian *kontradans* spread prolifically and evolved into the local genre *contradanza* (*habanera*). *Contradanza* was exported to Puerto Rico by the late nineteenth century and became simply *danza.*

15. Apart from church records, which do not mention music and dance, virtually no written records remain in Carriacou from this era. My research relies on archival newspapers and documents housed in the Grenada National Archives and other institutions, and I assume that what transpired in Grenada also occurred, at least in part, in Carriacou as well.

16. Several theories surround the reason for the migration of Scots to Carriacou. One is that in 1859, Governor Hincks of Barbados tried to resettle some of his poor white population elsewhere. While these people, reportedly descendants of indentured laborers sent out from the United Kingdom in the seventeenth and eighteenth centuries, played an important role in the economic life of Barbados and contributed to its militia and its emancipation, they had nevertheless been dispossessed of their land holdings and soon sank into poverty. Hincks hoped to alleviate their financial distress. This massive relocation was never officially undertaken, but between 1861 and 1871, 20,400 "poor whites" migrated from Barbados to Trinidad, St. Vincent, Grenada, Tobago, and St. Lucia (Steele 1974: 29). It is conceivable that a number of these migrants chose to settle in Windward. A second theory asserts that a ruinous blaze in Bridgeton, Barbados, toward the end of the eighteenth cen-

tury leveled parts of the city, and the forebears of the Carriacou Scots fled Barbados in boats, settling in Windward. A final theory is that Scottish boat builders in search of work were simply attracted by Windward's sheltered harbors.

17. In a brief handwritten history of Windward Village in the Carriacou Historical Society, local Windward historian Briget Rao writes: "Today, however, we have seen dances like the quadrille, lancers, and polka which were so popular with our ancestors, faded and die."

18. The integration and adaptation of European musical and dance genres into the social and aesthetic lives of slave cultures is not limited to the Caribbean. During the nineteenth century in the United States, enslaved black musicians routinely provided music for ballroom dances for the white upper class; black dance fiddlers, in particular, were in great demand (Southern 1997: 136). The fiddle was an extremely popular instrument among slave musicians, and the playing style was often "Africanized" to include a second layer of rhythm (Szwed and Marks 1988: 32). Works Progress Administration interviews from the 1930s with former slaves in the United States indicate that the dances most often remembered from the days of slavery included the quadrille, contradances, square dances, waltzes, and choreographies performed with distinctly African American footwork, such as juba, buck-dancing, and so on (Winans 1982: 4). In addition, it is documented that freedmen and the urban enslaved in the southern United States routinely attended formal balls at which dance suites were performed, and, as Szwed and Marks write, "Just how important and widespread these dances became is shown by the fact that the ex-slaves who were repatriated back to Liberia beginning in 1820 took the quadrille with them; and when they became the ruling elite of that country, they made it into something of a national dance. It continued to be popular at least well into the 1950s" (1988: 31).

19. Caribbean sociologist M. G. Smith's *Kinship and Community in Carriacou* (1962) supports the contentious notion of Carriacou being a classless society. Other scholars, such as Angela Lorna McDaniel, refute this, arguing that the Scottish descendants in Windward form "a class, differentiated not by wealth, but by a self-imposed culture concept" (McDaniel 1986: 185).

20. Figuratively, "We is one family" refers to an ongoing Kayak commitment to one other, which is manifested through myriad social expectations such as the frequency of gift giving, communal work projects, volunteerism, and so on. It also recognizes that an underlying level of social if not economic parity exists precisely due to this sense of familial bond.

21. For specific arguments concerning the alleged privileged treatment of enslaved Carriacouans, see Smith 1962: 24. Other scholars note that Iberian and French colonists might have been more tolerant than the British of neo-African expressive culture among the enslaved (Manuel 1995). In this regard, Carriacou would seem to be an exception, as the strongly West African Big Drum ceremony survived and thrived despite years of British rule. It is thus hard to judge exactly the conditions endured by enslaved Kayaks.

22. Late Big Drum practitioner Sugar Adams sings this nation song on Alan Lomax's 1998 recording *Carriacou Calaloo* (Rounder Records, 11661–1722–2).

23. Written information on the performance practice of quadrille music and dance in Carriacou in the second half of the twentieth century is scant. I base my research primarily on oral histories and on ethnographies (Hill 1997; Smith 1962) as well as on archival recordings (see Lomax 1962).

24. A similar tradition of bouquet balls existed in pre-emancipation Trinidad. Enslaved Trinidadians from different estates took turns hosting the event, and at each ball a "king and queen of the night" presented a nosegay of flowers to a couple from another estate who would preside at the next dance in the same capacity (Rohlehr 1990: 12–13).

25. Catholic Church interest in quadrille had many precedents. Plantation owners in the Americas had largely suppressed African music and dance among slaves, and the church shared their prejudice. A 1798 issue of the *St. George's Chronicle and Grenada Gazette* reports that slave owners sought to replace neo-African drumming with "a fiddle or two," believing that eventually the fiddle would become "more pleasing" (cited in McDaniel 1986: 130). Winston Fleary observes that by the 1960s the Catholic Church again sought to encourage quadrille at the expense of African-derived expressive forms: "I guess the priests and so on . . . gave more patronage to the quadrille and the violin . . . as opposed to the drums. They were viewing the African feasts as pagan" (interview, 1997).

26. This system of rewarding those students who are able to stay in school is largely in place today. A holdover from the British colonial educational system, which systematically denied education past Class Five, the Carriacou public education system tends to disregard academic achievement when a family cannot pay annual school fees or book and uniform costs. Furthermore, students must pass national exams after elementary school and then again after the first year of secondary school. If they fail to pass either exam, or simply cannot afford the fees, they must leave school and their formal education is effectively over.

27. While Grenada does not enjoy a large tourism industry in comparison to other Caribbean nations, its annual number of visitors has been on the rise, increasing from 30,000 in 1984 to 110,000 in 1996. Tourism took a nosedive after Grenada was devastated by Hurricane Ivan in September 2004. Since then, tourism has been steadily rebuilt through local and national initiatives.

28. Since the early 1960s L'Esterre has been home to many social clubs. The L'Esterre Cultural Club was formed in 1974; its sister social club, the L'Esterre Folk Group, was organized soon after and excelled in quadrille. Both groups organized the youth of L'Esterre and presented concerts, plays, and other events, many of which drew on African themes and images of contemporary Carriacouan life (C. Bristol, interview, 1997). Both groups have since folded; however, the L'Esterre South Striders Sports and Cultural Club today furthers the aims set forth by its predecessors.

29. An interesting parallel tradition is the Haitian-derived Cuban *tumba*

francesa, in which participants also dance in figures and wear European-style suits and gowns.

30. Dress did vary at the old time bouquet dances, ranging from street clothes to what some remember as their Sunday best: "In the '60s, 1965, when I left here, when the people go to dance, the women go to dance formally, as if they going to a wedding. Dressed like that. And the gentlemen in their tie and their . . . hat" (W. Fleary, interview, 1997).

31. Jocelyne Guilbault (1984) notes that *kwadril* dancers in St. Lucia also view this form both as a European genre inherited from the plantocracy and as a contemporary expressive art form that they now control.

32. The nine types of Nation Dances include Cromanti, Banda, Igbo, Manding, Kongo, Moko, Chamba, Arada, and Temne.

4. FRIDAY NIGHT: THE HOSANNAH BAND COMPETITION (PAGES 99–122)

1. Popularized in the United States and England in the 1870s by the evangelist Dwight Lyman Moody (1837–1899) and his musical partner, Ira David Sankey (1840–1908), these hymns have been widely distributed around the world via inexpensive hymnals. Sankeys were probably brought to Carriacou during the late 1800s by missionaries and/or via hymnals exported from the United States (Hill 1999b). Sankeys quickly became popular first in Protestant congregations and later in Catholic congregations. In contrast to Protestant hymns, the texts of sankeys are repetitive in structure and somewhat more secular, addressing one's fellow man rather than centering primarily on the sacred. Sankeys also feature more upbeat rhythms and tempi than Protestant hymns, which tend to be slower and more drawn out. The melodies of sankeys rarely exceed the range of an octave, whereas other hymns often cover a wider range and are therefore more difficult to sing (see Guilbault 1984: 188).

2. Several residents of Mount Royal—formerly an Afro-French village—are known as composers of hymns in a style reminiscent of the historical *cantique.* The remnants of French hymnody, *cantiques* were sung throughout the French Caribbean. In Carriacou, this tradition was once prevalent at wakes and prayer services (Hill 1999; see also McDaniel 1998: 128).

3. Donald Hill (1980) collected a variant of Lendore's toast in Carriacou in 1970 from Gordon Cayanne that can be heard on *The Big Drum and Other Ritual and Social Musics of Carriacou* (Smithsonian/Folkways Records): "I hung my jawbone on a fence./Someone pass and took it./My jawbone eat,/My jawbone talk,/My jawbone eat with knife and fork" (that is, you don't have to teach people to eat). The folklore of the jawbone as possessing powerful and magical qualities originates in the Old Testament, where it is written that Samson slew ten thousand Philistines using the jaw of an ass. Reiterated throughout African American and Anglo-American oral traditions in the southern United States, variants of Lendore's toast probably moved into Kayak oral tradition via seafarers from the United States and/or Canada who sailed to Carriacou during the nineteenth century. (Conversely,

records from the British Merchant Marine indicate that after emancipation in 1834, deepwater seafaring was an important alternative to plantation labor for Kayaks and other West Indians, and cultural exchange on board these vessels would have been inevitable [Cobley 2004].) Indeed, Lendore's toast is uncannily similar to many versions of a popular old-time sung fiddle tune from the southeastern United States, such as this version, entitled "Jawbone" and recorded on February 6, 1928, by Popes' Arkansas Mountaineers:

> *Jawbone walk and jawbone talk,*
> *jawbone eat with a knife and fork.*
>
> *(Chorus) Walk jawbone, and walk away,*
> *walk jawbone both night and day.*
>
> *My wife died in Tennessee,*
> *left that jawbone back to me.*
>
> *Hung my jawbone on a fence,*
>
> *Haven't seen nothing but the jawbone since.*
> *(Echoes of the Ozarks, vol. 1, CO-CD 3506)*

4. This line is a direct quotation from the poem "Casabianca" by Felicia Dorothea Hemans (1793–1835).

5. The effect of television on modern communication has been well documented (see, for example, Postman 1986). With the arrival of cable television in Carriacou in the mid-1990s, TV's effects on the population are clear: teacher/musician Albert Fortune notes that his students' attention spans have dwindled substantially (Fortune, interview, 1997). Similarly, I noticed that many of my Carriacouan friends, particularly women and their children, preferred to discuss the content of something they viewed on television the night before rather than the local happenings, as had been the case before the arrival of television.

6. Before telephones were widespread throughout the island, Carriacouans wrote short notes to each other, sending them to their neighbors in the care of children.

7. In addition to rehearsals, preparation for the Hosannah band competition involves the women members of the group sewing their costumes and organizing the men's costumes (each group sports a different set of matching costumes for the test and choice pieces). Hosannah band members must also build stage props that will dramatize the meaning of each carol.

8. The involvement of researchers as insiders to the community under study has long been discussed among scholars whose main source of data is ethnographic fieldwork (see, for example Bogdan and Biklen 1998; Narayan 1997). Many ethnomusicologists and anthropologists have had similar direct involvment with the group they are documenting. See, for example, Gregory Barz's (2003) account of his participation as a coach for and performer in a Tanzanian *kwaya* (choir); Carol Babiracki's (1997) experiences as an instrumentalist and dancer while researching

gender and performance in Bihar, India; and Steve Taylor's (2003) dual role as ethnographer and lead guitarist in the punk band that he writes about.

9. Another instance of outsiders assisting Kayaks with musical activities turned into one of our nicest experiences in Carriacou. My husband, Tom Randall, was asked by the fundamentalist Church of Christ to teach congregants how to read music so that they could make better use of their hymnals. Tom had been volunteering in the Hillsborough Secondary School as a music teacher; his reputation thus established, the church pastor, the Reverend Philip Mendes, asked Tom to teach his congregation on a weekly basis. Because playing musical instruments is forbidden in the Church of Christ, Tom relied on ear training and a modified form of solfege; my role was to help the sopranos and altos with their parts.

10. The judge in question told me that he also coached the Grenadian Hosannah band, One Love, assisting them with diction and intonation.

11. I was often mistaken for a volunteer teacher in Carriacou. In 1996–97, my husband, as I mentioned, in fact volunteered as a music teacher.

12. While Carriacou teachers use primarily Metropolitan English in the schools, most Kayaks who speak it lived abroad. Often Carriacouans speak both. As I became a more familiar presence in Carriacou, people increasingly spoke to me in Creole, a language that took me several months to fully understand. For more on Carriacou Creole English, see Kephart 2000.

13. Competition is generally common throughout Carriacou. Many sporting and cultural events throughout the year are competitive, including calypso and soca contests, beauty pageants, and carnival-time Mas' (costume) contests. The annual August Regatta features sailing and boat racing contests as well as land and water sports contests.

14. Much has been written on the role of race and racial relations in musical performance among Caribbean populations. For example, Paul Austerlitz (1997) examines how race and racial distinctions have influenced the performance and consumption of merengue music in the Dominican Republic. Similarly, Katherine Hagedorn (2001) uses Cuban constructions of race to interrogate the rise of interest in folkloric Afro-Cuban music and dance there.

15. The Westernization of folk musics that are undergoing a conscious revival elsewhere in the world is well documented (see, for example, Cooke 1986, Henry 1989, Blaustein 1993). However, whereas these revived folk traditions—in the Shetland Islands, Ireland, and the southern United States—have moved toward a more homogenized, "Western"-sounding aesthetic, they have also flourished as community-based traditions, not competitions.

5. BREAK-AWAYS, *LAVWAYS*, CALYPSO, AND MORE: AN ETHNOGRAPHY AND SOCIAL HISTORY OF CARRIACOU STRING BAND MUSIC (PAGES 123–62)

1. The term "maroon" generally refers to runaway slaves or to the descendants of escaped slaves. In Carriacou, a *maroon* is a village celebration, most often a har-

vest festival for wet-season crops or an opportunity for fishermen to give thanks for bountiful catches from the sea. Donald Hill (1977) classifies *maroons* in Carriacou by their primary function as folk social organizations and as a means by which the community can maintain contact with their deceased ancestors (as in the Big Drum Dance tradition).

2. This pattern of appropriation follows, in part, Philip Richardson's notion of the trajectory of social dances. He writes that popular elite dances and their accompanying music often originated as peasant dances, then were modified in aristocratic circles and urban elite society (Richardson 1960: 18). As a form became popular, it spread to other regions, sometimes due to colonialism. Once in the new country, the forms filtered back "down" to the peasants again.

3. The term "break-away" was commonly used to refer to the Spanish *paseo*, a type of parang music played in Trinidad during the first half of the twentieth century. According to Krister Malm (1978: 44), the Trinidadian break-away had a profound influence on the development of the calypso between 1910 and 1950.

4. This transcription only approximates Mr. Joseph's performance. A consummate master of the *cuatro*, he played very rapidly yet with a great economy of hand motion, making an entirely accurate transcription of his playing virtually impossible.

5. This transcription also features the guitar playing of Welcome Cummins (another retiree who had recently returned from years in England) and my husband, Tom Randall.

6. Canute Caliste's version of "Whispering Hope" as the second figure in the English quadrille, played during a wedding reception in L'Esterre, can be heard on the recording *The Big Drum and Other Ritual and Social Music of Carriacou* (Hill 1980).

7. Trinidadian string bands are also related to the particular ensembles that perform at Venezuelan *velorio* (funeral customs), which include the *cuatro, cinco* (five-string guitar), guitar, *tiple* (small guitar), *bandore* or *pandora* (mandolin-like instrument), flute, maracas, *perdero* (tambourine), drum, bass drum, *furuco* (friction drum), and *charrasca* (scraper made from a bull's horn) (see Girard 1980).

8. Soca calypso is a popular music from the Anglo-Caribbean that focuses less on political or social messages and more on creating a "jump up" or party atmosphere (see Dudley 1996).

9. There is little extant scholarship on Carriacou string band music with the exception of Donald Hill's work (1977) describing string band music from the early 1970s; Hill also produced an excellent documentary recording of Carriacou music from this period (1980). Cuban ethnomusicologist Rolando Pérez Fernández (1983) also recorded string band music in Carriacou during the early 1980s. M. G. Smith (1962) makes passing mention of string band musicians, as do Lorna McDaniel (1986) and Christine David (1985).

10. A 1971 Sunblisters performance of the calypso "Raycan" at the Carnival calypso finals at Hillsborough Secondary School can be heard on *The Big Drum and Other Ritual and Social Music of Carriacou* (Hill 1980). This recording documents

one of the last performances of the original Sunblisters, as most of the members, including Poco Joseph, emigrated that year to New York City or Canada. Additionally, Donald Hill's monograph includes a photograph of a poster advertising an upcoming dance in Hillsborough featuring the music of the Sunblisters (1977: 323).

11. Although there were a few cars in Carriacou as early as the 1940s and 1950s, it has only been since the 1970s that vehicles have proliferated on the island. In 1971, there were fewer than fifty, most of them taxis, but even then the number had begun to grow rapidly.

12. Lyrical variants of "Magica Polka" are widespread in the Caribbean and have been recorded often on 78rpm phonograph records. The song might have originated in Carriacou or been introduced to Kayaks via these recordings.

13. Many calypsos and soca tunes from Grenada and Trinidad employ sexual imagery and allusion, as does their performance practice (singers are well known for their pelvic thrusts and explicit dance moves). In 1995 string bands adapted the popular calypso "Miss Daisy's Car," by Grenadian calypsonian Peter Humphries. A parody of the movie *Driving Miss Daisy,* the song ostensibly is about a car speeding through a crowded neighborhood, running red lights and careening out of control. The female passenger in the car tells the male driver,

> *No, no, no, not so fast!*
> *don't come so fast,*
> *I want it last.*
> *(I'm saying) No, no, no, not so fast,*
> *don't come so fast,*
> *I want it last.*

Note that Grenadians and Carriacouans sometimes use the verb "to come" in place of "to go." Also, native speakers eschew the infinitive form of the verb, so that "to last" becomes simply "last."

14. Lyrics reprinted with kind permission from The Alan Lomax Archive, New York City. Many of Lomax's 1962 recordings can be heard on three CD releases contained in the series *The Alan Lomax Collection: Caribbean Voyage; The 1962 Field Recordings* (Rounder Records 11661–1727–2; 11661–1726–2; and 11661–1722–2). A fourth CD in this series, entitled *Music for Work and Play,* is forthcoming and features Lomax's recording of "Magica Polka," quadrille music from both L'Esterre and Windward, pass play songs, sea chanteys, and other genres of vocal and instrumental music.

15. *Manicou* is a local term for opossum; *callaloo* is a dark, leafy green vegetable that is traditionally cooked into a thick soup or stew.

16. Donald Hill notes in the early years of the twentieth century, one type of *lavway* in Trinidad was termed the "leggo," a "street song for people who 'let go' toward the end of Carnival" (1993: 4). In Carriacou, the dry season (from February to roughly June) is referred to as the "leggo" season, when livestock are freed to wander to find water and graze wherever they can.

17. Mills established KYAK in 1996. A play on the name "Kayak," the radio station was funded entirely by Mills, who saw a need to get information out to Carriacouans quickly and efficiently (Mills, interview, 2001). Broadcasts from his radio station include live performances from Carriacou Carnival and the Parang Festival as well as the latest reggae, soca, calypso, and ragga hits from elsewhere in the Anglo-speaking Caribbean. In fact, KYAK is now heard almost everywhere in Carriacou, blasting from the minivans that serve as public transportation around the island and playing through speakers in rum shops and elsewhere as part of the island's soundscape.

18. Petit St. Vincent is the southernmost island of St. Vincent. In 1965, Hazen Richardson of Essex, Connecticut, purchased the island from Lily Bethel, a resident of Petit Martinique, for a reported sum of $80,000 (U.S. currency). Richardson has since turned the island into one of the Eastern Caribbean's most exclusive resorts.

19. Sources: String band musicians Maitland Coy and Lawrence Chase; Mike Taylor, Captain of the *Mandalay*.

20. Source: Judy Bullen, former manager of Silver Beach Resort, Carriacou.

21. Source: Hazen Richardson, owner/manager of Petit St. Vincent.

22. Source: Captain Mike Taylor, the *Mandalay*.

23. Source: Hazen Richardson.

6. *MELÉE!:* THE SUNDAY EVENING STRING BAND COMPETITION (PAGES 163–215)

1. "Shtoops" are sounds made by sucking one's front teeth. Shtooping is a widespread expression throughout Carriacou and the English-speaking Caribbean to signify disgust or annoyance. In this instance, it is unclear whether the assembled musicians are annoyed with the Hosannah singer's comment, the issues around tourism, or the possibility of dressing in a Middle Eastern–style costume.

2. Images of race and culture are increasingly contested in the popular media in Carriacou and elsewhere in the Caribbean. In 1996, for example, a popular reggae version of the holiday standard "White Christmas" adapted the lyrics as "I'm dreaming of a Black Christmas."

3. During the early 1970s, Calypsonians routinely tested their tunes and lyrics out on audiences several months prior to the competition to see what worked best (Hill 1980: 5). This previewing is even more involved and expensive today, as calypso singers might prerecord highly produced, arranged, and orchestrated versions of their calypsos. Indeed, in 1997 Kayak calypsonians complained in the *Grenadian Voice* about the "high economic times of today" and the fact that they "may not be able to deliver audio material for radio promotional purposes" due to the enormous expense.

4. String bands routinely incorporate polyrhythms into the *lavway* portion of their choice piece, usually between the solo and the rhythm instruments. The Ghetto Boys' mandolinist, Rhyno, for example, often moves into triple meter against a stable duple meter (see transcription 11, measures 1–9), a destabilizing rhythmic gesture

that can also be heard in quadrille violinist Canute Caliste's music (see chapter 3). Similarly, Big Drum musicians temporarily create a contrasting metrical feel during *cutter* drum solos over a bed of the two *boula* drums, the latter of which provides the basic rhythm specific to each African Nation Dance (McDaniel 1998: 86). Adding drive and syncopation, these temporary polyrhythms act as a musical meme or blueprint, a sort of performance trope heard throughout all of Carriacou's musics.

5. Parang business jingles are reminiscent of early-twentieth-century calypso performance practice in Trinidad (Hill, personal communication, 1999).

6. The exception to this is One Love, the single band that travels from Grenada to compete in Carriacou Parang. Their *lavway* is strictly religious, and they always place last or second to last.

7. During the Parang Festival in 1996, competing bands played the first part of their choice piece fairly fast (quarter note = 96–126) in contrast to the second part (the *melée*) (quarter note = 94–100). By way of comparison, a typical parang song from Trinidad is much faster (quarter note = 144). While the dominant meter in Trinidadian parang music is a fast 6/8 that is clearly derived from Venezuelan sources, the first part of Carriacou choice pieces are most often in 4/4.

8. Gossip and ribald humor can easily turn vulgar, as was the case in 1991, when a parang band from Petit Martinique was censored because their lyrics were "slack" (obscene). This judgment was not limited to the Parang Committee; other musicians, such as Harrison Fleary of the Central Serenaders, threatened to not participate the next year if the offending band's lyrics were not censored (H. Fleary, interview, 1995).

9. My husband is a luthier and was given the guitar to repair, which he did, much to Canute Caliste's delight.

10. I use a pseudonym here in deference to the man named explicitly by the Ghetto Boys.

11. The use of song and music to record and report events is common to various West African cultures; Mandingo griots or *jalis,* for example, are charged with the preservation and recitation of the history of the Mande people. Many Caribbean cultures use song in a similar manner, particularly in Puerto Rico, where *plena* musicians relate the local news and lore of their community through songs accompanied by large frame drums called *panderettas.*

12. Sale of Carriacou land to foreigners represents, for some, a source of quick wealth, but others see it as a shortsighted decision that inevitably will result in unaffordable land prices for future generations. Senator Elvin Nimrod, Minister of Carriacou and Petit Martinique Affairs, stressed the need to educate Carriacouans regarding the implications of land sale:

> It is very difficult for the government to come and tell a private citizen, don't sell your land. . . . But the people themselves must know that there is a limit. . . . If a regular Carriacouan, a Kayak so to speak, approaches a land owner: "I want to buy this half an acre of land, $3.50 a square foot, that's

what I think it's worth," but at the end of the day, a foreigner comes and offers $4.00 U.S. per square foot. You know what would happen? This person would go with the foreigner.... But until people understand that the money is not all the same and, at the same time,... government understands that people are hungry and they have land and they want to sell ... it's unreasonable to tell a person you can't sell your land if that person wants to finance their children's education, build a new home, whatever it is. (Interview, 1997)

Senator Nimrod notes that alternatives do exist, such as longterm leasing, whereby after ten or fifteen years the land would revert back to the Kayak family. Thanks to legislation regarding Grenadian land policy, Nimrod is optimistic that Carriacou will not follow the many other Caribbean islands that are essentially owned by foreign investors.

13. The ejaculation *weeha* or *wayha* is a time-honored expression throughout the Caribbean. Common to Afro-French music, *wayha* can often be heard in calypso songs recorded as early as the 1920s (Hill 1999).

14. One of Trinidad's most famous calypsonians was known as "Roaring Lion." The image of the donkey is common to calypso as well as to other parang songs.

15. In 2001, the prize for first place was $2,400; second place, $2,000; third place, $1,700. There is also a consolation prize of $500, a "best-dressed" prize of $300, and a $100 prize for "best-rendered test piece."

7. "WESELF AS ONE PEOPLE": LOCAL IDENTITY/REGIONAL BELONGING (PAGES 215–21)

1. In recent years, Parang has garnered funding from the Grenadian government and major Grenadian businesses. Often, however, governmental support is tangential to the Parang Festival itself (in 1997, for example, the Grenadian government donated money to support the refurbishing of the Tennis Courts). The extent of this financial support is reflected in written acknowledgments in printed festival materials and publicity and through expressions of gratitude from the stage each evening by the head of the Parang Committee.

2. The increasing power of the MRPYM parallels, up to a point, the growth of the grassroots democratic New Jewel Movement that ultimately became the People's Revolutionary Government. In the case of the PRG, the acquisition and centralization of power would ultimately spell the demise of Grenada's experiment in socialism, as Tony Thorndike notes: "As centralization grew apace, so a paternalistic socialism emerged, capped by an authoritarian and undemocratic core, where dissent could [be], and was, met with severe punishment, as Bishop himself was to experience" (Thorndike 1990: 47).

References

BOOKS AND ARTICLES

Aberdeen, Michael.
   1986. *Grenada under the P.R.G: The Real Reason for the US Military Invasion.*
   Trinidad: The PPM.
Adedeji, J. A.
   1967. "Form and Function of Satire in Yoruba Drama." *Odu* (University of Ife,
   Ife-Ife, Nigeria) 4, no. 1: 61–72.
Adkin, Major Mark.
   1989. *Urgent Fury: The Battle for Grenada.* Lexington, Mass.: Lexington Books.
Agovi, Kofi.
   1995. "A King Is Not Above Insult: The Politics of Good Governance in Nzema
   Avudwene Festival Songs." In *Power, Marginality, and African Oral Literature,*
   ed. Graham Furniss and Liz Gunner. Cambridge: Cambridge University
   Press. 47–64.
Alexander, Jeffrey C.
   2004. "Toward a Theory of Cultural Trauma." In *Cultural Trauma and Collec-
   tive Identity,* Jeffrey C. Alexander, Ron Eyerman, Bernard Giesen, Neil J.
   Smelser, and Piotr Sztompka. Cambridge: Cambridge University Press.
   1–30.
Alvarez, Julia.
   1998. *Something To Declare.* New York: Penguin Books.
Anonymous.
   1979. Grenada Document GD 002378. Handwritten memorandum entitled
   "Some Proposals Arising from Today's Meeting." May.
Apter, Andrew.
   1991. "Herskovits's Heritage: Rethinking Syncretism in the African Diaspora."
   Diaspora 1, no. 3: 235–60.
Austerlitz, Paul.
   1997. *Merengue: Dominican Music and Dominican Identity.* Philadelphia: Temple
   University Press.
Averill, Gage.
   1997. *A Day for the Hunter, A Day for the Prey: Popular Music and Power in Haiti.*
   Chicago: University of Chicago Press.
Babiracki, Carol M.
   1997. "What's The Difference? Reflections on Gender and Research in Village
   India." In *Shadows in the Field: New Perspectives on Fieldwork in Ethnomusi-
   cology,* ed. Gregory F. Barz and Timothy J. Cooley. New York: Oxford Uni-
   versity Press. 121–38.

Barz, Gregory F.
   2003. *Performing Religion: Negotiating Past and Present in Kwaya Music of Tanzania.* Amsterdam: Rodopi.
Beaudry, Nicole.
   1997. "The Challenges of Human Relations in Ethnographic Inquiry: Examples from Arctic and Subarctic Fieldwork." In *Shadows in the Field: New Perspectives for Fieldwork in Ethnomusicology,* ed. Gregory F. Barz and Timothy J. Cooley. New York: Oxford University Press. 63–83.
Berlin, Ira, Marc Favreau, and Steven F. Miller.
   1998. *Remembering Slavery: African Americans Talk About Their Personal Experiences of Slavery and Emancipation.* New York: The New Press.
Bilby, Kenneth.
   1999. "'Roots Explosion': Indigenization and Cosmopolitanism in Contemporary Surinamese Popular Music." *Ethnomusicology* 43, no. 2 (Spring/Summer): 256–96.
Bishop, Maurice.
   1979a. "In Nobody's Backyard." In *Maurice Bishop Speaks: The Grenada Revolution, 1979–83.* New York: Pathfinder Press (1983). 26–31.
   1979b. "Education in the New Grenada." In *Maurice Bishop Speaks: The Grenada Revolution, 1979–83.* New York: Pathfinder Press (1983). 42–47.
   1981. "The Present Stage of the Grenada Revolution." Interview in *Granma Weekly Review* (July 12). Reprinted in *Maurice Bishop Speaks: The Grenada Revolution, 1979–83.* New York: Pathfinder Press (1983). 174–98.
   1982. "'A New Oneness': An Interview with Comrade Maurice Bishop." In *Carriacou and Petite [sic] Martinique: In the Mainstream of the Revolution,* ed. Chris Searle. St. George's, Grenada: Fedon Publishers. 16–25.
   1983. *Why the U.S. Invaded Grenada: Maurice Bishop Speaks to U.S. Workers.* New York: Pathfinder Press.
Bissio, Roberto Remo, editor.
   1988. *Third World Guide 89/90: Facts, Figures, Opinions.* Montevideo, Uruguay: ACU S.A.
Blaustein, Richard.
   1993. "Rethinking Folk Revivalism: Grass-Roots Preservationism and Folk Romanticism." In *Transforming Tradition: Folk Music Revivals Examined,* ed. Neil V. Rosenberg. Urbana: University of Illinois Press. 258–74.
Bogdan, Robert C., and Sari Knopp Biklen.
   1998. *Qualitative Research and Education.* 3rd ed. Boston: Allyn and Bacon.
Bourguignon, Erika Eichhorn.
   1951. "Syncretism and Ambivalence in Haiti: An Ethnohistoric Study." Ph.D. dissertation, Northwestern University.
Brinkley, Frances.
   1978. "An Analysis of the 1750 Carriacou Census." *Caribbean Quarterly* 20, nos. 1, 2 (March, June): 44–60.

Brisk, William J.
  1969. *The Dilemma of a Ministate: Anguilla*. Columbia: Institute of International Studies, University of South Carolina.
Bristol, Cosmos.
  1996. Recitation from Hosannah Band Competition, Parang Festival.
Brizan, George.
  1984. *Grenada: Island of Conflict, From Amerindians to People's Revolution, 1498–1979*. Bath, England: Zed Books, Ltd.
Callender, Randolph "Baboo."
  1982. "We Going Good, Man!" In *Carriacou and Petite [sic] Martinique: In the Mainstream of the Revolution,* ed. Chris Searle. St. George's, Grenada: Fedon Publishers. 61–64.
Caruth, Cathy, ed.
  1995. *Trauma: Explorations in Memory*. Baltimore: The Johns Hopkins University Press.
Catlin, Roger.
  2000. "Relaxed Hart Truckin' with International Sounds." *Hartford Courant,* February 3, 2000, Life 2–3 Section, pg. 1.
Chernoff, John Miller.
  1979. *African Rhythm and African Sensibility*. Chicago: The University of Chicago Press.
Cobley, Alan.
  2004. "Black West Indian Seamen in the British Merchant Marine in the Mid-Nineteenth Century." *History Workshop Journal* 58: 259–74.
Collins, John, and Paul Richards.
  1989. "Popular Music in West Africa." In *World Music, Politics, and Social Change,* ed. Simon Frith. Manchester, England: Manchester University Press. 12–46.
Cooke, Peter.
  1986. *The Fiddle Tradition of the Shetland Islands*. Cambridge: Cambridge University Press.
Coy, Milton.
  1991. "Carriacou Parang: An Experience." In "M.R.P.Y.M. Presents Carriacou Parang '91." Newsletter. Carriacou: Anansi Publications.
Crum, Ellis J.
  1960. *Sacred Selections for the Church*. Kendallville, Ind.: Chancel Music.
Danticat, Edwidge.
  1994. *Breath, Eyes, Memory: A Novel*. New York: Vintage Books.
Dash, J. Michael.
  1996. "Psychology, Creolization, and Hybridization." In *New National and Post-Colonial Literatures: An Introduction,* ed. Bruce King. Oxford: Clarendon Press. 45–57.
David, Christine.
  1982. "Let The Drums Beat!" In *Carriacou and Petite [sic] Martinique: In the*

Mainstream of the Revolution, ed. Chris Searle. St. George's, Grenada: Fedon Publishers. 85–95.

1985. *Folklore of Carriacou.* Barbados: Coles Printery Limited.

Devas, Raymund P.

1932. *Conception Island, or the Troubled Story of the Catholic Church of Grenada.* London: Sands and Co.

1974. *A History of the Islands of Grenada, 1498–1796, with Some Notes and Comments on Carriacou and Events of Later Years.* St. George's, Grenada: Carenage Press.

Domínguez, Luis Arturo.

1960. *Veloria de Angelito.* 2nd ed. Caracas: Ediciones del Ejecutivo del Estado Trujillo.

Du Bois, W. E. Burghardt.

1969. *The Souls of Black Folk.* New York City: Signet Classics.

Dudley, Shannon.

1996. "Judging 'By the Beat': Calypso Versus Soca." *Ethnomusicology* 40, no. 2: 269–98.

Dujmovic, Nicholas.

1988. *The Grenada Documents: Window on Totalitarianism.* Special Report. A Publication of the Institute for Foreign Policy Analysis, Inc. Washington: Pergamon Brassey's.

Eyerman, Ron.

2001. *Cultural Trauma: Slavery and the Formation of African-American Identity.* Cambridge: Cambridge University Press.

2004. "Cultural Trauma: Slavery and the Formation of African American Identity." In *Cultural Trauma and Collective Identity,* Jeffrey C. Alexander, Ron Eyerman, Bernard Giesen, Neil J. Smelser, and Piotr Sztompka. Berkeley: University of California Press. 60–111.

Fanon, Frantz.

1963. *The Wretched of the Earth.* New York: Grove Press.

Feintuch, Burt.

1993. "Musical Revivalism as Musical Transformation." In *Transforming Tradition: Folk Music Revivals Examined,* ed. Neil V. Rosenberg. Urbana: University of Illinois Press. 183–93.

Fernández, Rolando Pérez.

1983. *Folk Music of Carriacou.* LP. C-001. Havana: Empresa de Grabaciones y Ediciones Musicales.

Frazier, E. Franklin.

1957. *The Negro in the United States.* New York: Macmillan.

Gates, Henry Louis Jr.

1988. *The Signifying Monkey: A Theory of African-American Literary Criticism.* Oxford: Oxford University Press.

Gilroy, Paul.
  1993. *The Black Atlantic: Modernity and Double Consciousness.* Cambridge, Mass.: Harvard University Press.
Girard, Sharon.
  1980. *Funeral Music and Customs in Venezuela.* Tempe, Ariz.: Center for Latin American Studies, Arizona State University.
Guilbault, Jocelyne.
  1984. "Musical Events in the Lives of the People of a Caribbean Island, St. Lucia." Ph.D. dissertation, University of Michigan.
  1985. "St. Lucian *Kwadril* Evening." *Latin American Music Review* 6, no. 10: 31–57.
Hagedorn, Katherine Johanna.
  1995. "*Anatomía del Proceso Folklórico:* The 'Folkloricization' of Afro-Cuban Religious Performance in Cuba." Ph.D. dissertation, Brown University.
  2001. *Divine Utterances : The Performance of Afro-Cuban Santeria.* Washington, D.C.: Smithsonian Institution Press.
Heine, Jorge.
  1990. "The Hero and the Apparatchik: Charismatic Leadership, Political Management, and Crisis in Revolutionary Grenada." In *A Revolution Aborted: The Lessons of Grenada,* ed. Jorge Heine. Pittsburgh: University of Pittsburgh Press. 217–56.
Henry, Edward O.
  1989. "Institutions for the Promotion of Indigenous Music: The Case for Ireland's Comhaltas Ceoltoiri Eiréann." *Ethnomusicology* 33: 67–95.
Henry, Paget.
  1983. "Decolonization and Cultural Underdevelopment in the Commonwealth Caribbean." In *The Newer Caribbean: Decolonization, Democracy, and Development,* ed. Paget Henry and Carl Stone. Philadelphia: Institute for the Study of Human Issues.
  1990. "Socialism and Cultural Transformation in Grenada." In *A Revolution Aborted: The Lessons of Grenada,* ed. Jorge Heine. Pittsburgh: University of Pittsburgh Press. 51–82.
Herskovits, Melville J.
  1937. *Life in a Haitian Valley.* New York: Alfred A. Knopf.
  1941. *The Myth of the Negro Past.* Boston: Beacon Press.
Hill, Donald R.
  1973. "'England I Want to Go': The Impact of Migration on a Caribbean Community." Ph.D. dissertation, Indiana University.
  1974. "More on Truth, Fact, and Tradition in Carriacou." *Caribbean Quarterly* 20, no. 1: 44–59.
  1977. *The Impact of Migration on the Metropolitan and Folk Society of Carriacou, Grenada.* Anthropological Papers of the American Museum of Natural History 54, part 2. New York: American Museum of Natural History.

1980. *The Big Drum and Other Ritual and Social Music of Carriacou.* LP. Folkways Records FE 34002. Washington, D.C.: Smithsonian/Folkways Records.

1993. *Calypso Calaloo: Early Carnival Music in Trinidad.* Gainesville: University Press of Florida.

Huntley, Earl.

2005. "The Treaty of Basseterre & OECS Economic Union." Publication of the Organization of Eastern Caribbean States (OECS).

James, C. L. R.

1967. "Black Power and Stokely." In *The C. L. R. James Reader,* ed. Anna Grimshaw. Oxford: Basil Blackwell, 1992. 362–74.

Joefield-Napier, Wallace.

1990. "Macroeconomic Growth under the People's Revolutionary Government: An Assessment." In *A Revolution Aborted: The Lessons of Grenada,* ed. Jorge Heine. Pittsburgh: University of Pittsburgh Press. 83–120.

Kay, Frances.

1987. *This Is Carriacou.* St. George's, Grenada: Carenage Press.

Kephart, Ronald.

1985. "'It Have More Soft Words': A Study of Creole English and Reading in Carriacou, Grenada." Ph.D. dissertation, University of Florida.

2000. *"Broken English": The Creole Language of Carriacou.* New York: Peter Lang Publishers.

Kincaid, Jamaica.

1990. *Lucy.* New York: Penguin Books.

Koetting, James T.

1992. "Africa/Ghana." In *Worlds of Music,* ed. Jeff Todd Titon. 2nd ed. New York: Schirmer Books. 67–105.

Lamb, Andrew.

1980. "Lancers" and "Quadrille." Entries in *The New Grove Dictionary of Music and Musicians,* ed. Stanley Sadie. London: Macmillan Publishers, Ltd.

Lazarus-Black, Mindi.

1994. *Legitimate Acts and Illegal Encounters.* Washington, D.C.: Smithsonian Institution Press.

Ledeen, Michael, and Herbert Romerstein.

1984. *Grenada Documents: An Overview and Selection.* Washington, D.C.: Department of State and the Department of Defense.

Levine, Lawrence W.

1977. *Black Culture and Black Consciousness: Afro-American Folk Thought from Slavery to Freedom.* New York: Oxford University Press.

Lewis, Gordon K.

1987. *Grenada: The Jewel Despoiled.* Baltimore: The Johns Hopkins University Press.

Lomax, Alan.

1962. Unpublished Folksong Recording Project notes, July 30, 1962, Carriacou, Grenada. American Folklife Center at the Library of Congress.

1999. *The Alan Lomax Collection: Caribbean Voyage, the 1962 Field Recordings; Carriacou Calaloo.* LP. Rounder Records 11661–1722–2.

2000. *The Alan Lomax Collection: Caribbean Voyage, the 1962 Field Recordings; Saraca: Funerary Music of Carriacou.* LP. Rounder Records 11661–1726–2.

2001. *The Alan Lomax Collection: Caribbean Voyage, the 1962 Field Recordings; Tombstone Feast, Funerary Music of Carriacou.* Rounder Records 11661–1727–2.

Forthcoming. *The Alan Lomax Collection: Caribbean Voyage, the 1962 Field Recordings; Music for Work and Play in Carriacou.* Rounder Records.

MacDonald, Scott B.

1986. *Trinidad and Tobago: Democracy and Development in the Caribbean.* New York: Praeger Publishers.

Malm, Krister.

1978. "The Parang of Trinidad: A Case of Transformation through Exploitation." *Antropologiska Studier* 25–26: 42–49.

1993. "Music on the Move: Traditions and Mass Media." *Ethnomusicology* 37, no. 3: 339–52.

Mandle, Jay R.

1985. *Big Revolution, Small Country: The Rise and Fall of the Grenada Revolution.* Lanham, Md.: North-South Publishing Company.

Manuel, Peter.

1994. "Puerto Rican Music and Cultural Identity: Creative Appropriation of Musical Sources from *Danza* to *Salsa*." *Ethnomusicology* 38, no. 2: 249–80.

Manuel, Peter, with Kenneth Bilby and Michael Largey.

1995. *Caribbean Currents: Caribbean Music from Rumba to Reggae.* Philadelphia: Temple University Press.

Mapp, Catherine.

1982. "Freedom as Wide as You Could Think about It." In *Carriacou and Petite [sic] Martinique: In the Mainstream of the Revolution,* ed. Chris Searle. St. George's, Grenada: Fedon Publishers. 108–10.

Marshall, Paule.

1983. *Praisesong for the Widow.* New York: Penguin Books.

Martin, Denis-Constant.

1991. "Filiation or Innovation?: Some Hypotheses to Overcome the Dilemma of Afro-American Music's Origins." *Black Music Research Journal* 11, no. 1: 19–38.

Martin, Von.

1982. "Merry Christmas Parang Style." Documentary aired on National Public Radio's *Horizons.*

Masi, Vincent, compiler.

18[??]. *The Cotillion Party's Assistant, and Ladies Musical Companion. Containing Six New Sets of Cotillions, and six Contra-Dances in a new style; With the Original Music For the Violin, German Flute, and adapted to the Piano Forte. For the Use of the Ladies.* Boston: The Compiler.

McAlister, Elizabeth.
2002. *Rara!: Vodou, Power, and Performance in Haiti and Its Diaspora.* Berkeley: University of California Press.
McCoy, James A.
1968. "The *Bomba* and *Aguinaldo* of Puerto Rico as They Have Evolved from Indigenous, African, and European Cultures." Ph.D. dissertation, Florida State University.
McDaniel, Angela L.
1986. "Memory Songs: Community, Flight, and Conflict in the Big Drum Ceremony of Carriacou, Grenada." Ph.D. dissertation, University of Maryland.
McDaniel, Lorna.
1992. "The Concept of Nation in the Big Drum Dance of Carriacou, Grenada." In *Musical Repercussions of the 1492 Encounter,* ed. Carol Robertson. Washington, D.C.: Smithsonian Institution Press.
1998. *The Big Drum Ritual of Carriacou: Praisesongs in Rememory of Flight.* Gainesville: University Press of Florida.
McIntosh, Norma A.
1955. *Hurricane Janet in Grenada and Carriacou, British West Indies: Complete Story and Pictures of the "Night of Terror," September 22, 1955.* Bridgetown, Barbados: Advocate Co., Ltd.
Miller, Rebecca S.
1996. "Irish Traditional and Popular Music in New York City: Identity and Social Change, 1930–1975." In *The New York Irish: Essays Towards a History,* ed. R. H. Bayor and T. J. Meagher. Baltimore: The Johns Hopkins University Press. 481–507.
2000. "'The People Like Melée': The Parang Festival of Carriacou, Grenada." Ph.D. dissertation, Brown University.
Mintz, Sidney W.
1974. *Caribbean Transformations.* New York: Columbia University Press.
Mintz, Sidney W., and Richard Price.
1992. *The Birth of African-American Culture: An Anthropological Perspective.* Boston: Beacon Press.
Mount Royal Progressive Youth Movement.
1990. "M.R.P.Y.M. Presents Carriacou Parang '91." Program booklet.
Mursell, James L.
1960. *Music around the World, Book Six.* Morristown, N.J.: Silver Burdett and Company.
Narayan, Kirin.
1997. "How Native Is a 'Native' Anthropologist?" In *Situated Lives: Gender and Culture in Everyday Life,* ed. Louise Lamphere, Helena Ragune, and Patricia Zavella. New York: Routledge. 23–41.

Nelson, George.
   1982. "Weself as One People." In *Carriacou and Petite [sic] Martinique: In the Mainstream of the Revolution,* ed. Chris Searle. St. George's, Grenada: Fedon Publishers. 72–73.
Okpewho, Isidore.
   1992. *African Oral Literature: Backgrounds, Character, and Continuity.* Bloomington: Indiana University Press.
Payne, Anthony, Paul Sutton, and Tony Thorndike.
   1984. *Grenada: Revolution and Invasion.* New York: St. Martin's Press.
Pearse, Andrew C.
   1956a. "Carnival in Nineteenth-Century Trinidad." *Caribbean Quarterly* 4, nos. 3–4: 175–93.
   1956b. Liner notes to the LP *The Big Drum Dance of Carriacou.* Ethnic Folkways Library P1011.
Piersen, William D.
   1977. "Puttin' Down Ole Massa: African Satire in the New World." In *African Folklore In The New World,* ed. Daniel J. Crowley. Austin: University of Texas Press. 20–34.
Postman, Neil.
   1986. *Amusing Ourselves to Death: Public Discourse in the Age of Show Business.* New York: Penguin Books.
Price, Sally, and Richard Price.
   1980. *Afro-American Arts of the Suriname Rain Forest.* Berkeley: University of California Press.
Rice, Timothy.
   1997. "Towards a Mediation of Field Methods and Field Experience in Ethnomusicology." In *Shadows in the Field: New Perspectives for Fieldwork in Ethnomusicology,* ed. Gregory Barz and Timothy Cooley. New York: Oxford University Press. 101–20.
Richardson, Philip J. S.
   1960. *The Social Dances of the Nineteenth Century in England.* London: Herbert Jenkins.
Ricoeur, Paul.
   1976. *Interpretation Theory: Discourse and the Surplus of Meaning.* Fort Worth: Texas Christian University Press.
Rodney, Walter.
   1969. *The Groundings with My Brothers.* London: Bogle D'Ouverture.
Rohlehr, Gordon.
   1990. *Calypso Society in Pre-Independence Trinidad.* Port of Spain, Trinidad: Gordon Rohlehr, Publisher.
Ryan, Selwyn.
   1990. "The Restoration of Electoral Politics in Grenada." In *A Revolution Aborted:*

The Lessons of Grenada, ed. Jorge Heine. Pittsburgh: University of Pittsburgh Press. 265–88.

Said, Edward W.

1994. *Culture and Imperialism.* New York: Vintage Books.

Sandburg, Carl.

1927. *The American Songbag.* New York: Harcourt, Brace & Co.

Sealey, John, and Krister Malm.

1982. *Music in the Caribbean.* London: Edward Arnold.

Searle, Chris.

1983. *Grenada: The Struggle Against Destabilization.* London: Writers and Readers Publishing Cooperative Ltd.

1984a. *Words Unchained: Language and Revolution in Grenada.* London: Zed Books Ltd.

1984b. *In Nobody's Backyard: Maurice Bishop's Speeches, 1979–1983; A Memorial Volume.* London: Zed Books Ltd.

Searle, Chris, ed.

1982. *Carriacou and Petite [sic] Martinique: In the Mainstream of the Revolution.* St. George's, Grenada: Fedon Publishers.

Sekou, Lasana M., ed.

1992. *Fête: Celebrating St. Martin's Traditional Festive Music.* St. Martin: House of Nehesi Publishers.

Singer, Roberta.

1988. "Puerto Rican Music in New York City." *New York Folklore* 14, nos. 3–4: 139–50.

Singham, A. W.

1968. *The Hero and the Crowd in a Colonial Polity.* New Haven, Conn.: Yale University Press.

Slobin, Mark.

1992. "Micromusics of the West: A Comparative Approach." *Ethnomusicology* 36, no. 1: 1–88.

Smelser, Neil J.

2004. "Epilogue: September 11, 2001, as Cultural Trauma." In *Cultural Trauma and Collective Identity,* Jeffrey C. Alexander, Ron Eyerman, Bernard Giesen, Neil J. Smelser, and Piotr Sztompka. Berkeley: University of California Press. 264–82.

Smith, M. G.

1962. *Kinship and Community in Carriacou.* New Haven, Conn.: Yale University Press.

1965. *The Plural Society in the British West Indies.* Berkeley: University of California Press.

Southern, Eileen.

1997. *The Music of Black Americans: A History.* 3rd ed. New York: W. W. Norton and Co.

Spottswood, Richard K.

    1988. Liner notes to *L'Ame Negre en exit: Au Bal Antillais. Franco-Creole Biguines from Martinique, Early Recordings of Caribbean Dance Music*. LP. Folklyric Records 9050.

Starbird, Ethel A.

    1979. "Taking It as It Comes: St. Vincent, The Grenadines, and Grenada." *National Geographic* 156, no. 3 (September): 398–425.

Steele, Beverley A.

    1974. "Grenada, an Island State: Its History and Its People." *Caribbean Quarterly* 20, no. 1: 5–43.

Stiell, Edwin ("Fries").

    1982. "Carriacou: Revolutionary Sister." In *Carriacou and Petite [sic] Martinique: In the Mainstream of the Revolution*. St. George's, Grenada: Fedon Publishers. 26–40.

Stuempfle, Stephen.

    1995. *The Steelband Movement: The Forging of a National Art in Trinidad and Tobago*. Philadelphia: University of Pennsylvania Press.

Sunshine, Catherine A.

    1982. *Grenada, the Peaceful Revolution*. Washington, D.C.: EPICA Task Force.

    1985. *The Caribbean: Survival, Struggle, and Sovereignty*. An EPICA Publication. Boston: South End Press.

Szwed, John F., and Morton Marks.

    1988. "The Afro-American Transformation of European Set Dances and Dance Suites." *Dance Research Journal* 20, no. 1 (Summer): 29–36.

Taylor, Daphne Pawan.

    1977. *Parang of Trinidad*. National Cultural Council of Trinidad and Tobago.

Taylor, Steven.

    2003. *False Prophet: Fieldnotes from the Punk Underground*. Middletown, Conn.: Wesleyan University Press.

Tegg, Thomas.

    1825. *Analysis of the London Ball-Room: In Which Is Comprised, The History of the Polite Art, from the Earliest Period, Interspersed with Characteristic Observations on each of its Popular Divisions of Country Dances, which contain a selection of the most Fashionable and Popular; Quadrilles . . . and Waltzes . . . Calculated for The Use of Domestic Assemblies, and Arranged for the Piano-Forte*. London: R. Griffin and Co.

Thomas, Bentley.

    1982. "A New Trust." In *Carriacou and Petite [sic] Martinique: In the Mainstream of the Revolution,* ed. Chris Searle. St. George's, Grenada: Fedon Publishers. 116–18.

Thompson, Robert Farris.

    1966. "An Aesthetic of the Cool: West African Dance." *African Forum* 2, no. 2 (Fall): 85–102.

1984. *Flash of the Spirit: African and Afro-American Art and Philosophy.* New York: Vintage Books.

Thorndike, Tony.

1985. *Grenada: Politics, Economics, and Society.* Boulder, Colo.: Lynne Rienner Publishers.

1990. "People's Power in Theory and Practice." In *A Revolution Aborted: The Lessons of Grenada,* ed. Jorge Heine. Pittsburgh: University of Pittsburgh Press. 29–50.

Walters, Keith.

1999. "'He Can Read My Writing But He Sho' Can't Read My Mind': Zora Neale Hurston's Revenge in *Mules and Men.*" *Journal of American Folklore* 112, no. 445: 343–71.

Warner, Keith Q.

1982. *Kaiso! The Trinidad Calypso.* Washington, D.C.: Three Continents Press.

Warner-Lewis, Maureen.

1986. "The Influence of Yoruba Music on the Minor Key Calypso." In *Papers: Seminar on the Calypso.* St. Augustine, Trinidad: University of West Indies/ISER.

Waterman, Christopher Alan.

1990. *Jùjú: A Social History and Ethnography of an African Popular Music.* Chicago: University of Chicago Press.

Waterman, Richard Alan.

1952. "African Influence on the Music of the Americas." In *Acculturation in the Americas: Proceedings of the 29th International Congress of Americanists, Vol. 2,* ed. Sol Tax. Chicago: University of Chicago Press. 207–18.

Wilcken, Lois.

1998. "The Changing Hats of Haitian Staged Folklore in New York City." In *Island Sounds in the Global City: Caribbean Popular Music and Identity in New York,* ed. Ray Allen and Lois Wilcken. New York: The New York Folklore Society and the Institute for Studies in American Music, Brooklyn College.

Winans, Robert B.

1982. "Black Instrumental Music Traditions in the Ex-Slave Narratives." *Black Music Research Newsletter* 5, no. 2 (Spring): 2–5.

Yih, Yuen-Ming David.

1995. "Music and Dance of Haitian Vodou: Diversity and Unity in Regional Repertoires." Ph.D. dissertation, Wesleyan University.

NEWSPAPERS

Grenada Free Press and Public Gazette, vol. 2, no. 146, November 26, 1828; July 13, 1831; vol. 6, no. 355, November 28, 1832.

St. George's Chronicle and Gazette, vol. 15, April 14, 1857.

Grenadian Government Gazette no. 22, May 16, 1894.

Grenadian Voice, vol. 15, no. 2, January 13, 1996; vol. 16, no. 4, p. 15, January 25, 1997; vol. 17, no. 33, August 15, 1998; vol. 17, no. 51, December 19, 1998; vol. 18, no. 36, September 4, 1999.

New York Times, November 2, 1983.

INTERVIEWS AND PERSONAL COMMUNICATIONS

(All took place in Carriacou unless otherwise indicated.)

Adams, Gus, 1995

Alexander, Clemencia, 1995, 1997 (pc)

Allert, Sonnelle, 1997

Bullen, Glenna, 1997

Bullen, Judy, 1995

Bullen, Lyle, 1997

Bullen, Mario, 1997 (St. George's, Grenada)

Bristol, Bernice, 1997

Bristol, Cosmos, 1997

Callender, Randolph "Baboo," 1997

Caliste, Canute, 1995, 1997

Charles, Augustin, 1997

Chase, Lawrence, 1996 (pc)

Clouden, Derick, 1997 (St. George's, Grenada)

Collins, Wallace, 1997

Collins, Godwin, 1997

Coy, Milton "Tailor," 1996 (pc)

De Rochet, Lucy, 1995

Doherty, Tom, 1986 (Brooklyn, N.Y.)

Fleary, Harrison, 1995, 1997

Fleary, Winston, 1996

Fortune, Albert, 1997

Frazier, Malcolm, 1997 (pc)

George, Norris, 1997

Gerstin, Julian, 1998 (pc) (via email)

Guyan, Captain, 1997

Henry, Paget, 1997 (pc) (Providence, R.I.)

Hill, Donald R., 1999 (pc) (via email)

Ingram, Amelia, 2005 (pc) (via email)

James, Anselm, 1996 (pc)

Jerome, Theo, 1997

Joseph, Curtis, 1997

Joseph, Dennis, 1997

Joseph, Kenly "Rhyno," 1997

Largey, Michael David, 2007 (pc) (via email)
Lendore, Bernadette, 1997 (pc)
Lendore, Brian, 1996
Lendore, Linton, 2007 (pc)
MacFarlane, Gaby, 1997
Mathison, Andy "Leftist," 1997
McGillivary, Jerry, 1997
McQuilkin, Elwyn, 1997 (St. George's, Grenada)
Mills, Kimberlin, 2001
Moses, Godwin, 1995 (pc)
Nimrod, Senator Elvin G., 1997, 2001
Quashie, Peter, 1996 (pc)
Richardson, Hazen, 1996 (Petit St. Vincent, St. Vincent)
Sarah (bursar on *The Mandalay*), 1995 (pc)
Stiell, Eslyn "Tateen," 1997
Stiell, Kervin, 1996 (pc)
Stiell, Lionel, 1997
Stiell, Thora, 1997 (pc)
Taylor, Captain Mike, 1995
Thomas, Bentley, 1999 (London via telephone)
Woolf, Andy, 1999 (pc) (Massachusetts)

Index

verbal art: open vs. indirect criticism, 52,
58–59; *picong* (satirical) speech, 192–93,
214; sexuality in expressive culture, 141–
42; "shtooping," 166, 212, 215, 237n1;
signifying, 213; "toasts" during Hosannah band performances, 102–3, 232–
33n3. *See also* language
village as sociopolitical unit: Bishop administration's conception of, 167; cultural
identity of villages, 119–20; Hosannah
band competition inter-village rivalry,
29, 119–20; local affiliation of bands,
167; Parang Festival organization and,
167–68; string band competition inter-
village rivalry, 11–12, 163–64
violin: absence in *lavway* competition, 177;
Canute Caliste style, 72–73, 74, 75–76,
228n10; in Carriacou string bands, 125,
136, 138; early importation to islands,
81; Kayak violin style, 24; as lead instrument, 70–71, 73; performance of break-
aways, 126; in serenading bands, 147; as
slave instrument, 230n18; in Trinidad
string bands, 134, 223n7

Wallis, Roger, 155
waltz: popularity in Carriacou, 228n12; at
quadrille events, 68, 77, 81; in string
band repertoire, 126; Transcription 5
("Windward Waltz"), 138–39, *139–40,*
Warner, Mr. (pseudonym), 197–98, 238n10

Warner-Lewis, Maureen, 151
Waterman, Christopher, 206
weddings, 143–46, *144, 146,* 155
West London (England), 4
"wetting of the ring" ritual, 60–61, 66–67,
227n4
"Whispering Hope," 126, 129–30, 235n6
Wilcken, Lois, 64
Williams, Eric, 14, 226n10
Windward (Carriacou): Catholic Church
promotion of quadrilles in, 88; Hosannah singing tradition in, 104; Lomax
visit to, 138; public services, 32–33;
quadrille dance in, *66,* 230n17; recollec-
tion of bouquet dances in, 86; Scottish
boat-builder settlers in, 6, 80, 120, 138,
229n16, 230n19; sea chanteys in, 10;
string band music in, *137–38,* 138; village cultural identity of, 119–20
"Windward Waltz," *137–38,* 138–39
women: as calypso subjects, 206; Carriacouan emigration to England and, 105;
fieldwork experiences with, 26–27; gender relations in wedding symbolism,
145; in Hosannah bands, 101, 105; in
serenading bands, 147–48; in string
band music, 26, 124

X-Trak, 110, 118

youth groups, 33–34, 47–50, 226n9, 226n11

MUSIC / CULTURE

A series from Wesleyan University Press
Edited by Deborah Wong, Sherrie Tucker, and Jeremy Wallach

The Music/Culture series has consistently reshaped and redirected music scholarship. Founded in 1993 by George Lipsitz, Susan McClary, and Robert Walser, the series features outstanding critical work on music. Unconstrained by disciplinary divides, the series addresses music and power through a range of times, places, and approaches. Music/Culture strives to integrate a variety of approaches to the study of music, linking analysis of musical significance to larger issues of power—what is permitted and forbidden, who is included and excluded, who speaks and who gets silenced. From ethnographic classics to cutting-edge studies, Music/Culture zeroes in on how musicians articulate social needs, conflicts, coalitions, and hope. Books in the series investigate the cultural work of music in urgent and sometimes experimental ways, from the radical fringe to the quotidian. Music/Culture asks deep and broad questions about music through the framework of the most restless and rigorous critical theory.

MUSIC/CULTURE FALL 2024

Benjamin Barson
Brassroots Democracy: Maroon
Ecologies and the Jazz Commons

Donna Lee Kwon
Stepping in the Madang:
Sustaining Expressive Ecologies
of Korean Drumming and Dance

Sumarsam
The In-Between in Javanese
Performing Arts: History and Myth,
Interculturalism and Interreligiosity

A COMPLETE LIST OF SERIES TITLES CAN BE FOUND AT
https://www.weslpress.org/search-results/?series=music-culture

About the Author

Rebecca S. Miller is professor of music at Hampshire College, a public sector folklorist/documentary maker, and an accomplished traditional fiddler.